# AMERICAN APOCALYPSE

# American Apocalypse

## Yankee Protestants and the Civil War

## 1860-1869

James H. Moorhead

New Haven and London   Yale University Press

1978

Awarded the 1976 Frank S. and Elizabeth
D. Brewer Prize of the American Society of Church
History.

Designed by John O. C. McCrillis
and set in Press Roman type.
Printed in the United States of America by
The Alpine Press, Inc., S. Braintree, Ma.

Published in Great Britain, Europe, Africa, and
Asia (except Japan) by Yale University Press,
Ltd., London. Distributed in Latin America by
Kaiman & Polon, Inc., New York City; in
Australia and New Zealand by Book & Film
Services, Artarmon, N.S.W., Australia; and in
Japan by Harper & Row, Publishers, Tokyo
Office.

Library of Congress Cataloging in Publication Data

Moorhead, James H.
    American apocalypse.
    Originally presented as the author's thesis, Yale,
1975.
    Bibliography: p.
    Includes index.
    1. Millennialism—History. 2. Messianism,
American—History. 3. Protestant churches—United
States—History. 4. United States—History—Civil
War, 1861–1865—Religious aspects. I. Title.
BR525.M56    1978    280'4'0973    77–14360
ISBN 0-300-02152-6

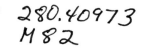
To Cynthia
and the memory of her father,
Frank W. Stephens (1912-1975)

Compassion and pragmatism, wit and purpose—in
rare compact, these were the
measure of the man.

# Contents

Preface                                                    ix

Introduction: The Millennium and the Republic              1

1  From Confusion to Crusade                               23

2  The Armageddon of the Republic                          42

3  Slavery and the Kingdom                                 82

4  The Crucible of Folk Loyalty                           129

5  Search for the Jordan                                  173

6  "Wanted—A Moral Purpose"                               218

Epilogue: American Protestantism in the Gilded Age        236

Bibliography                                              245

Index                                                     271

# Preface

On a Sunday afternoon in October 1862, the Congregational Church in a small New Hampshire village was filled with blue-coated men. A company of Union volunteers about to depart for the front listened as the Reverend William Gaylord predicted a glorious destiny for America once the war was ended.

> Oh! what a day will that be for our beloved land, when carried through a baptism of fire and blood, struggling through this birth-night of terror and darkness, it shall experience a resurrection to a new life, and to a future whose coming glory already gilds the mountain tops. That day of future glory is hastening on. That day of a truer and deeper loyalty to God and to country—that day when the oppressor's rod shall be broken, when the sigh of no captive spirit shall be heard throughout all our fair land.... The day of the Lord is at hand![1]

A generation steeped in the imagery of the Bible needed no reminder that "the day of the Lord" was a prophetic pseudonym for that time when catastrophic judgment would announce the final realization of God's purpose on earth. Gaylord was claiming an audacious significance for the Civil War, and Northern congregations heard similar messages on other Sundays throughout the 1860s. Although no churches formally altered their confessional statements, it was an unofficial article of Protestant faith that the current struggle would prove the decisive point of American—indeed, of world—history. Singing the strident cadences of Julia Ward Howe's "Battle Hymn of the Republic," thousands believed their eyes were seeing "the glory of the coming of the Lord."

These grand hopes pointed to a long-standing tradition that placed America within an apocalyptic framework of universal history. The

---

1. William L. Gaylord, *The Soldier God's Minister*, "A Discourse Delivered in the Congregational Church, Fitzwilliam, N.H., Sabbath Afternoon, October 5, 1862, on the Occasion of the Departure of a Company of Volunteers for the Seat of War," pp. 19–20.

Puritan colonists, nurtured in the providential assumptions of the English Reformation, brought to these shores an acute millennial consciousness; and early in the life of the young republic that heritage became part of a widely held belief in the religious-political mission of the United States. America was a new Israel, a chosen people set before the nations as an exemplary society and commissioned to lead them to the latter-day glory. This faith was significant not only as a datum of church history but also as a crucial mode whereby nineteenth-century Americans defined their national identity.

The Civil War provides an important field for the study of these themes. Although a portion of the clergy invoked providence to bless national arms in previous conflicts, no war since the Revolution had aroused anything approaching universal clerical support or ardor. In fact, numerous Protestants argued that the policies of Madison in 1812 and of Polk in 1846 perverted America's special mission. What makes the 1860s especially interesting is the sheer intensity and virtual unanimity of Northern conviction that the Union armies were hastening the day of the Lord—indeed that the war was not merely one sacred battle among many but was the climactic test of the redeemer nation and its millennial role. Though scarcely surprising in the context of a struggle for national survival, these sentiments marked a crucial reappraisal of the United States' destiny. During the seventy years prior to secession, except for the two momentary and partial spasms of war fever, the churches overwhelmingly believed America's mission to be one of moral persuasion with evangelical piety and democratic institutions offering a contagious example to the rest of the world. This vision by no means expired with the war, but after Fort Sumter fell, Protestants hopelessly confused the weapons of the saints with the Union's military power and awaited the first signs of the millennium in the exploits of the Army of the Potomac. These grandiose expectations, incapable of realization in any event, contributed to a simplistic assessment of national problems and were among the many roots of America's unpreparedness to deal responsibly with Reconstruction or the legacy of slavery, let alone the other strange and bewildering difficulties on the far side of Appomattox.

This book is both more and less than a survey of millennialism. I have looked at only one aspect of the diverse millennial tradition in America: its use in the major Protestant denominations of the North to ascribe a special mission to the Republic. Not every enthusiast for the millennium gave this central distinction to the United States, nor was such interest confined to the evangelical mainstream. Antebellum America had proliferated a multitude of sects and communitarian movements, many of which drew inspiration from their own eccentric readings of the Apocalypse. A complete history of millennialism in the United States, even for the single decade of this study, would have to travel down these exotic byways, and the result would be a book considerably longer than this monograph. Yet if the views here discussed were only one variant of a species, they were still, in James F. Maclear's words, "so common as to be almost canonical."[2] An examination of this particular millennial strand inevitably leads beyond itself. As they portrayed the movement of American history toward the Kingdom of God, Protestants used the Scriptures eclectically, often juggling clearly eschatological ideas with other biblical motifs such as national election, covenant, or prophetic jeremiad. They also spoke of providential destiny in the context of contemporary problems. Their attitudes, for example, about slavery and the nature of democracy formed—and in turn were formed by—their understanding of America as a redeemer nation. Accordingly these broader issues also figure prominently in my narrative.

This book is not about the much-discussed civil religion, not if that phrase is defined in the terms proposed by Robert Bellah in his now celebrated article. I am concerned primarily with ecclesiastical attitudes rather than with a national faith existing "alongside of and rather clearly differentiated from the churches."[3] Nevertheless this inquiry is written in the belief that evangelical Protestantism was one of the prime shapers of American identity and purpose. To affirm this conviction is not to deny the crucial importance of other forces or traditions or to ignore the extent to which subsequent history has diluted the original impulse and given it a life independent of de-

2. James F. Maclear, "The Republic and the Millennium," in *The Religion of the Republic,* ed. Elwyn A. Smith, p. 184.
3 Robert N. Bellah, "Civil Religion in America," *Daedalus* 96 (Winter 1967): 1.

nominational religion. Still less do I espouse a celebrationist account of our past. In spite of the pluralism of American life, our corporate symbols have often lacked the universality claimed for them, and perhaps, as Charles Long recently suggested, they still fail to address a sizable minority of citizens.[4] To study the churches during the Civil War is in part to make a troubling assessment about the sources of that parochialism.

This study focuses on the four major Protestant denominations of the North: Baptists, Congregationalists, Methodists, and Presbyterians (Old and New Schools). In the mid-nineteenth century these four groups were virtually the Protestant establishment, wielding great social power and successfully molding the national ethos. Their story during the Civil War and Reconstruction is, in large measure, the story of the North itself. The Afro-American churches, Roman Catholicism, and Judaism possess significant histories during the decade of the rebellion, and the Southern white denominations drew upon the common evangelical heritage to develop the notion of a new Confederate Israel. None of these, however, set the moral tone of the victorious Union, and they are accordingly not direct subjects of this study.

I have tried to relate the narrative without bias and to cite representative rather than extreme voices. In most instances, many similar unquoted sources stand behind the one cited in the text. Without ignoring the weighty theological quarterlies, I have devoted particular attention to pamphlet sermons and the popular religious press as a gauge of rank-and-file opinion. The evangelical weeklies exerted a public influence that the editors of today's denominational papers must surely envy. In a study of New York in the mid-nineteenth century, Whitney Cross discovered that religious periodicals made up over a quarter of the newspaper circulation in the state, and one cannot escape the conclusion that many found in this press a chief source of information and views.[5] Since both the journals and

4. Charles Long, "Civil Rights—Civil Religion: Visible People and Invisible Religion," in *American Civil Religion,* ed. Russell E. Richey and Donald G. Jones, pp. 211–21.

5. Whitney R. Cross, *The Burned-over District: The Social and Intellectual History of Enthusiastic Religion in Western New York, 1800–1850,* p. 104.

weeklies espoused divergent views on numerous questions, I have sampled opinion from varying persuasions. In many cases the affiliation of a particular paper is apparent by title; where this information is not clear, it is provided in a brief annotation to the bibliographic entry.

This book was originally a doctoral dissertation submitted to Yale University in 1975. To Sydney E. Ahlstrom, who was the director of the thesis, I owe my chief academic debt. Despite an arduous schedule, he provided constant encouragement and criticism. C. Duncan Rice graciously interrupted a leave of absence to read the entire manuscript and to offer valuable counsel. Alan C. Thomson, Richard Warch, and William G. McLoughlin also reviewed the text and saved me from several errors. Lefferts A. Loetscher, whose classes first awakened my interest in American religious history, did the same. Correspondence or conversation with C. Conrad Wright, Daniel W. Howe, W. Lawrence Highfill, Obie Wright, Jr., Albert Raboteau, and Christine Heyrman also helped to sharpen my thinking.

The staffs of two Yale libraries, the Robert E. Speer Library in Princeton, New Jersey, and the D. H. Hill Library in Raleigh, North Carolina, rendered expert aid. E. Richard McKinstry of the New Jersey Historical Society gave proof of our long friendship by searching diligently for germane sources. Financial assistance was provided by a Whiting Fellowship during the 1974-75 academic year. For the supportive environment provided by my colleagues at North Carolina State University, I am also thankful, especially for the aid of Robert O. Tilman and Robert S. Bryan—dean of the School of Liberal Arts and head of the Department of Philosophy and Religion, respectively—who made available the resources of their offices to speed preparation of the final manuscript. Glena Ames and Evelyn Wilson performed the unenviable task of translating my erratic typing into readable copy.

I am grateful to the American Society of Church History, which awarded my dissertation the Frank S. and Elizabeth D. Brewer Prize for 1976, and for the material assistance the prize entails.

Without Cynthia Stephens Moorhead, I might have written this study; but the work would have lost much of its soul and inspiration. Our son Evan added the saving grace of perspective, the spontaneity of the toddler reminding his father that scholarship is only one part of life. To Robert and Tina Moorhead as well as Frank and Jean Stephens, I am thankful for parental encouragement. It is an occasion of deep lament that my father-in-law, who took keen interest in this project, did not live to see its completion.

Raleigh, N.C.
May 1977

# Introduction:

# The Millennium and the Republic

Harriet Beecher Stowe, in her 1878 novel *Poganuc People*, reconstructed an antebellum Fourth of July celebration in Connecticut. Among the prayers on this occasion were "petitions for the glorious future of the United States of America—that they might be chosen vessels, commissioned to bear the light of liberty and religion through all the earth and to bring in the great millennial day, when wars should cease and the whole world released from the thralldom of evil, should rejoice in the light of the Lord."[1] This exhilarating

---

1. Harriet Beecher Stowe, *Poganuc People: Their Loves and Their Lives*, p. 197. Literature dealing with millennialism in America is extensive and growing. Ernest L. Tuveson, *Redeemer Nation: The Idea of America's Millennial Role*, which builds on his older *Millennium and Utopia: A Study in the Background of the Idea of Progress*, was the first effort to present millennialism as a leitmotiv in American nationalism. Though written from broader interpretive frameworks, several other recent accounts of American religion shed considerable light on Protestant conceptions of the nation's millennial destiny: Sydney E. Ahlstrom, *A Religious History of the American People;* Conrad Cherry, ed., *God's New Israel: Religious Interpretations of American Destiny;* Robert T. Handy, *A Christian America: Protestant Hopes and Historical Realities;* Winthrop S. Hudson, ed., *Nationalism and Religion in America: Concepts of American Identity and Mission;* Martin E. Marty, *Righteous Empire: The Protestant Experience in America;* and Cushing Strout, *The New Heavens and the New Earth: Political Religion in America.* A few of the significant published works treating aspects of millennialism in the United States include Cross, *Burned-over District;* Oliver W. Elsbree, *The Rise of the Missionary Spirit in America;* Edwin S. Gaustad, ed., *The Rise of Adventism;* Alan E. Heimert, *Religion and the American Mind: From the Great Awakening to the Revolution;* Perry Miller, *The Life of the Mind in America: From the Revolution to the Civil War;* and Timothy L. Smith *Revivalism and Social Reform: American Protestantism on the Eve of the Civil War.* The studies of C. Norman Kraus, *Dispensationalism in America: Its Rise and Development,* and Ernest L. Sandeen, *The Roots of Fundamentalism: British and American Millenarianism, 1800-1930,* indicate the significance of premillennialism to the beginnings of Fundamentalism. LeRoy Edwin Froom, *The Prophetic*

hope was sounded from pulpits throughout the nation in the decades before the Civil War, for it had become an unofficial Protestant tenet that the United States would play a unique role in the coming of the Kingdom of God. How this ancient Christian vision was claimed as the special property of America is one of the most significant stories of modern Western thought.

The roots of this belief can be traced to the eschatological revolution spurred by the Reformation. For hundreds of years before that upheaval, the apocalyptic hope of the primitive church had been in official disfavor. The dramatic scenario of St. John's Revelation—angels pouring out vials of wrath and announcing calamities to precede Christ's millennial reign on earth—was something of an embarrassment to a church that had made its peace with the world. Following Augustine, most Christian leaders rejected a temporal Kingdom of God yet to come and argued that the millennium was a spiritual rule already begun at the Resurrection. During the medieval period, chiliastic excitement had flourished from time to time in popular religion and among sectarians, but the church frowned upon it. Protestantism began a reversal of the prevailing attitude. Although the major reformers deplored the radical millenarianism of certain Anabaptists and adhered to much of the traditional

---

*Faith of Our Fathers*, is a veritable encyclopedia of primary millennial sources, but since Froom writes from an avowedly Adventist bias, his study must be used cautiously. Helpful articles include Christopher M. Beam, "Millennialism and American Nationalism, 1740–1800," *Journal of Presbyterian History* 54 (Spring 1976): 182–99; Ira Brown, "Watchers for the Second Coming: The Millennial Tradition in America," *Mississippi Valley Historical Review* 39 (December 1952): 441–58; C. C. Goen, "Jonathan Edwards: A New Departure in Eschatology," *Church History* 28 (March 1959): 25–40; Nathan O. Hatch, "The Origins of Civil Millennialism in America: New England Clergymen, the War with France, and the Revolution," *William and Mary Quarterly,* 3d ser. 31 (July 1974): 407–30; James F. Maclear, "New England and the Fifth Monarchy: The Quest for the Millennium in Early American Puritanism," *William and Mary Quarterly,* 3d ser. 32 (April 1975): 223–60; Maclear, "The Republic and the Millennium"; and David E. Smith, "Millenarian Scholarship in America," *American Quarterly* 17 (Fall 1965): 535–49. For perspectives transcending the American scene, consult Norman Cohn, *The Pursuit of the Millennium;* Sylvia L. Thrupp, ed., *Millennial Dreams in Action;* and George Hunston Williams, *Wilderness and Paradise in Christian Thought.* Recent literature is surveyed in Hillel Schwartz, "The End of the Beginning: Millenarian Studies, 1965–1976," *Religious Studies Review* 2 (July 1976): 1–15.

Augustinian view, they frequently showed interest in the apocalyptic portions of the Bible, most commentators agreeing with Luther that these scriptures identified the papacy and Romanism as the Antichrist, foretold their demise, and predicted the triumph of a reformed Christianity. By the seventeenth century, many Protestants openly revived the primitive hope of a future millennium, perhaps soon to arrive. These speculations suited Protestant experience well. Aside from providing good propaganda against Catholicism, they made sense of a chaotic age and explained how God could allow an apostate church to persecute his saints for so long: all was part of a hidden plan whereby war, corruption, and terrible judgments would lead to the eventual triumph of righteousness.[2]

In England this reawakened millennial consciousness acquired peculiar intensity. John Foxe's influential *Acts and Monuments Most Special and Memorable* (1563)—better known to posterity as the *Book of Martyrs*—identified Rome with the apocalyptic beast in whose destruction the English nation and church were to play an especially honorable role. After 1600 numerous pamphlets expounding the Revelation poured from the presses, and by the time of the English Civil War millennial fervor and a conviction of national election were widespread.[3]

The Puritans who left this environment to colonize America quite naturally envisioned their errand into the wilderness in similar terms. As their predilection for Old Testament names testified, they saw themselves as a covenanted people, a new Israel, destined to build up the waste places of Zion in preparation for the latter-day glory. Their opportunity and responsibility alike were staggering. "For your full assurance," Edward Johnson reminded them in 1653, "know this is the place where the Lord will create a new Heaven and a new earth. . . , new Churches and a new Commonwealth together."[4] Although these sentiments were most pronounced in

2. See especially Tuveson's *Millennium and Utopia* and *Redeemer Nation,* pp. 1–25.

3. B. S. Capp, *The Fifth Monarchy Men: A Study in Seventeenth-century English Millenarianism;* Peter Toon, ed., *Puritans, the Millennium and the Future of Israel: Puritan Eschatology, 1600–60;* and John F. Wilson, *Pulpit in Parliament: Puritanism during the English Civil Wars, 1640–1648.*

4. Edward Johnson, *Wonder-Working Providence,* ed. J. Franklin Jameson, p. 25.

the New England colonies, the idea of providential mission was not limited to the region north of Long Island Sound. Most British immigrants, including the Anglicans of Virginia, had been at least partially shaped by the Puritan Protestant impulse and spiritually nourished amid the dreams that inspired Foxe's *Book of Martyrs.* Nevertheless, it was from New England that the most articulate statements of America's millennial role were to come.[5]

These early settlers also hastened a momentous cultural transformation. In its drive to remake church and commonwealth, Puritanism proved to be a veritable "revolution of the saints," which in spite of contradictory elements helped to loosen traditional restraints and create a new kind of society. In conjunction with other forces, this dynamic movement played a major role in the rise of political and economic individualism; and well before 1776, British America was already becoming something its founders never imagined or desired: a bourgeois democracy.[6]

As colonial society matured, new ideas softened the rigors of Puritanism. Early in the eighteenth century a prosperous people began to absorb Enlightened theories about human rights and the nature of government. From English libertarians, colonists learned to think as radical Whigs.[7] These developments did not mean, however, that a religious sense of mission had disappeared. Rather, old commitments and new together refashioned American identity to meet the realities of the present. The Great Awakening marked an important stage in that process. For a few years after 1739, the colonies went on a revivalistic binge that left an immense imprint upon the emerging national consciousness. Critics might later remember the Awakening as a time when "multitudes were seriously, soberly, and solemnly out of their wits"; but to at least some of its defenders—most notably Jonathan Edwards—the spiritual enthusi-

5. See, for example, Perry Miller, *Errand into the Wilderness,* pp. 99–140.
6. Michael Walzer, *The Revolution of the Saints: A Study in the Origins of Radical Politics,* and David Little, *Religion, Order, and Law: A Study in Pre-Revolutionary England,* are particularly helpful recent studies on the revolutionary implications of Puritanism.
7. Bernard Bailyn, *The Ideological Origins of the American Revolution.* On the influence of the Enlightenment, see Henry F. May, *The Enlightenment in America.*

asm offered the tantalizing hope that the millennium would begin in America.[8] Subsequent revolutionary nationalism was not, of course, the inevitable or logically necessary result of this excitement, but there was between the two phenomena a substantial, if more subtle, connection. Once the war for independence was underway, the colonists' traditional sense of providential destiny, heightened by the revivals, lent a peculiar urgency to revolutionary ideology. Patriotic addresses took on what Gordon Wood calls a "millennial tone," some advocates suggesting the imminence of the Kingdom and virtually all regarding the new Republic as the start of a new epoch in world history.[9] As early as 1765 John Adams portrayed the colonial struggle for liberty in images borrowed from biblical prophecy. Americans, he said, continued the contest of the Protestant reformers against "the man of sin, the whore of Babylon, the mystery of iniquity."[10]

This weaving of secular and religious motifs into one holy history became commonplace after independence. From Ezra Stiles's *The United States Elevated to Glory and Honor* (1783) to Philip Schaff's *America* (1855), the advance of God's Kingdom was intimately connected with the progress of democracy, and both were believed best exemplified in the United States. As one clergyman put the matter, America was leading the world toward a "millennium of republicanism."[11] After the wrenching debates about the propriety of the War of 1812 had passed, hopeful sentiments gained especial credibility because their chance of fulfillment appeared bright.[12] While the American republic expanded vigorously during

8. Ezra Stiles quoted in Carl Bridenbaugh, *Mitre and Sceptre: Transatlantic Faiths, Ideas, Personalities, and Politics, 1689-1775,* p. 9; Goen, "Jonathan Edwards."

9. Gordon S. Wood, *The Creation of the American Republic, 1776-1787,* p. 117. See also Hatch, "Origins of Civil Millennialism." Heimert, *Religion and the American Mind,* makes an important but overdrawn case for the significance of the Awakening as a transformer of American consciousness.

10. Charles Francis Adams, ed., *The Works of John Adams,* 3: 453.

11. B. F. Telft, "Progress of Society," *Ladies' Repository* 8 (June 1848): 186.

12. The divisive effect of the War of 1812 on the churches is chronicled in William Gribbin, *The Churches Militant: The War of 1812 and American Religion.*

a heyday of revivalism and evangelical enterprise, periodic cries for liberty and reform unsettled Europe's old order. In China and the Near East, native governments succumbed to Western gunboats, commerce, diplomacy, and missionaries. Thus the Kingdom—the Gospel together with republican civilization—bid fair to radiate outward, as if by concentric circles, from a spiritual center in the United States. In 1850 a Methodist monthly for women analyzed the significance of the invention of the telegraph for American destiny, and the conclusion evoked the essence of the religious and cultural expectations with which Protestants had invested their national Union:

> This noble invention is to be the means of extending civilization, republicanism, and Christianity over the earth. It must and will be extended to nations half-civilized, and thence to those now savage and barbarous. Our government will be the grand center of this mighty influence. . . . The beneficial and harmonious operation of our institutions will be seen, and similar ones adopted. Christianity must speedily follow them; and we shall behold the grand spectacle of a whole world, civilized, republican, and Christian. Then will wrong and injustice be forever banished. Every yoke shall be broken, and the oppressed go free. Wars will cease from the earth. Men "shall beat their swords into plough shares, and their spears into pruning-hooks. Nation shall not lift up sword against nation; neither shall they learn war any more"; for each man shall feel that every other man is his neighbor—his brother. Then shall come to pass the millennium, when "they shall teach no more every man his neighbor, and every man his brother, saying Know ye the Lord; for all shall know him, from the least of them unto the greatest."[13]

### PROBLEMS AND ANXIETIES

All was not well within God's new Israel. Optimism was tempered by the realization that serious problems had to be resolved if the nation were to enter the latter-day glory; and even as the clergy speculated about the millennial implications of the telegraph, agitation

13. Joseph Brady, "The Magnetic Telegraph," *Ladies' Repository* 10 (February 1850): 61–62.

over the slavery question rent America. Other dilemmas vexed Protestants as well. Materialism threatened republican simplicity, partisanship debased political integrity, and the frontier seemed easy prey to what Horace Bushnell called "the bowie knife style of civilization."[14] Amid these signs of social decay, supposed conspiracies threatened the nation, although the candidate for chief demon varied according to one's preference—Roman Catholicism, the slave power, abolitionism, Mormonism, or freemasonry.[15]

The conviction of a great work to be done prompted an unprecedented exertion of religious zeal. In the first quarter of the nineteenth century emerged the so-called evangelical united front whose efforts were ramified through a vast network of tract, Bible, temperance, missionary, and other benevolent societies.[16] Protestants

14. Horace Bushnell, *Barbarism the First Danger*, p. 20.

15. The fear of conspiracy in America is suggestively analyzed by David Brion Davis in several works: "Some Themes of Countersubversion: An Analysis of Anti-Masonic, Anti-Catholic, and Anti-Mormon Literature," *Mississippi Valley Historical Review* 47 (September 1960): 205–25; *The Slave Power Conspiracy and the Paranoid Style;* and *The Fear of Conspiracy: Images of Un-American Subversion from the Revolution to the Present.* Also important is Richard Hofstadter, *The Paranoid Style in American Politics.* On the basis of these works and of Bailyn's, it is possible to suggest plausible sources of this mentality. Bailyn has disclosed the centrality of the English libertarian heritage as epitomized in such people as John Trenchard (1662–1723) and Thomas Gordon (d. 1750), to American Revolutionary thought. It was a cardinal doctrine of these pamphleteers that liberty is a tenuous possession, ever won anew from the encroachments of conspiratorial power. If Bailyn's thesis is correct, one might surmise that succeeding generations of Americans have seen themselves as reenacting this primal struggle and thereby assuming the mantle of their ancestors. Also, the relative mobility and freedom from institutional control within American life may have contributed to a corporate identity crisis, a cultural anomie, in the midst of which conspiratorial modes of thought provided a comforting sense of order and meaning. Finally millennialism itself appears conducive to the paranoid style. If history is one struggle of the forces of God against Satan, it is natural for the adherents of the Kingdom to perceive a coherent, sinister intelligence animating the various problems they encounter.

16. See the following works: John R. Bodo, *The Protestant Clergy and Public Issues, 1812–1848;* Charles C. Cole, Jr., *The Social Ideas of the Northern Evangelists, 1826–1860;* Ellsbree, *Rise of the Missionary Spirit in America;* Collin Brummit Goodykoontz, *Home Missions on the American Frontier, with Particular Reference to the American Home Missionary Society;*

consciously employed these tools to build a Christian America, and they frequently drew encouragement from their hope that the Kingdom of God was coming. "Soon the whole earth," wrote William Cogswell of the American Education Society in a treatise on the millennium, "will chant the praises of the Redeemer, and the song of salvation will echo from shore to shore. But in order to this [sic], there must be more fervent prayer, more abundant labors, more enlarged charities. In this conquest of the world to Christ, the church must become a well disciplined army, and every member of it must know her place and duty."[17]

That the church could thus win victory in the world was a hopeful doctrine deserving further comment, for biblical prophecies do not automatically yield such cheering prospects. "Woe unto you that desire the day of the Lord!" Amos had written. "The day of the Lord is darkness and not light"—an opinion surely corroborated by the gruesome calamities to which the Book of Revelation points as signs of the end.[18] The millennial hope is a paradoxical one, making the persecution of the saints essential to their victory and a time of judgment the precondition to an age of fulfillment. From this ambiguous conjunction of themes and obscure images one can extrapolate a dismal or optimistic view of history, encompassing temporal disasters, or progress, or both. Accordingly one's activity in the world can be equally varied. Efforts to seize the Kingdom by violence, passive withdrawal from corruption to await the Second Coming or melioristic reform efforts—all these and other responses have been adduced from eschatological symbols.[19]

---

Charles I. Foster, *An Errand of Mercy: The Evangelical United Front, 1790–1837;* Clifford S. Griffin, *Their Brothers' Keeper: Moral Stewardship in the United States, 1800–1865;* and Smith, *Revivalism and Social Reform.* The least pleasant aspect of Protestant social activism is told in Ray A. Billington, *The Protestant Crusade, 1800–1860: A Study in the Origins of American Nativism.*

17. William Cogswell, *The Harbinger of the Millennium,* pp. 299–300. For other samples of Protestant thinking on the millennium, consult Joseph Emerson, *Lectures on the Millennium,* and Samuel Hopkins, *A Treatise on the Millennium.*

18. Amos 5:18

19. I am greatly indebted to James W. Davidson, "Eschatology in New England: 1700–1763" (Ph.D. diss., Yale University, 1973), for his treatment

In an effort to understand what was hidden in the counsel of God, most antebellum expositors turned to postmillennialism, the technical term designating the belief that Jesus will return to earth after the millennium. Jonathan Edwards was among the first prominent Americans to espouse this point of view, and by 1859 one writer asserted without fear of contradiction that the theory was "the commonly received doctrine" in the United States.[20] As usually interpreted in the mid-nineteenth century, this idea meant that the millennial age would not be utterly new but would arise out of the present labors of the church. Advocates argued that this promise of success gave impetus to every good work, and they believed that the Kingdom was already growing in the contemporary triumphs of missions, social reform, science, the arts, and democracy. Within the major denominations were also a few premillennialists who taught that Jesus must return in the flesh before the golden age. Although critics argued that this position destroyed the motive for action—after all, why struggle for a victory that cannot be won until Christ comes back?—its partisans, unlike such radical adventists as the Millerites, did not withdraw into an isolated posture and were not laggards in support of the same evangelical causes that the majority endorsed. Thus, except for the sectarian movements, George Marsden's observation is generally accurate: "The differences between the millennial views in the pre–Civil War era appear to have been less important than the similarities of the militant apocalyptic imagery shared by most American Protestants."[21]

of the ambiguities inherent in millennial symbolism. See also Sylvia Thrupp's introductory essay in *Millennial Dreams in Action*, pp. 11–27.

20. "History of Opinions Respecting the Millennium," *American Theological Review* 1 (November 1859): 655.

21. George M. Marsden, *The Evangelical Mind and the New School Presbyterian Experience: A Case Study of Thought and Theology in Nineteenth-Century America*, p. 197. In contradistinction to the few premillennial spokesmen in the major denominations, most radical sectarian adventists do appear to have adopted a pessimistic and apolitical stance vis-à-vis the Republic. Even here, however, one must qualify the argument carefully. In his splendid essay "Adventism and the American Experience" in *Rise of Adventism*, ed. Gaustad, Jonathan M. Butler shows how post-Millerite Adventism gradually emerged from a withdrawn posture to espouse a more positive view of American culture and to participate more actively therein. The scholarship of Butler, David-

Yet their activism and general optimism notwithstanding, the churches did not completely forget the darker side of the Apocalypse. National sins provoked warnings that the day of the Lord would bring wrath as well as deliverance and that America could become a fearful example of retribution unless it repented. But the United States might stand above the travail by turning to God. Surveying the condition of the world in 1827, Lyman Beecher concluded that "revolutions and convulsions are doubtless indispensable" to the coming of the millennium. "He that sitteth upon the throne must 'overturn and overturn' before his rights and the rights of man will be restored. Revolutions, of course, are predicted such as shall veil the sun, and turn the moon into blood, and shake the earth with the violence of nation against nation, until every despotic government shall be thrown down and chaos resume its pristine reign, and the Spirit of God shall move again upon the face of the deep and bring out a new creation." Gloom and doom certainly abound here; but Beecher quickly moved on to note that America, if faithful to its calling, would escape the cataclysm for God had appointed the Republic to be the lofty example by which the broken fragments of the former order would be reconstituted.[22] When revivalist Lorenzo Dow discussed contemporary signs that the woes of the Apocalypse were being fulfilled, he too held out the hope that the United States might be spared tribulation. "I do not believe," he concluded, "that a country was ever given up to the sword and destruction where *pure religion* was on the progression; therefore, we need to pray for peace that we may be kept from the deluge of the *old* world which is fast progressing."[23] The millennium, in short, was viewed simultaneously as promise and as

---

son, and Marsden provides a needed caution against drawing too neat a dichotomy between a hopeful, activistic postmillennialism and a pessimistic, socially disengaged premillennialism. Although that typology works relatively well in many instances, especially in the context of nineteenth-century American evangelicalism, we need, in Butler's words, "more subtle models" if we are to understand better the nuances of millennialism.

22. Lyman Beecher, "The Memory of Our Fathers," quoted in Hudson, ed., *Nationalism and Religion in America,* p. 101.

23. Lorenzo Dow, *History of Cosmopolite: or the Writings of Rev. Lorenzo Dow,* p. 537.

threat: a special mission awaited the redeemer nation, but it would suffer wrath if it proved false to its vocation. The intense evangelical enterprise of the antebellum period was thus an expression of anxiety as well as hope.

The method of that endeavor was to make the American people fit for their high responsibilities and for republican society through moral persuasion. In his classic *Religion in America* (1844), Robert Baird asserted that men "must first acquiesce with submission in the government of God before they can yield a willing obedience to the requirements of human government."[24] No postulate was more fundamental to Protestant social thought, and its logic deserves close attention. Every society requires defined rules of order. Under an authoritarian regime, these limits can largely be enforced by fiat or external coercion; but where citizens rule themselves, the only effective constraint demands voluntary acceptance. Unchristianized, the people of a democracy easily fall prey to natural depravity and make liberty the occasion of anarchy. Thus the evangelical community believed that republicanism was viable only where the citizenry was internally disciplined by the moral sanctions of religion. According to Philip Schaff, the secret of American greatness lay in the fact that "the impulse towards freedom and the sense of law and order are inseparably united, and both rest on a moral basis."[25] Voluntary submission to the government of God provided the common ground upon which liberty and order might join hands. How to advance the government of God was not, however, a subject of universal agreement.

Protestants often suggested that evangelism alone would alleviate all social ills. In a widely read devotional tract, Baptist Henry Clay Fish argued: "The Gospel comes to one alone, and saves that single man, and holds him responsible for certain duties. It converts the individual. Other religions seek to convert men by masses. Resort is had to the edict, and the sword, that as nations they may at once submit. But the religion of Christ converts men one by one,— sanctifying a single heart, reforming a single life, elevating a single

---

24. Robert Baird, *Religion in America*, ed. Henry Warner Bowden, p. 153.
25. Philip Schaff, *America: A Sketch of Its Political, Social, and Religious Character*, ed. Perry Miller, p. 47.

character,—and thus operates upward and outward through the mass of humanity, just as the particle of leaven to which it is likened operates upon the particle lying next to itself, and it upon another, until the whole lump is leavened."[26] Once citizens were inspired by religion to act morally, every person would do his duty, and the social order, like a well-constructed machine with each part in place, would function properly. Sidney Mead has aptly character- ized this attitude as the "principle of automatic harmony"—faith that no ultimate conflict could exist among free people constrained by the Spirit.[27] By this logic, tinkering with the social order was unnecessary. In 1849 the *Christian Advocate and Journal* ridiculed Fourierist socialism and kindred reform schemes because they assumed that the human condition might be bettered by eliminating the "artificial and unnatural construction" of the social order. To the *Advocate* this attitude was nonsense. Since the dislocations of society sprang from the "depravity of its members," evangelism alone was "God's instrumentality" to remedy these ills. Once human nature was set right, institutional equilibrium would follow automatically. "When society is imbued with the spirit of Chris- tianity," said the editor, "*it will come to order*—wrong and oppres- sion of every kind, with all arbitrary and unnatural distinctions will be annihilated."[28]

The commitment to build a republic of free people, each made suitable for democracy by inward submission to the divine will, could move with equal logic in another direction. In exalting the direct reign of God in the hearts of men, Protestants implicitly dethroned all intermediate authorities. Here was a potential rationale for assault against all arbitrary barriers and customs that impeded the society of free people.[29] Edward Beecher suggested in 1835

26. Henry C. Fish, *Primitive Piety Revived, or the Aggressive Power of the Christian Church*, p. 195.

27. Sidney E. Mead, *The Lively Experiment: The Shaping of Christianity in America*, p. 100. Mead borrows the concept from Paul Tillich. For additional thoughts on the relationship of the free individual to the social order, see Ralph Henry Gabriel, *The Course of American Democratic Thought*, esp. pp. 12–39.

28. *Christian Advocate and Journal*, July 5, 1849, p. 106.

29. My thoughts concerning this ambivalence within antebellum Protestant- ism have been greatly provoked by Lewis Perry, *Radical Abolitionism: Anar-*

that the Christian's task was "not merely to preach the gospel to every creature, but to reorganize human society in accordance with the law of God. To abolish all corruptions in religion and all abuses in the social system and, so far as it has been erected on false principles, to take it down and erect it anew."[30] As Charles G. Finney explained in his *Lectures on Revivals of Religion,* the conversion of sinners did not mark the end of the Christian life but rather the beginning of a career of practical service to further God's

_____

*chy and the Government of God in Antislavery Thought.* Perry argues that stress upon the "pre-emptive sovereignty of God" created an ambiguity within abolitionist thought. On one hand, radical antislavery spokesmen rejected the peculiar institution as an instance of the illegitimate coercive government of men. This aspect of the abolitionist critique led to nonresistance, anarchism, and the rejection on principle of all political solutions to social problems. On the other hand, the concept of the reign of God raised troublesome questions about the validity of an idealistic anarchism. In a yet imperfect world, rejection of human government might increase arbitrary, lawless power and thus actually drive the political order even further from the divine rule. Furthermore, hostility to a particular instance of coercion—namely, slavery—increasingly made millennial utopianism into a secular reform movement that could not avoid the programmatic issue of means, including possible violence. In short, the belief in God's sovereignty yielded contradictory prescriptions for the diseases of society.

The similarity (as well as the difference) between Perry's model and my own is readily apparent. We both see tensions within the doctrine of the moral government of God as the source of contrary solutions to the problems of the social order, but our focuses of study are different. Perry is preoccupied with the minority antislavery vanguard, and thus for him the central dynamic is between a radical utopian rejection of human government and a compromising acceptance of political tools as necessary to secular reform. Since my concern is mainline Protestantism, a somewhat different debate arises. No significant voices within the major denominations attacked the validity of human government; rather the issue was how the political order could be made subject to the reign of God. Did the Christian fulfill his responsibility by evangelism, or was he also obliged to agitate for the reform of specific evils? Although advocates sometimes took one position to the exclusion of the other, these answers should generally be conceived as the poles of a continuum, most churchmen placing themselves at some point between the extremes. As Perry notes in his concluding remarks, the running argument between Billy Graham and his liberal critics (pp. 306–07), indicates the perennial relevance to social thought of the ambiguities within the doctrine of the "pre-emptive sovereignty of God."

30. Quoted in Smith, *Revivalism and Social Reform,* p. 225.

Kingdom. "Young converts should be taught to do all their duty," he opined. "They should never rest satisfied till they have done their duty of every kind. . . . They should set out with a determination to aim at being useful in the highest degree possible."[31] To add specificity to his admonition, Finney noted those social evils to whose eradication "useful" work would address itself—among others, slavery, intemperance, and inadequate education. Finney remained primarily a winner of souls until his life's close and never connected himself with the various reform movements that owed so much to his influence, but he had sketched in almost classic form the evangelical imperative for social activism: that the moral energy unleashed by Christianity had to be channeled into the reform of specific abuses.

The ambiguity within the churches' program for the Kingdom can be traced along another divide: whether the citizen's duty was to maintain the Constitution and the political unity of the United States or to apply a higher moral standard to the nation's life.[32] Because it embodied the hopes of humanity, the Union became for many an object of transcendent worth to be preserved at all costs. According to this view, the patriot should seek to protect America's political institutions, not to reform them by ill-advised schemes that might jeopardize the precious good already achieved. On the death of President William Henry Harrison, Bishop Leonidas L. Hamline of the Methodist Church assessed the citizen's responsibility in these terms: "No government excels our own. Its prominent features are so nearly what one might desire that there is small chance for improvement. . . . It is clearly inferred that we have no acquisition to make on this score. Yet there is something for us to do. Our office is to preserve, not to create. This last our fathers did. Sacred be the work of their hands. Heaven grant us the wisdom and

31. Charles Grandison Finney, *Lectures on Revivals of Religion*, ed. William G. McLoughlin, pp. 403–04. A classic study of the indebtedness of antislavery thought to evangelical Protestantism is Gilberts Hobbs Barnes, *The Anti-Slavery Impulse, 1830–1844*.
32. This dichotomy is traced in Paul C. Nagel, *This Sacred Trust: American Nationality, 1798–1898*, pp. 129–93. For a more detailed account of the rise of the conception of the Union as an object of transcendent worth, see Nagel's *One Nation Indivisible: The Union in American Thought, 1776–1861*.

the grace not to destroy what they constructed."[33] Some Protestants, however, were restive as keepers of the ark of the Union. Gilbert Haven, a coreligionist of Hamline, observed caustically at the passage of the Fugitive Slave Act: "It has become too much the fashion of late to center all moral excellence and national prosperity in the Constitution. . . . In Christ, not in the Constitution, must we put our trust."[34] Not many Protestants were willing to go all the way with William Lloyd Garrison and denounce the federal government as a compact with the devil; but leaders such as Haven represented a growing sentiment, particularly in the last decade before the Civil War, that mere survival of the United States intact did not constitute a patriotism lofty enough to command respect. America bore the promise of the millennium not as a perfected social order but rather as a principle in the process of realization. To fulfill its destiny, the United States first had to subject itself to that higher law which alone gave meaning to national election. Anything could be sacrificed to preserve the Union, said Francis Wayland, except "truth and justice and liberty. When I must surrender these as the price of the union, the union becomes at once a thing I abhor."[35]

The tragedy of American patriotism in the waning years of the antebellum period was the increasingly fierce controversy "among those claiming that stewardship meant unquestioning acceptance of America as a system and those who demanded a stewardship aggressive in behalf of cherished values and principles."[36] In the congressional debates before the passage of the Compromise of 1850, Daniel Webster urged mutual conciliation as a way to save the sacred federal compact, but William Seward replied that above the Constitution was a higher law prohibiting deviation from principle. The two senators spoke past one another, and their impasse symbolized the dilemma of the entire nation. If the Union had to be main-

33. F. G. Hibbard, ed., *Works of Rev. Leonidas Hamline, D.D.: Sermons,* pp. 399–400.

34. Gilbert Haven, *National Sermons,* pp. 28–29. The significance of Haven's life and work is analyzed in a recent study by William Gravely, *Gilbert Haven, Methodist Abolitionist: A Study in Race, Religion, and Reform, 1850–1880.*

35. Quoted in Cole, *Social Ideas of the Northern Evangelists,* p. 216.

36. Nagel, *This Sacred Trust,* p. 131.

tained inviolate to preserve America as an instrument for mission, it could be asked with equal justice what mission remained to a people that prostituted itself to the service of ignoble ends.

These tensions within the conception of national purpose were exacerbated by sectionalism and the debate over slavery within the churches. Between 1837 and 1845 the Presbyterian, Methodist, and Baptist denominations were split, although for the Presbyterians the slavery question was intermixed with complex issues of theology and church polity.[37] In each schism the spirited argument about the South's peculiar institution revealed the divided mind of Protestantism on the propriety of denouncing particular social abuses. An allied question, particularly significant in the Old School-New School clash within the Presbyterian Church, concerned the role of the interdenominational voluntary societies. Conservatives resisted what they deemed the irresponsible activities of the "united front," and their objection raised pointedly the issue of the church's role in society: was its function merely to provide an ecclesiastical roof for various reform enterprises or to evangelize the nation through the established ministries of preaching and the sacraments? These divisions within the churches reflected the fundamental dilemma of broadly representative denominations within a free society. On controversial issues, these bodies could move neither too far ahead nor lag too far behind their constituencies lest disaffected minorities secede. In a time of general agreement, the problem might be minimal, but in an era of contradictory commitments, unity could be purchased only by moral platitudes and purity by schism. The inability of Protestants to agree whether the American promise was a sacred polity to be preserved or a higher law to be obeyed represented the impotence of moral suasion in face of the crisis besetting the nation.

Although denominational disagreements occurred primarily along North-South lines—the Presbyterian rupture is an exception—the schism was reenacted in varying ways among Northern churchmen. Charles I. Foster has spoken of the disintegration of the evangelical

37. For accounts of these schisms, see Marsden, *Evangelical Mind*, pp. 59–87; Donald G. Mathews, *Slavery and Methodism: A Chapter in American Morality, 1780–1845*, esp. pp. 246–82; and Robert G. Torbet, *A History of the Baptists*, rev. ed., pp. 282–97.

united front after 1837.[38] That diagnosis is misleading if it is taken to suggest that the array of benevolent activities that distinguished Protestant life in the three preceding decades disappeared. The tract, missionary, and reform societies for the most part maintained their work; and where they faltered, the slack was taken up by denominational agencies. In fact, much of the work that had been done on an interdenominational basis was undertaken after 1840 by the communions themselves.[39] What was disappearing was the integrating center that gave a sense of participation in one united evangelical crusade to bring in the millennium. The hosts of the Lord had divided. After the 1830s the major denominations could be certain of internal strife over the issue of slavery; and the large voluntary associations encountered strident opposition to their policy of avoiding the question. For example, in 1844 the American Missionary Association was founded by a group of abolitionists no longer willing to accept what they regarded as the time-serving policies of the American Board of Commissioners for Foreign Missions, and the American Tract Society was subjected to a steady drumfire of criticism for its failure to issue an antislavery statement.[40]

Even among the outspoken critics of slavery, the process of disintegration took place. The original American Anti-Slavery Society

38. Foster, *Errand of Mercy*, pp. 249–74.

39. After 1837 the amity between Presbyterians and Congregationalists— the spirit of the 1801 Plan of Union—was severely strained. See Marsden, *Evangelical Mind*, pp. 104–41, and Williston Walker, *A History of the Congregational Churches in the United States*, pp. 370–426. The effect of this development upon the Home Mission movement is traced in Goodykoontz, *Home Missions on the American Frontier*, pp. 298–301. A mark of the time was the organization by Baptists of their own Bible Society in 1837. See Torbet, *History of the Baptists*, p. 279. Methodists after 1844 became increasingly absorbed in denominational squabbles with their Southern brethren over the fate of the Border State Conferences and the disposition of their publishing house. This story is told in Emory Stevens Bucke, ed., *The History of American Methodism*, 2: 159–67, 177–81.

40. On the AMA, see Augustus Field Beard, *A Crusade of Brotherhood: A History of the American Missionary Association*, pp. 1–32. A good example of the pressure to which the American Tract Society was subjected is found in Robert M. York, *George B. Cheever, Religious and Social Reformer, 1807–1890*, pp. 156–57.

lasted intact only seven years until 1840 witnessed the departure of its more conservative and church-oriented wing. In the two succeeding decades, the moral passion of abolitionism spilled over into political action in the form of the Liberty, the Free Soil, and finally the Republican party; but commitment to moral suasion as the appropriate path to reform was so deeply imbedded in the American conscience that the translation of the struggle into the slippery realm of electoral politics prompted soul-searching debate.[41] The slavery question, of course, was not the only issue that polarized conflict between the supporters of moral versus political reform. The discontent of many friends of the temperance movement when former colleagues launched a campaign for prohibitory legislation is a case in point.[42] Nevertheless, the arguments among antislavery leaders illustrate most clearly the divided mind of antebellum reform and suggest the pervasive uncertainty about the meaning and future of American nationality. That the millennium was coming few would question. What citizens should do in the interim, however, had become an open question.

Political events after 1840 deepened the agony. The Texas question and the war with Mexico severely divided the country. Although some Northern Protestants endorsed the conflict heartily, much ecclesiastical support was lukewarm or perfunctory, and a sizable number unsparingly denounced "the present unrighteous war" as a ploy for the expansion of slave territory.[43] After Congress passed the Fugitive Slave Act in 1850, hundreds of clergy—many previously untainted with abolitionism—vowed disobedience to

41. Among the many works on the antislavery movement, the following have been particularly helpful to me: Martin Duberman, ed., *The Antislavery Vanguard: New Essays on the Abolitionists;* Louis Filler, *The Crusade Against Slavery, 1830-1860;* Aileen S. Kraditor, *Means and Ends in American Abolitionism: Garrison and His Critics on Strategy and Tactics, 1834-1850;* Perry, *Radical Abolitionism;* and Bertram Wyatt-Brown, *Lewis Tappan and the Evangelical War Against Slavery.*

42. John Allen Krout, *The Origins of Prohibition,* esp. pp. 153-81.

43. Resolution of the New School Presbyterian Synod of Indiana as quoted in Clayton Sumner Ellsworth, "The American Churches and the Mexican War," *American Historical Review* 45 (January 1940): 301-26. See also Bodo, *Protestant Clergy and Public Issues,* pp. 216-32.

this statute requiring the return of escaped bondsmen.[44] In this situation, the darker elements of biblical prophecy acquired new timeliness, and many spoke of judgment, catastrophe, and conflict rolling toward climactic resolution. In her conclusion to *Uncle Tom's Cabin*, Harriet Beecher Stowe surveyed the paralysis of the national will in the face of slavery and concluded that the "wrath of Almighty God" would soon descend upon America if it did not respond to the brief "day of grace" that yet remained. Using the eschatological imagery of Malachi 3, she urged the religious community to discern the lateness of the hour: "O Church of Christ, read the signs of the times! Is not this power the spirit of HIM whose kingdom is yet to come, and whose will is to be done on earth as it is in heaven? But who may abide the day of his appearing? 'For that day shall burn as an oven: and he shall appear as a swift witness against those that oppress the hireling in his wages, the widow and the fatherless, and that turn aside the stranger in his right: and he shall break in pieces the oppressor!'"[45]

The succeeding years of crisis, marked off by the Kansas-Nebraska question, the Dred Scott decision, and John Brown's raid scarcely diminished the force of Stowe's prophecy; by the end of the decade the notes of the last trumpet were heard by many churchmen. In early 1859 a writer in the *American Theological Review* concluded: "The plot of the world's great drama has long been thickening: but everything indicates that its denouement is at hand. And it would seem probable that it will be made in this land. Here probably is to be fought the great battle of principles—not merely for ourselves, but for the world; freedom struggling against arbitrary power; learning with ignorance and superstition; and spiritual religion, with that which is formal and false. The aspect of the times, also, indicates that the struggle may reach its culminating point during this century. Already we hear the roll of the drum, the clangor of the trumpet, and the shout of captains, concentrating and marshal-

44. The effect of the Fugitive Slave Act upon Northern Protestant opinion is discussed in Chester A. Dunham, *The Attitude of the Northern Clergy Toward the South, 1860–1865*, pp. 28–34.

45. Harriet Beecher Stowe, *Uncle Tom's Cabin*, p. 476. Mrs. Stowe's use of Malachi 3 is a paraphrased abridgment.

ling the hosts."[46] A special burden had always rested upon God's model republic, but now the supreme test in which its destiny would be finally vindicated or forever lost loomed in view. "Every citizen, every lover of his country, every man of God," announced the Reverend D. W. Clark, "must gird himself for the contest" in the awesome knowledge that here "in our land and in our age" the forces of righteousness will "achieve their grandest triumph or experience their most disastrous defeat."[47]

God himself appeared to pour out his Spirit to prepare his people for the test. In the midst of a severe economic reversal in late 1857, noonday prayer meetings sponsored by the New York YMCA in the Fulton Street Dutch Reformed Church began drawing overflow crowds. The success of these services prompted their imitation in churches throughout the city and, soon, the United States. By spring the press carried daily accounts of a nationwide revival of unprecedented character. Unlike earlier seasons of the spirit, which had erupted into divisiveness, this revival won the endorsement of virtually the entire clergy, and every denomination from the Presbyterian (Old School) to the Unitarian experienced significant awakenings in its midst.[48] Protestants later recalled these tokens as a "providential preparation for the Civil War," and that interpretation is largely faithful to the eschatological significance that its contemporaries attached to the revival.[49] One commentator in the *National Preacher* assessed the awakening's significance in these terms: "God is only waiting to see us ready for the march. Much territory is yet to be possessed. One strong, united earnest effort to return to God in the spirit of a true consecration, and the voice of God is ready to break out from the mercy-seat, saying: 'Rise and go forward!'

46. "The United States a Commissioned Missionary Nation," *American Theological Review* 1 (January 1859): 172.

47. D. W. Clark, "Educate the People," *Ladies' Repository* 20 (October 1860): 592.

48. For further information on the prayer meeting revival, see Russell E. Francis, "Pentecost: 1858" (Ph.D. diss., University of Pennsylvania, 1948), and Carl L. Spicer, "The Great Awakening of 1857 and 1858" (Ph.D. diss., Ohio State University, 1935). A good synopsis of the revival is found in Smith, *Revivalism and Social Reform,* pp. 63–69.

49. Frank Grenville Beardsley, *A History of American Revivals,* 3d ed., p. 238.

Now, let my Spirit go forth. Let souls be awakened. Let the Jordan be crossed. Let the tall Anakims be slain. Let Christ have his inheritance and my people their millennium."[50] After 1858 Protestants sang a new hymn inspired by the revival. George Duffield, Jr., summoned his fellow Christians to the final impending conflict.

> Stand up, stand up for Jesus,
> The trumpet call obey;
> Forth to the mighty conflict
> In this His glorious day.
>
> Stand up, stand up for Jesus,
> The strife will not be long
> This day the noise of battle;
> The next the victor's song.[51]

What the trumpet call ordered was far from clear, and the prayer meetings shed little light upon the subject. The YMCA advertised its services with the slogan, "No controverted points discussed"—a restriction scrupulously observed by leaders who excluded the slavery question from the revival hall.[52] Its indeterminate character allowed one to see in the awakening whatever vision he wished for the American future. Horace Greeley and Harriet Beecher Stowe might regard the spiritual excitement as the genesis of an abolitionist uprising, but a conservative Democrat like publisher John W. Forney of Pennsylvania could believe with equal justice that "the present great awakening" would "harmonize sectional differences" and thereby save the Union from destruction by fanatics.[53]

50. E. S. Wright, "The Cloud and the Tabernacle," *National Preacher*, n.s. 2 (March 1859): 84.
51. See Edward S. Ninde, *The Story of the American Hymn*, pp. 215–22. Duffield was inspired to write the hymn by the dying words of his friend and fellow participant in the revival, the Reverend Stephen H. Tyng, Jr.: "Tell them, 'Let us all stand up for Jesus.'" During the Civil War this song was one of the favorites of the Union troops. Although Duffield was a premillennialist, the wide popularity of the hymn testifies that its affirmations were not considered incompatible with the crusading postmillennialism of the Protestant majority.
52. C. Howard Hopkins, *History of the Y.M.C.A. in North America*, p. 82.
53. Francis, "Pentecost: 1858," pp. 99, 166–67.

This ambiguity was symptomatic of the national mood in the twilight of the antebellum years. Everyone sensed the imminence of crisis, perhaps of catastrophe, but there were no commonly accepted marching orders as struggle loomed in view. The situation represented a failure for the churches. They had launched evangelical crusades to make the United States a fit millennial instrument and had hoped to turn aside the divine judgments that harried other peoples; but after seven decades under the federal Union, their efforts had not prevented moral confusion and political disorder. Thus the Lord of hosts would himself have to intervene in a dramatic and perhaps terrible way if the Kingdom of God were to come in America. Years later in his portrait of Lincoln's Sangamon County in the late 1850s, Francis Grierson recalled a time of hope, mingled with uncertain fear, as his countrymen awaited an answer to the unresolved problem of American nationality.

> In the late 'Fifties the people of Illinois were being prepared for the new era by a series of scenes and incidents which nothing but the term "mystical" will fittingly describe. Things came about not so much by preconceived method as by an impelling impulse. The appearance of "Uncle Tom's Cabin" was not a reason, but an illumination; the founding of the Republican party was not an act of political wire-pulling, but an inspiration; the great religious revivals and the appearance of two comets were not regarded as coincidences, but accepted as signs of divine preparation and warning. . . . It was impossible to tell what a day might bring forth. The morning usually began with new hope and courage; but the evening brought back the old silences, with the old, unsolved questionings, strange presentiments, premonitions, sudden alarms.[54]

Before the "new era" came, those "unsolved questionings" would grow yet more acute.

54. Francis Grierson, *The Valley of Shadows: Recollections of the Lincoln Country, 1858–1863,* pp. 1–2.

# 1

# From Confusion to Crusade

By the winter of 1860–61 the plight of the nation had become fully apparent. The Democrats were hopelessly divided into Northern and Southern wings, and the Republican party had elected its first president on a purely sectional basis. Although Lincoln tempered his opposition to the extension of slavery by a promise to respect the institution where it already existed, the South regarded such assurances as illusory. On 20 December South Carolina seceded. and by late February six more states had withdrawn from the Union to form the Confederate States of America. The federal government was paralyzed by the crisis. Alternately lecturing the South on the illegality of secession and wringing his hands because he had no authority to stop it, President James Buchanan successfully alienated almost every sector of public opinion. Senator John Crittenden of Kentucky suggested the restoration of the Missouri Compromise, and others proposed a constitutional convention. These were futile gestures, for the departed states had already made an irrevocable choice, and the incoming administration was uninterested in any compromise that might repudiate the platform on which it had come to power. When Lincoln assumed office on 4 March 1861, he pledged his government to enforce the laws "in all the States." Beyond this aim, he would attempt no coercion. "There will be no invasion," said the president.[1] It was, however, not clear how the first item could be achieved without resort to the second.

The cautious policy of the central government under two presidents reflected the lack of a national consensus that would sustain military action against the Confederacy. Many citizens, especially those in large metropolitan business firms with Southern invest-

1. Roy P. Basler, ed., *Abraham Lincoln: His Speeches and Writings*, p. 583.

ments, advocated sectional conciliation, and that policy received venerable support from the Websterian notion of a sacred Union worthy of any compromise. On the other hand, a majority within the free states had voted for a presidential candidate opposed to the extension of slavery, and they were not willing to throw away their victory. Confident that secession had been the work of a small conspiracy, they believed that a show of Yankee determination would bring the Southern majority to its senses and that the Confederacy would collapse without the firing of a shot. The few who did contemplate a permanent dismemberment of the Union wondered if the result might not prove a disguised blessing, freeing the North from the taint of slavery. A divided public, in short, could agree on only one point: the inadvisability of armed intervention in the South. The restrictions imposed by popular opinion and the need to secure the loyalty of the border states effectively limited the president's options to tactical maneuvers. Lincoln strove to ensure that if war did come, its terms might promote Northern unanimity. Whether by artifice or bungling, he accomplished this goal. Northern unity and a holy crusade emerged out of the mouth of a cannon in Charleston harbor.[2]

### INITIAL RESPONSES TO SECESSION

During the presidential interregnum, the threat of national dismemberment prompted numerous clerical pleas for reason and forbearance. "The Union," explained Henry A. Boardman to his Philadelphia congregation, "is too sacred a trust to be sacrificed except upon the most imperative grounds. It has cost too much blood and treasure: it is freighted with too much happiness for this great nation: it is too closely linked with the cause of human liberty, and with the salvation of the world. To destroy it at the bidding of passion; to destroy it until every practicable means for preserving it has

2. Of the many works available on this subject, see especially, William R. Brock, *Conflict and Transformation: The United States, 1844–1877*, pp. 170–215; David M. Potter, *Lincoln and His Party in the Secession Crisis;* and Kenneth W. Stampp, *And the War Came: The North and the Secession Crisis, 1860–1861.*

been tried and exhausted, would be a crime of appalling turpitude against patriotism, against religion, and against humanity."[3]

To avoid that disaster, would-be conciliators offered various remedies to mollify the South. A circular letter signed by various clergy in the New York-Philadelphia area decried the inflammatory rhetoric that supposedly characterized many pulpits, North and South, and urged Southern Christians to join in an open-minded and conciliatory regard for the feelings of those in all sections of the country.[4] A widely disseminated sermon by Old School Presbyterian Henry J. Van Dyke of Brooklyn branded abolitionism as "the great mischief maker between the North and the South, . . . the great stumbling block in the way of a peaceful settlement of our difficulties." Although he professed loyalty to the principle of free speech, Van Dyke proposed rigorous slander laws to bridle the "utterance of libellous words" from antislavery zealots. Such would be a minor sacrifice compared to the imminent dissolution "amid confused noise, and garments rolled in blood" of the "brightest prospect the world ever beheld."[5] Others suggested that the North might demonstrate good faith by altering the laws that the South deemed a violation of its constitutional rights. Several free states had adopted so-called personal liberty laws that forbade state officials from enforcing the Fugitive Slave Act. The *Presbyterian* observed: "If our present government is to be perpetuated, nullification, in all its forms, must be abandoned on all sides. The few Northern states which have adopted personal liberty bills, thereby, to all intents and purposes, setting at naught the provision of the Constitution guarantying protection to the South, should recede from this legis-

3. Henry A. Boardman, *What Christianity Demands of Us at the Present Crisis,* "A Sermon Preached on Thanksgiving Day, November 29, 1860," p. 27.

4. Lewis G. Vander Velde, *The Presbyterian Churches and the Federal Union, 1861–1869,* pp. 32–33.

5. Henry J. Van Dyke, *The Character and Influence of Abolitionism* "A Sermon Preached in the First Presbyterian Church, Brooklyn, on Sabbath Evening December 9th, 1860," pp. 26–28, 35, 38. For further discussion, see my "Henry J. Van Dyke, Sr.: Conservative Apostle of a Broad Church," *Journal of Presbyterian History* 50 (Spring 1972): 19–38.

lation. They must revert to the Constitution as it is, or not complain
if the South, in equal disregard of the Constitution, should take
measures to protect itself."[6] If this measure should prove insufficient, a few were prepared to move to the ultimate compromise:
a constitutional convention that would ensure the perpetuity of
slavery where it already existed. No sacrifice could be too great,
in the words of a New Hampshire clergyman, for a Union that was
"the palladium of your political safety and prosperity."[7]

The advocates of compromise believed that disunionists, whether
of the Garrisonian or Confederate variety, were a small, self-serving
band who could be isolated by a prudent majority. In an article
published in the *Methodist Quarterly Review* shortly before the
November election, Reverend J. Townley Crane offered the conservative analysis: "In our national legislature there is a little faction
of agitators, who aim at the dismemberment of the Union. They are
not numerous, or influential, nor do they represent any important
division of the nation."[8] As secession began this reassuring argument
was reiterated to suggest that the movement was a minority effort
destined to failure unless the North foolishly provoked Southern
feeling. The best counsel for the present, asserted the *Presbyterian,*
was to avoid any action that might lead to confrontation: "If South
Carolina in its ill-judged enterprise is determined to set up a government for itself, and if, through her example, several other States
should also prove recreant, it is a question whether they should not
be foreborne with without conceding the right of secession, while
they try their impracticable experiment, and wait for the inevitable
disastrous results of it, rather than precipitate a war, which might
involve the Border states that we might readily retain. Such forbearance, in the long run, would promote and strengthen our future
union."[9]

From our vantage point the deep-seated sectional animosities may
appear to have predetermined an irrepressible conflict before which

6. *Presbyterian,* December 15, 1860, p. 198.

7. Nathaniel Bouton, *Days of Adversity,* "A New Year's Sermon Preached
in Concord, N.H., January 6, 1861," p. 20.

8. J. Townley Crane, "Party Politics," *Methodist Quarterly Review* 42
(October 1860): 577.

9. *Presbyterian,* January 12, 1861, p. 6.

the optimism of the *Presbyterian* and kindred spokesmen looks naive; but in the winter of 1860, a people desperate for hope could see an inviting plausibility to this logic. Pockets of nationalist sentiment had been disclosed in most of the seceded states; and until Lincoln requested volunteers after the bombardment at Fort Sumter, only seven states in the Deep South had left the Union. Had the Confederacy not been ultimately strengthened by the addition of the Upper South, primarily Virginia, it would have remained a weak, truncated political unit with a doubtful future. After a trip through the South in these months, the aging Methodist preacher Heman Bangs surveyed the uncertainties of the moment and summed up the conservative credo: avoid "rash judgment" and await the decision of God in future events.[10]

This call fell upon a Protestant community impatient with further accommodation. Numerous churchmen believed that a Union purchased at the price of another compromise with slave interests would forfeit the respect of true patriots. Few used stronger language than Lester Williams, Jr., of Holden, Massachusetts. Commenting upon President Buchanan's January 4 Fast Day, Williams noted acerbically:

> For the continuance of this Union we are exhorted to pray. Can we do it? Can we in conscience? Let us see. Once the Union of the States meant something. It meant fraternity, mutual regard, forbearance, sympathy, brotherly help. . . . What is the Union worth to-day? Every good thing pertaining to it is sacrificed to *one* thing in one half of the country. Trade, Friendship, Comity, Religion, Honor, Civilization, all yield to the clamors of slavery, and are brushed away before it. It is the Dagon god of the South to which everything else must fall down. The wrathful cry is, "Slavery shall have new and stronger guarantees, or the Union shall be dissolved." The Union if it exists, must be made to bear slavery on its shoulders, and so become a bond of iniquity. Shall we be called upon to pray for *such* a Union? I don't believe God can regard with complacency such a prayer. It is too repulsive

10. Heman Bangs, *The Autobiography and Journal of Rev. Heman Bangs,* p. 323.

to all Christian faith to think it. I could as soon pray that Satan might be prospered and his kingdom come.[11]

The sacred trust as defined by the tradition of Webster was now perceived in many quarters as an instrument of evil.

In these polemics the essence of American nationalism was defined as adherence to righteous principles requiring every iniquity to be purged from the land. At a Thanksgiving service in Ellenville, New York, the Reverend Edward Bentley told the Methodist and Dutch Reformed congregations that perpetual "agitation is the inevitable consequence" of the national faith. "This is a Christian nation. It has avowed the Lord to be its God. It has deliberately made God's revealed will its standard of morality, and this agitation is but the utterance of a Christian desire that its conduct should conform to its standard. 'Stop this agitation!' As well command, the national pulse to stop its beating, or the national conscience to sheathe its stings." Bentley was certain that this "throbbing" of the "national heart" would not cease "till this crowning curse and sin is wiped from our national fame."[12]

To persons of Bentley's opinion, the United States represented commitment to a universal ideal. True loyalty to the Republic meant devotion to the mission of spreading freedom and religion throughout the world, and unless the Union promoted these high aims, it ceased to be a legitimate object of reverence. "God is rebuking our idolatry of the Union," Joseph P. Thompson told his audience in the Broadway Tabernacle in New York City. "I value the Union of these States as a means of peace and prosperity to them all. I value the Union and Constitution, as ordained for freedom and justice, and capable of bringing out the highest development of self-government under recognized law." American nationality, however, had become sadly debased; what God intended as a vehicle of his grace was worshipped in its own right. "But some, instead of valuing the Union as the means to the great ends of order, freedom, and peace, have

11. Lester Williams, Jr., *Freedom of Speech and the Union,* "A Discourse Delivered December 30, 1860, at Holden, Mass.," p. 11.

12. Edward W. Bentley, *The Lord Our National God,* "A Sermon Preached Before the United Congregations of the Methodist Episcopal and Reformed Dutch Churches, in the M. E. Church, Ellenville, N.Y., Thursday, November 29th, 1860," pp. 7–8.

glorified it as in itself an END, and have vaunted the Constitution above the 'higher law' of God. When the advocates of Slavery have demanded some palpable wrong under the threat of breaking up the Union, these worshippers of the Union, as such, have conceded the wrong to save the Union. . . . We have assumed that the Union was the perfection of human government, and necessary to the advancement of religion in the world. God is rebuking our pride and idolatry. He is teaching us that no human agency is indispensable to his plans, and that He can overthrow our Constitution with a breath."[13] Thompson, one of the editors of the *Independent*, had for years maddened abolitionist zealots by his cautious antislavery position.[14] His harsh rhetoric indicated the rapidly failing appeal of further political accommodation.

Mere disapproval of slavery did not alone make Northern moderates adamant against further compromise. Although ever larger numbers of Protestants had come to detest the institution as a barbaric anachronism, they were willing to tolerate it, within present limits, in the confidence that it would collapse from internal weakness. Horace Bushnell suggested that the economic unprofitability of slavery would gradually float the system away, and others agreed that if shut up to its present domains, the peculiar institution would be set, in Lincoln's evocative phrase, in the course of ultimate extinction.[15] Northern churchmen were aroused from these optimistic slumbers by the conviction that the South had adopted a concerted rule-or-ruin policy. Unwilling to accept the existing confines of slavery, the Southern leadership demanded that it have unlimited access to all portions of the nation and the unqualified sanction of the federal government. The correspondence of the Northern perception of a slave power conspiracy with the actuality of Southern intention is dubious; and, of course, the latter's counterbias that a sinister cabal of abolitionist forces directed Northern policy departs even further from reality. These beliefs cannot be dismissed as to-

---

13. Joseph P. Thompson, *The President's Fast*, "Preached in the Broadway Tabernacle Church, January 4, 1861," pp. 18–19.

14. Louis Filler, "Liberalism, Anti-Slavery and the Founding of the Independent," *New England Quarterly* 27 (September 1954): 291–306.

15. Horace Bushnell, *The Census and Slavery*, "A Thanksgiving Discourse Delivered in the Chapel at Clifton Springs, N.Y., November 29, 1860."

tally mythic constructions, however. Repeated accusations of malevolence heightened sectional estrangement, drove some to extreme positions, and thus gave the dire warnings a measure of self-fulfillment.[16] The issue for most Northern Protestants had ceased to be whether slavery as a local institution should be grudgingly endured. The struggle now concerned the very core of American nationality: whether the South should be allowed to foist its iniquity upon the entire nation. The answer seemed clear.

D. D. Whedon, the editor of the *Methodist Quarterly Review,* epitomized the shift in mood. In earlier years a conciliator willing to mute his antislavery convictions, he now believed that the nation had been summoned to an irrevocable moral Rubicon. In the April 1861 issue of the *Review,* he tried to set the problem in historical perspective. When the Constitution was adopted, freedom was held to be the normal condition of man, "slavery the dark and terrible exception." Initially all Americans, including Southerners, had accepted this doctrine; but at length the South had sought to make slavery a permanent national institution to which all other interests must submit. Disregarding the threat for decades, the North had finally roused itself from its torpor to save the nation from total humiliation at the hands of the slavocracy.

> But one more national victory of the proslavery Democracy [the Democratic party], and the decision of the Lemmon case would have opened the door to the remanding of slavery to the free states. But one turn still farther of the judicial screw, and emancipation even in our Northern states would have been decided to be subversive of the rights of property and contrary to the Constitution, and the plot would have been completed. Slavery would have been pronounced national; abolitionists and anti-slavery men would have been lynched and hung as freely in New England as in Carolina, and Senator Toombs [of Georgia] might have built his slave-pen under the shadow of Bunker Hill. To such a denouement were we firmly and rapidly marching. From it we were saved, not by the advocates of compromise and pseudo-conservatism, but by fearless hearts and unshrinking voices; by men in Church and State who breasted the

16. For a suggestive analysis of this problem, see Davis, *Slave Power Conspiracy and the Paranoid Style,* esp. pp. 3–31.

brunt of battle and won the victory that culminated in the election of Abraham Lincoln.

The issue had been fairly joined, and no further conciliation could be honorable. Either the North would yield no further ground to the South, or it would submit to "complete subjugation" by the slave power. The latter alternative might indeed preserve the political unity of the nation but it would do so "at the expense of all that renders the Union dear."[17]

A more remarkable conversion occurred in an even less likely quarter. Throughout his long career Charles Hodge, the doyen of Old School Presbyterianism, had vehemently opposed abolitionism and had urged ecclesiastical silence on such secular matters. Yet in the January 1861 issue of the *Princeton Review,* he indicated that his patience, too, had worn thin. Having dominated the national government during most of the Republic's history, Southerners now decided that they could not bear the loss of one election and that they could not "live in any political community which they do not control." This attitude, he concluded, was "unrighteous and unreasonable," a constitutional "impossibility." Hodge insisted that he still abhorred abolition and favored just compromise, but he believed that the South had drawn a line that could not be honorably crossed. Southern intransigence had transformed an essentially political question into a moral imperative. "There are occasions," he suggested, "when political questions rise into the sphere of morals and religion; when the rule for political action is to be sought not in the considerations of state policy, but the law of God."[18] The present crisis was such an occasion. As he prepared his article for the printer, Hodge wrote to his brother that he had become thoroughly disgusted with the "poltroonery of Northern men" who "go down on their knees" before the South. The time had come to take "just ground, and take it firmly."[19]

17. D. D. Whedon, "The State of the Country," *Methodist Quarterly Review* 43 (April 1861): 313–14.

18. Charles Hodge, "The State of the Country," *Biblical Repertory and Princeton Review* 33 (January 1861): 1–36.

19. Archibald Alexander Hodge, *The Life of Charles Hodge, D.D., LL.D.,* p. 463. Although Hodge was fast becoming hardened against the South's position—he voted for both Frémont and Lincoln—his conviction that the church qua church should not address controversial political issues led him to

This attitude indicated a negative program more than a positive one. The opponents of further compromise knew fairly well what they did not want: personal liberty laws should not be rescinded, the Crittenden proposal should be rejected, and the Constitution should not be altered.[20] Left undetermined was what policy the government should pursue in regard to the seceded states: whether they should be permitted to depart in peace, or whether coercion should be employed to retain them.

This painful question was blunted by the continued faith in America's providential mission. When Protestants examined world events, they saw everywhere evidence that the Kingdom of God was hastening among men. Cavour and Garibaldi led the Italian risorgimento that would usher in a democratic era in that land, the papal states teetered on the verge of collapse, and heathen powers relaxed barriers to the missionary. "The redemption of the world draws nigh," observed the *Christian Watchman and Reflector,* "and if our faith and labors go hand in hand, it may be given to our generation to see the knowledge of the Lord covering the earth as the waters cover the sea."[21] With all omens pointing to the progress of Christian civilization, it was inconceivable that the United States should be left behind. Heman Humphrey, one of Congregationalism's most venerable pastors, queried: "Would He have brought us hither and given

---

oppose the 1861 General Assembly's resolution supporting the federal government. Hodge admitted that the Bible enjoined obedience to the "powers that be" but insisted that it did not give the church mandate to determine which of rival claimants to authority was legitimate. Since the Old School Assembly still nominally contained Southern as well as Northern members, he believed that the judicatory was proposing to settle a case belonging in this latter category. At the same time, Hodge avowed that he personally agreed with the sentiments of the resolution and that if it were moved in a lower church court—for example, in his own Synod of New Jersey where churchmen agreed that the Union was the rightful authority—he would vote for it! The unpopularity and complexity of his stand remained a source of embarrassment to Hodge throughout the war. His definitive apologia for his wartime views can be found in "The *Princeton Review* on the State of the Country and the Church," *Biblical Repertory and Princeton Review* 37 (October 1865): 627–57.

20. For representative comments on these issues, see *Christian Advocate and Journal,* January 21, 1861, p. 28, and *Independent,* January 3, 1861, p. 4.

21. *Christian Watchman and Reflector,* February 18, 1861.

us so much work in prospect for bringing in the millennium, if He had intended to pluck us up, just as we are entered upon the work?"[22]

Viewed from this perspective, disunion appeared to be the dying gasp of an exhausted despotism. After the election of Lincoln, Gilbert Haven predicted that the South's intransigence would soon be overcome and that its people would soon breathe "the summer morning air of freedom." "The day is nigh at hand. It has already dawned. It shall speedily arise." And then with the benediction to the Apocalypse, Haven concluded: "Surely I come quickly. Amen! Even so, come, Lord Jesus!"[23] In similar language the *Independent* predicted that Southern resistance presaged the early collapse of the slave power. "Slavery rocks and reels with the premonitory symptoms of its overthrow. If we hold fast our faith in God, we shall see 'greater things than these'—the Son of Man taking to Himself the power over the nations."[24] A few weeks later in opposing the Crittenden compromise, the paper suggested: "This is the last hope of the slave power. After the fourth of March the cry of compromise will be heard no more; the necessity for compromise will be felt no more, the Government will go forward in the exercise of all its Constitutional functions, the slave power will know its place; and, by degrees, business and public affairs will return to their accustomed channels."[25]

As it became clear that the affairs of state would not return to "accustomed channels," many clergy began to suggest that dismemberment of the Union might bring unexpected benefits. D. D. Whedon remarked: "Even disunion has its compensations. It will make us what we have never yet been, fully and consistently a FREE nation. Countless will be the blessings of a full emancipation from the dread evils not only of slavery domination but of union with slaveholders. That disunion will hasten the downfall of slavery and perhaps a reconstruction on a free basis."[26] Cut loose from the

22. Heman Humphrey, *Our Nation,* "A Discourse Delivered at Pittsfield, Mass., January 4, 1861," p. 36.
23. Haven, *National Sermons,* pp. 198, 212.
24. *Independent,* January 3, 1861, p. 4.
25. *Ibid.,* January 31, 1861, p. 4.
26. Whedon, "State of the Country," 321.

burden of a union with the South, suggested Zachary Eddy of Northampton, Massachusetts, the remainder of the nation might more fully "develop all the forces of a high, Christian civilization."[27] According to the Reverend Sefferenas Ottman of Branchport, New York, there existed the additional consolation that the system of human bondage would die soon whether the Union persisted or not. "In the Union or out of it, Slavery must die. God has written upon it its inevitable doom; and universal civilization has pronounced against it."[28]

A clean break with decades of Union sentiment was not easy, but the step was being taken. In January, for example, the *Independent* urged the nation to bear any "extremity" for the maintenance of the Union; by February the paper concluded that coercion would be unwise.

> God, who controls the destiny of nations, is opening a new chapter in the history of the world's wickedness. He has permitted the apostasy of Southern Christianity and the incendiary sophistry of Southern politics to work out their results. He has permitted that revolutionary frenzy to sweep over so many states. *Quis vult perdere, dementat.* It is for us to accept the fact. Those states must be permitted to work out their own destruction under that retributive Providence which is ordering their dreadful destiny. . . . Let the boundaries between them and the United States be defined by negotiation and peaceful agreement, if possible; and then let their destiny and ours be developed.[29]

Even those advocating coercion suggested a minimum response. The *Christian Watchman and Reflector* favored reinforcement of arsenals in Southern territory, blockades of the region's ports, and a suspension of the postal service, but the paper explicitly insisted that

27. Zachary Eddy, *Secession: Shall It Be Peace or War?* "A Fast Day Sermon Delivered in the First Church, Northampton, April 4, 1861," p. 20.

28. S. Ottman, *God Always for the Right and against Wrong,* "A Discourse Delivered on the Occasion of our National Fast, January 4, 1861, to the Presbyterian Church at Pultney, New York," p. 14.

29. *Independent,* January 17, 1861, p. 4, February 14, 1861, p. 4.

such was "the only force we advocate." The editor hoped to maintain the laws, without a full-scale invasion of the South, until the "disaffected States" could be legally dismissed from the Union.[30]

By April 1861 it was clear the the churches were inching into the future cautiously and uncertainly. Although many continued to exalt the Union as the zenith of value, a majority of clergy insisted that American nationality was essentially commitment to an ideal that could admit no further compromise. Most, of course, hoped that the harsh choice between liberty and Union would not be forced upon them. The South—pacified according to some, treated firmly according to others—would perhaps come scurrying back to the fold; and if that happy end did not result, a few concluded that disunion was not the unbearable option that a generation of Americans had thought. In spite of millennial rhetoric about a coming conflict, Protestants were not yet prepared to fight that battle with the weapons of the flesh.

### THE HOLY CRUSADE

After December 1860 federal property within the territory of seceded states presented a dilemma to both the United States and to the fledgling Confederacy. The problem was focused by the existence of Fort Sumter in the harbor of Charleston, South Carolina. By early April it was apparent that the garrison could not hold out much longer without resupply. A decision not to provision Sumter would signal a tacit recognition of disunion, and Lincoln therefore informed the governor of South Carolina on 6 April that fresh supplies would shortly be sent. The Southern government saw in this action the threat of an indefinite federal presence astride one of its leading ports—a situation that President Jefferson Davis believed could not be endured if the Confederacy's independence were to be credible. Accordingly he decided on 12 April to demand the surrender of Sumter and, when this ultimatum was rejected, to seize the arsenal by force. After a few hours of token resistance, Major Robert Anderson surrendered the garrison. Several days later Lincoln issued a proclamation calling for 75,000 volunteers to suppress

30. *Christian Watchman and Reflector*, February 14, 1861.

the rebellion. Throughout the North the fall of Sumter was received as evidence that peaceful secession was impossible.[31]

The loyal states—their clergy not least among them—responded to the president's call with an éclat of patriotic devotion submerging the doubts and divisions of the previous weeks. A year later Unitarian Edmund Willson of Salem, Massachusetts, assessed the remarkable transformation in sentiment. "One week before all was uncertainty; there was apathy, doubt, gloom. The uncrystallized atoms floated loose and uncohesive. . . . [But in the wake of Sumter] the problem which no man could work out was solved. Deeplying affinities were found beneath all our repulsions; surface seams were healed; and we were one people"—one people, he might have added, firmly committed to restore the Union by force of arms.[32]

Conservatives recently dallying with conciliation turned upon the South with the anger of friends betrayed. "When the first indications of this conflict made their appearance," explained Dr. Gardiner Spring of New York's Brick Presbyterian Church, "all my prepossessions, as is well known, were with the Southern states. If their leading statesmen had conducted themselves like Christians and as friends of peace—for myself, I would have been the advocate of some amicable arrangement rather than have been forced to the arbitrament of the sword. But when I hear so few kind words, and these suppressed by violence or fear; when crafty politicians eager for fame, and panting for place and power, blind and enslave the minds of the people; when I learn that this secession was preconcerted and determined in years gone by, and was only biding its

31. The burst of patriotic ardor that followed Sumter is analyzed in Thomas J. Pressly, *Americans Interpret Their Civil War,* pp. 27–52. This book remains the best single treatment of interpretations of the Civil War. For an overview of the ecclesiastical response to the war, see Ahlstrom, *Religious History of the American People,* pp. 670–97; William Clebsch, "Christian Interpretations of the Civil War," *Church History* 30 (June 1961): 212–22; and Dunham, *Attitude of the Northern Clergy.* Useful denominational studies include William Warren Sweet, *The Methodist Episcopal Church and the Civil War,* and Vander Velde, *Presbyterian Churches and the Federal Union.* Those interested in the reaction of Southern clergy to the war may find a helpful introduction in James W. Silver, *Confederate Morale and Church Propaganda.*

32. Edmund B. Willson, *Reasons for Thanksgiving,* "A Sermon Preached in the North Church, Salem, April 20, 1862," pp. 6–7.

time, . . . when I see these things my convictions are strong that we have reached the limit beyond which forbearance may not be extended."[33] It was, in fact, Spring who introduced in the May session of the Old School General Assembly a motion that firmly allied the denomination with the federal cause. Passed after considerable debate about their propriety, the so-called Spring resolutions marked a significant departure from the Old School's often reaffirmed policy of not pronouncing upon secular issues.[34]

Enraged conservatives now believed that previous talk of a diabolical slave power conspiracy had proven all too accurate. The Baptist *Christian Review* had previously sidestepped political issues for the sake of sectional amity, but now the journal pictured a fiendish South greedy for every inch of Northern territory, and it called for the military obliteration of the Confederacy.[35] Bishop Thomas A. Morris, a Southerner by birth and a sectional peacemaker by conviction, insisted in an open letter to border state Methodists that treason foreclosed all alternatives to an unsparing "destruction of its authors."[36] As Henry Boardman explained, it was no longer possible to maintain any sympathy for those by whom "this rebellion was concocted many years ago." A "cumulative series of proofs" had unmasked the utter duplicity of the Southern leadership. More than any other factor, said Boardman, this revelation of Southern character "has brought the prudent and conservative classes of society into full sympathy with this war for the defence of the Union. . . . And now, that the treachery is laid open, and they see that all the while, the one cherished object of these men was to *destroy* the Union, they have the double mixture of personal wrong and public duty to inflame their zeal on behalf of the cause of their country."[37]

33. Gardiner Spring, *State Thanksgiving During the War,* "A Sermon Preached November 28, 1861," pp. 32–33, 34.

34. *Minutes of the General Assembly of the Presbyterian Church in the United States of America, Old School* (1861), 16:325, 336–44. See also Vander Velde, *Presbyterian Churches and the Federal Union,* pp. 42–87.

35. "The National Crisis," *Christian Review* 26 (July 1861): 491–521.

36. John F. Marlay, *The Life of Rev. Thomas A. Morris, D.D.,* p. 317.

37. Henry A. Boardman, *Thanksgiving in War,* "A Sermon Preached in the Tenth Presbyterian Church, Philadelphia, on the 28th Day of November, 1861," pp. 13–14.

The assault against the flag worked a different alchemy upon those who had rebuked the idolatry of the Union. Some of these people suggested that peaceful secession be allowed as a means of purging the nation of slavery. It will never be known whether they seriously wished this outcome or were instead expressing passionately a hypothetical possibility preferable to further compromise with the South. In any case, the outbreak of violent revolution cut short these speculations, and the proponents of the higher law enlisted with enthusiasm in the war for the Union. The *Independent* epitomized the new war spirit:

> The question of the hour is a new question. What is now to be decided is not the Nebraska question, nor the Lecompton question, nor the question of the fugitive slave law. The question is not whether the Union shall be divided. . . . Had the seceding states proposed a peaceable division of the Union, by any method consistent with the forms and spirit of the Constitution, the question now to be decided would not have arisen. . . . All other questions are now merged in one: Have we a Government? Is the Union of these states a solid reality, or only an airy vision? Can citizens of the United States make war upon the United States and not be guilty of treason? Shall the Government and Union of these states be defended against the enemies that have planned all this treason, and are now marching upon the capital? This is the question of the hour. Let all questions heretofore debated be foreborne.[38]

In short, the problem of slavery had been supplanted by the issue of constitutional legitimacy, and staple sermon texts shifted to Romans 13: "Let every soul be subject to the higher powers. For there is no power but of God: the powers that be are ordained of God."[39]

Protestants were convinced that failure to uphold the Union would set in motion centrifugal tendencies that would not halt until the nation and its cherished freedom were in ruins. The *Christian Watchman and Reflector* predicted that a United States which allowed revolution would recapitulate the history of Europe "with bitter local jealousies and antipathies, and large standing armies, and

38. *Independent,* April 25, 1861, p. 4.
39. For a further treatment of this issue, see chapter 4.

frequent wars and crushing debts."[40] The Reverend William Dwight of Portland, Maine, pushed the warning a step further: broken into a half-dozen or so confederacies, the former nation would lapse into the colonial orbit of England or France.[41] At stake, said A. L. Stone of Park Street Church in Boston, was the principle of law. If successfully challenged by the rebellion, legitimate authority would disappear, forcing Americans "back from friendships and brotherhoods and all alliances, to the instincts of the forest brute." Foreswearing momentarily his antislavery convictions, Stone urged citizens to "strike for Law and Union, for country and God's great ordinance of Government."[42]

It would not be accurate to infer that the claims of transcendent morality had been completely displaced in the clamor to maintain the Union. Rather, the preservationist rhetoric had itself been infused with a new moral significance. Formerly an argument in behalf of concession to the South, such language now summoned the nation to battle against an iniquitous slave power. The holy Union that Northerners defended was no longer the compromise-tainted object of earlier years; it was democratic civilization in collision with an alien way of life. Thus the Vermont Baptist Association declared in October 1861: "We witness the culmination of a strife which has long been progressing between the principles of freedom incorporated into the framework of our government and lying at the foundation of our national existence on the one hand, and the system of American slavery on the other."[43] In its Independence Day issue the *Christian Advocate and Journal* saw the conflict as the reflection of the universal struggle between aristocracy and democracy. After alluding to the economic and political differences between the two sections, the paper suggested that these were only surface difficulties: "But beneath all these is the predisposing cause. . . . The sentiment of the South is aristocratic, that of the North democratic. Its community is a rural aristocracy,

40. *Christian Watchman and Reflector,* July 25, 1861.

41. William T. Dwight, *The Nationality of a People Its Vital Element,* "An Oration Delivered in the New City Hall before the City Government and Citizens of Portland, July 4, 1861," pp. 24–25.

42. A. L. Stone, *The Divineness of Human Government,* "A Discourse Delivered in Park Street Church," pp. 9–10, 49.

43. *Christian Watchman and Reflector,* October 10, 1861.

resting like that of ancient Sparta, upon a helotry. Here lies the heart of our trouble." At a superficial glance the war might be called merely a struggle to vindicate legitimate government, but on the deeper level it was a great people's war for Christian democracy. As the editor of the *Advocate* expressed the matter succinctly, "Directly we are contending for government, but indirectly for freedom."[44]

The significance of such an ideological conflict could not be restricted to one nation alone, and Protestants asserted vigorously that in fighting the battle for liberty in America they were waging a war of universal significance. The *Independent* suggested that the war should not be categorized "with ordinary instances of international hostility." Unlike petty dynastic squabbles or commercial imbroglios, this struggle reached beyond local interests and constituted "a crisis in the world's history." By resolving a fundamental issue, the war would prove one of the "hinges on which the destiny of nations and of ages" turns.[45] That question was starkly simple: was democracy a viable form of government? "Free institutions," said Francis Wayland in a pamphlet for the American Tract Society, "have been established in this country under every advantage, and have achieved a material, social, and intellectual progress wholly without a parallel. If they cannot be maintained here, in the midst of a Protestant population, with a Bible in every house, and education as free as air, and in the enjoyment of 'perfect liberty in religious concernments,' then it may be reasonably believed that they can be sustained nowhere. Crushed and degraded humanity must sink down in despair, and centuries must elapse before this experiment can be made again under so favorable auspices."[46]

In the vanguard of the worldwide struggle for liberty, Americans bore a responsibility unlike that of any other people. They were in the deepest sense the representatives of humanity, and their government was the property of all. After a trip to the Levant in the spring of 1861, Daniel C. Eddy of Boston's Harvard Street Baptist Church was impressed anew by the unique position of the United States. "That flag belongs to the world; it is the ensign of the oppressed of

44. *Christian Advocate and Journal,* July 4, 1861, p. 212.
45. *Independent,* August 22, 1861, p. 4.
46. Quoted in *Christian Advocate and Journal,* September 26, 1861, p. 308.

all lands. The soil we tread! it is not yours or mine. It does not belong to the cotton lords of the South, nor to the merchant princes of the North. It belongs to constitutional government and human happiness."[47] The Union had to be preserved because it freighted the hopes of all people. Although narrow chauvinism contributed, as it does in all wars, to the burst of military ardor that followed the start of hostilities, the patriotic spirit of 1861 was nourished also by the conviction that the cause was mankind. America's sacred trust was holy because it was held for all humanity and not for America alone. As Albert Barnes, New School Presbyterianism's best-known spokesman, said: "Of all the civil and political trusts ever committed to any generation of men, that Constitution is the most precious, for it guards higher interests and secures richer blessings to the world than any other."[48]

By any standard of judgment, the metamorphosis of feeling in April 1861 was remarkable. The unthinkable war had become the irrepressible conflict in which the clergy eagerly volunteered their oratorical services. Conservatives who had urged conciliation set their faces against further compromise, and those who had talked glibly of sundering the nation suddenly bowed in reverence before the ark of the Union. As a symbol of political and religious meaning for all Protestants, the Union had been rehabilitated and suffused with new moral vitality. Virtually without exception, the clergy united with Zachary Eddy, whose conversion from an apostle of peaceful disunion to a drum major in the war effort was complete. "If the crusaders, seized by a common enthusiasm, exclaimed, 'IT IS THE WILL OF GOD! IT IS THE WILL OF GOD!'—much more may we make this our rallying cry and inscribe it on our banners."[49] The late 1850s witnessed an upsurge in the expectation of a titanic conflict; in 1861 that apocalyptic struggle started to assume tangible definition.

47. Daniel C. Eddy, *Our Country: Its Pride and Its Peril,* "A Discourse Delivered in Harvard Street Baptist Church, Boston, August 11, 1861, on the Return of the Pastor from Syria," p. 32.

48. Albert Barnes, *The Love of Country,* "A Sermon Delivered in the First Presbyterian Church, Philadelphia, April 28, 1861," p. 22.

49. Zachary Eddy, *A Discourse on the War,* "Preached to the Northampton Volunteers, Sunday Evening, April 28, 1861," p. 9.

# 2

## The Armageddon of the Republic

Several weeks after the surrender of Fort Sumter, the *Presbyterian* confessed its perplexity with the dark events that had befallen the Union. The United States had been "raised up and commissioned of God to serve as a light and a deliverer to those long down-trodden and degraded populations" of the earth. Yet at the very moment when democracy had taken root in Europe and ancient barriers to missions had begun to crumble, the nation destined to lead this world renovation had succumbed to internecine strife. That America should stumble when its golden hour had come, concluded the paper, "is surely one of the most lamentable, and one of the most inexplicable providences in the history of nations or of mankind."[1]

War forced the churches to reconsider their previous understanding of the manner in which the Kingdom of God would come. In spite of the growing sense of crisis in the 1850s, many had not given up hope that the United States might be spared tribulation and that its mission would be one of peace. In a sermon to the Foreign Missionary Society the week after Lincoln's election, the Reverend Walter Clarke summarized the role that churchmen expected to play in the transformation of the world. "The people of God have no need to assail the nations; they have no use for arms, and no license for invasion. They have only to keep their Christian virtues, and exercise them, and by this simple process they shall at length acquire a Kingdom. . . . And they are to do all this as the leaven does its transforming and restless work; by the secret infusion into all parts of the social organism, of the spirit of their master, the spirit of equity, and truth, and love."[2] Whatever wars might augur the Kingdom

1. *Presbyterian*, May 11, 1861, p. 74.
2. Walter D. Clarke, "The Reign of the Saints," *National Preacher*, n.s. 4 (February 1861): 51–52.

would likely fall upon the earth's benighted peoples, its victims of despotic princes and religious superstition; the American Republic, unperturbed in its peaceful mission, would be happily exempt from the travail. After 12 April 1861, however, these hopes were awash in a sea of blood. The *Christian Review* expressed the anguish of the religious community: "Coming into existence in an age and region remote from the political corruptions, the diplomatic intrigues, the hereditary feuds, and the traditionary abuses of the Old World, we had flattered ourselves that we should escape the desolating wars which have marked the fluctuating fortunes of the European Empire, and that in a pathway of unbroken peace we should sweep forward into the cloudless splendors of the Millenial [*sic*] era. . . . Our visions have been suddenly, rudely dispelled."[3]

Almost as soon as the first guns had fired, Protestants set about reevaluating their conception of the historical process and of national destiny. Drawing upon the Puritan tradition of pulpit jeremiads, the clergy suggested that the nation's hope had gone awry because the people had sinned. Since their virtue and piety had declined from the glorious example of their revolutionary ancestors. God demanded expiation in blood. Simultaneously Protestants concluded that the woes of the Apocalypse applied even to the United States. Here, too, the Kingdom could come only through travail and the clash of arms. God was violently overturning the old, corrupt order and was bringing the disparate forces of history to a climactic resolution in one place and time. It had been granted to Americans to fight the definitive battle that would ensure the future happiness of the nation and the world. The Armageddon of the Republic had begun.

## NORTHERN JEREMIADS

"No truth is more patent in American history," wrote Edward McNall Burns some years ago, "than the fact that this nation is an Old Testament people."[4] The chosen vessel of the millennium, the United States was also believed to be the modern successor to the ancient Jewish state. Herman Melville, far from the orthodox community, indicated the pervasiveness of this sentiment when he

3. "The National Crisis," *Christian Review* 26 (July 1861): 492.
4. Edward McNall Burns, *The American Idea of Mission: Concepts of National Purpose and Destiny*, p. 11.

observed, "We Americans are the peculiar, chosen people—the
Israel of our time; we bear the ark of the liberties of the world."[5]
As he had done with Israel, God entered into a special covenant
with the American people and conferred great blessings upon them.
A covenant, however, entails mutual obligations, and if either party
defaults, the agreement can be annulled. From the beginning of the
colonial enterprise, Americans sensed, albeit dimly at times, that
election thus carried a threat as well as a promise. Governor John
Winthrop of the Massachusetts Bay Colony gave classic expression
to this awareness in 1630 in his sermon to the immigrants on the
*Arbella:* "Thus stands the cause between God and us, we are entered
into Covenant with him for this work . . . ; but if we shall neglect
the observation of these Articles which are the ends we have pro-
pounded, and dissembling with our God, shall fall to embrace this
present world and prosecute our carnal intentions seeking great
things for our selves and our posterity, the Lord will surely break
out in wrath against us, be revenged of such a perjured people, and
make us know the price of the breach of such a Covenant."[6] As
Perry Miller has shown, later Puritan preaching virtually institutionalized this motif in a sermonic form, the jeremiad, which affirmed
that whatever evils befell the people came as punishment for the
transgression of the covenant.[7] The jeremiad was considerably modified during the Revolutionary and early National periods, but it
never fully disappeared as a theological rationale for the sufferings
of a chosen people.[8]

5. Quoted in Marty, *Righteous Empire,* p. 46.
6. Perry Miller and Thomas H. Johnson, eds., *The Puritans: A Sourcebook
of Their Writings,* 1: 198. I have modernized the spelling.
7. Perry Miller, *The New England Mind: From Colony to Province,* pp.
27–39.
8. Cf. Perry Miller, "From the Covenant to the Revival," in *The Shaping of
American Religion,* vol. 1 of *Religion in American Life,* ed. James Ward
Smith and A. Leland Jamison, pp. 322–68; and Gribbin, *The Churches Militant,* esp. pp. 129–55. See also Marvin Meyers, *The Jacksonian Persuasion:
Politics and Belief.* Meyers argues that the central ideological feature of Jacksonianism was its hankering after a lost agrarian simplicity now threatened by
corrupt and sinister forces—such as the Bank of the United States and Nicholas
Biddle. The conception of a decline from a golden age of republican virtue
into a time of corruption requiring political repentance bears an interesting
similarity to the jeremiadic format.

The tragedy of civil war reinvigorated the jeremiadic tradition, and these thunderings of judgment seemed peculiarly appropriate to the crisis. In an editorial early in the war, the *Presbyterian* investigated the theme: "Now, although God's covenant with his ancient people was in some points peculiar, we have no doubt that God has impliedly entered into a covenant with our American nation, whose main features are similar. His word of promise is unaltered, and his word of threatening is the same. . . . There underlies all this a very important question—have we maintained our fealty to God? Have we not grievously sinned, by forgetting the giver of all our mercies and by our ingratitude, pride, and hardness of heart forfeited all our privileges?"[9] At the national fast on 30 April 1863, Byron Sunderland framed the charge more sharply to his Washington, D.C., congregation: "We have sinned, while holding in trust the noblest heritage ever held by any people, while having charge in effect of the last and most precious hopes of human nature." Unless God stayed his wrath, the country would soon "sink into an abyss of shame and infamy such as no people ever contracted, not even the doomed and wandering house of Israel."[10]

False to its covenant bonds, the nation was summoned to hear anew the word of the prophets that the Lord is an avenging God. "The Old Testament, in our current notions and sympathies," suggested A. L. Stone, "has been almost outlawed from human affairs. We have turned its leaves for its curious and quaint old histories, but felt as though we were living under a new dispensation. And now the days have come upon us, for which these strong-chorded elder Scriptures have been waiting. Their representations of God, as the rewarder of the evil doer; the Avenger of the wronged, the Asserter of his own trampled prerogatives, . . . suit the day and hour of the intense present."[11] In similar spirit, Edwards Amasa Park analyzed the imprecatory psalms and concluded that the war was bringing out the "hidden uses of such parts of the Bible as had

9. *Presbyterian,* September 20, 1862, p. 150.

10. Byron Sunderland, *The Crisis of the Times,* "A Sermon Preached in the First Presbyterian Church, Washington, D.C., on the Evening of the National Fast, Thursday, April 30, 1863," p. 8.

11. A. L. Stone, *Emancipation,* "A Sermon Delivered in Park Street Church on Fast Day Morning, April 3, 1862," p. 4.

seemed antiquated."[12] Perhaps Levi Paine of Farmington, Connecticut, captured the mood most succinctly when he told his church that the mystery of God's present retribution could be unlocked only by a careful study of the similar "dealings of God with his chosen people, Israel."[13]

The sword had fallen upon the nation for sins that the entire people had committed, and the North was as much the object of divine wrath as was the South. "Let no one section of our common country," insisted Roswell Hitchcock of Union Seminary, "angrily upbraid another for its vices or crimes. We are offenders all of us, North and South, East and West."[14] According to Methodist George Peck, the meaning of the crisis could be learned from the actions of God during the Assyrian invasion of Judah, when the Lord raised up a heathen king to smite his own people for their wickedness. Thus "as God often uses one wicked people for the punishment of another, he is permitting this slaveholders' rebellion to inflict upon us terrible chastisement." The North similarly was being used by God to inflict a "judicial punishment" upon the South for its iniquitous slave system.[15] Unwittingly the two parties to the conflict had become the rods by which God was scourging both for their sins.

In lamentations over the state of the American Israel, the clergy compared the present citizenry unfavorably with the founding fathers. Unlike an earlier golden age, said Levi Paine, "we no longer have a class of men we can call by eminence, statesmen." America had entered an "era of demagogues and traitors and corrupt politicians" who willingly prostituted the nation to "the highest bidder."[16] In more sweeping terms, the *Independent* suggested that the history of the Republic had been that of a spiritual Babylonian captivity. "During this long seventy years—the very measure of the old Baby-

12. Edwards A. Park, "The Imprecatory Psalms Viewed in the Light of the Southern Rebellion," *Bibliotheca Sacra* 19 (January 1816): 165.

13. Levi Paine, *Political Lessons of the Rebellion,* "A Sermon Delivered at Farmington, Connecticut, on Fast Day, April 18, 1862," p. 5.

14. Roswell Hitchcock, "Our National Sin," *National Preacher,* n.s. 4 (November 1861): 328.

15. George Peck, *Our Country: Its Trial and Triumph,* p. 118.

16. Paine, *Political Lessons of the Rebellion,* pp. 17–18.

lonian captivity—we have sought to make up our radical and fatal treachery to God's trust by zeal in all collateral fields. We have planted schools, built churches, founded colleges and schools of theology, nourished revivals of religion, wept over the desolations of Zion in the Orient, and poured our wealth upon the heathen lands. But these were but so many ruffles and garments around Death!"[17] As Nathaniel Eggleston summarized the matter, the nation had departed from the "feeling of the fathers."[18]

Frequently these confessions enumerated alleged violations of virtually every prohibition in the Scriptures. George Duffield's widely circulated *God of Our Fathers*, for example, uncovered a catalog of transgressions among which were ingratitude, intemperance, violation of the Sabbath, infidelity, adultery, murder, unjust wars, and oppression.[19] In spite of their inclusivity, the jeremiads were not merely time-honored rhetorical broadsides lacking specific relevance to the contemporary situation. Clergy recognized that the manifold sins of the Republic were traceable to two chief moral failures: the toleration of slavery and the want of an effective internal discipline within American democracy.

For those who seriously pondered the American heritage, it was a scandal of shocking proportions that a people affirming certain inalienable rights for all should have so long endured human bondage in their midst. The Reverend M. L. P. Thompson of Cincinnati suggested that the nation's hypocritical retreat from its first faith had prompted the present judgment: "Like the Israelites taking possession of their promised land, who disobediently spared some of the idolatrous nations whom God had commanded them to drive out, and were ever after vexed by them in all their generations—so, we, denying in practice the holy doctrine of our Exodus, with which God accompanied us as a friend, and established us in our inheritance, left in the heart of our land the very flail with which he is

17. *Independent,* April 23, 1863, p. 4.
18. Nathaniel Eggleston, *Reasons for Thanksgiving,* "A Discourse to the Congregational Church and Society in Stockbridge, Mass., on the Day of Annual Thanksgiving, November 21, 1861," p. 17.
19. George Duffield, Jr., *The God of Our Fathers,* "An Historical Sermon Preached in the Coates' Street Presbyterian Church, Philadelphia, on Fast Day, January 4, 1861," esp. pp. 16–29.

now threshing us."[20] In this extremity, a cheap repentance could no longer suffice. Payment for slavery must be made, said Baptist minister George Ide, in "rivers of blood and oceans of treasure."[21] Another indictment explained the calamity: the people had succumbed to an overweening selfishness that threatened chaos. To many perceptive observers, it seemed that the young republic was a nation without internal cohesion. Relative social egalitarianism and economic mobility atomized the citizenry into competitive individuals, each striving for material gain and security. As Starr H. Nichols of the Congregational church in Mansfield, Ohio, suggested: "Being a people of the most enduring and versatile energy, and possessing a continent of the richest and most varied resources; having noble forests, large and navigable rivers, exhaustless mineral wealth in mines of gold and silver . . . , we swept forward upon a career of development and progress." Unfortunately tantalizing material possibilities had converted the United States into a country of headstrong children, "impetuous" and "defiant" of all restraint.[22] In more biting language, the Reverend Marvin Vincent suggested that the search for profit at any cost had run personal liberty into "wild and brutal license which has brought us well nigh to the brink of anarchy."[23]

In an address to the Plymouth Congregational Church of Milford, Connecticut, the editor of the *American Presbyterian and Theological Review* suggested that all the particular vices of the nation might be traced to this primal sin. Preoccupied with "style and luxury and extravagance," Americans had deserted the "republican simplicity" of the fathers. An undisciplined citizenry had given up politics to demagoguery, bribery, and interest groups. The practitioners of lynch law, radicalism, and utopian socialism had denigrated legitimate authority in the name of a spurious liberty. The end result of such disregard for order could be only that which the

20. M. L. P. Thompson, *Discourses*, "Preached in the Second Presbyterian Church, Cincinnati, Ohio, September 26 and November 28, 1861," p. 21.

21. George Ide, *Battle Echoes, or, Lessons from the War*, p. 94.

22. Starr H. Nichols, *Our Sins and Our Repentance*, "Preached September 26, 1861," pp. 7–8.

23. Marvin Vincent, *Our National Discipline*, "A Thanksgiving Sermon Preached in the First Presbyterian Church, Troy, N.Y., Nov. 26, 1863," p. 25.

nation was now experiencing—a bloody insurrection. The vital center of American nationality had been dissipated by unbridled individualism, and until this defect was remedied, "God will keep his hand heavy down upon us."[24]

However the sins be named, there was agreement that the hour for leisurely repentance had passed. As in the Old Testament, the Lord of Hosts had taken the sword to smite his people. "It is the year of recompense for the controversy of Zion," said the Reverend Henry Smith of Buffalo, New York. "The streams have been turned to pitch, and the dust into brimstone. God is treading the wine press alone. . . . For the day of vengeance is in his heart, and the year of his redeemed is come."[25]

### THE PURPOSE OF HISTORY

God's judgment upon the United States was not part of an endless cycle of sin and chastisement, for the divine wrath systematically moved toward a final victory over evil. Although the nations had indeed sinned repeatedly and received condign punishment, each convulsion marked the defeat of a particular iniquity, which, once vanquished, would never flourish again. George Prentiss of Union Seminary in New York remarked that current upheavals only appeared to replicate past ones. "A new cycle of events begins," he explained. "A fresh chapter is opened in history. Humanity takes a step never taken before toward the fulfillment of its grand destiny. The hand on the dial-plate of time is moved forward, and no mortal power is strong enough ever to put it back again."[26] According to the *Independent,* the deity of the Scriptures was the *deus eversor,* God the destroyer. Never content with the world as it was, he subverted, one by one, the barriers to the millennium. "This is the burthen [*sic*] of all prophecy—this the light that shines along the track of time, growing brighter as the world advances and God's

24. J. M. Sherwood, "The Moral Causes of Our National Calamity," *National Preacher,* 3d ser. 2 (June 1863): 147, 153.

25. Henry Smith, *God in the War,* "A Discourse Preached in Behalf of the U.S. Christian Commission on the Day of National Thanksgiving, August 6th, 1863," 3d ed., p. 20.

26. George L. Prentiss, "The National Crisis," *American Theological Review* 4 (October 1862): 692.

plan unfolds itself in history. God 'overturns, overturns, overturns';
one power after another, one nation after another, one mighty
iniquity after another, falls and is no more; while earth and heaven
are waiting till he shall come whose right it is to reign." And if such
were God's way of working, the American Christian could only
conclude of the Civil War: "We are in the midst of such an overturning."[27]

Protestants reasoned that the Kingdom would occasion more tur-
bulence than they had once hoped, and some looked back wistfully
to a former dream that moral example alone might redeem the
world. Dr. Prentiss spoke movingly of his own exuberance several
decades earlier.

> We, whose entrance into intellectual life was in those days,
> are not likely to forget what a fair bow of promise seemed to
> rest upon the future. . . . Never before, within the same period,
> were such varied and strenuous exertions put forth to diffuse
> useful knowledge, to elevate and educate the masses, to amelio-
> rate the condition of the indigent, neglected and unfortunate
> classes, to reform the vicious, to train up children in right paths,
> to popularize the highest truths of science and religion, to
> emancipate and dignify labor, to multiply the conveniences
> and comforts of life, to do away with slavery, war, intemper-
> ance, and the other giant evils which had so long preyed upon
> human happiness—in a word, to render the world the abode of
> industrious freedom, peace, domestic joy, and virtuous intelli-
> gence.[28]

Prentiss concluded sadly that the reformist zeal of the old evangelical united front had been fatuous optimism. The generation that was
expected to surrender its swords to the Prince of Peace had instead
given itself up to war: the 1848 revolutions in Europe, English imbroglios in India and China, the Crimean conflict, the Italian war
for unification, and now civil strife in America. "We can now see
plainly enough," he continued, "that the age which at Waterloo
seemed to be bidding adieu to the sword, was itself pregnant with

27. *Independent,* October 10, 1861, p. 4.
28. Prentiss, "National Crisis," p. 688.

the elements of titanic strife, . . . [and] that the occupation of the peace society is for the present gone."[29]

Prentiss's hard-nosed attitude did not indicate a loss of faith in the final triumph of God's purposes or a repudiation of the ultimate success of the United States. "Let us not only not despair of the Republic," he counseled, "but cherish unbounded faith in its heaven-appointed destiny. Hope is our American and Christian birthright. We belong to the future; and if the past was not a mockery, that future has in store for us unspeakable blessings. But we must prove ourselves worthy of them before they will be ours." To establish their worthiness Americans had to prove themselves in a "dreadful contest" on the field of battle—a war "like that waged in heaven" between the Archangel Michael and Satan in the Apocalypse. In short, Prentiss had not renounced his optimism, but he had tempered it with the realization that progress could be wrought only by blood and iron. The world would move forward, he said, "with confused noise and garments rolled in blood."[30]

Dr. George Ide repeated the assertion that violence was a necessary tool of the Kingdom of God. Although the "normal character of His dispensations" was found in the "persuasive ministry" of the Gospel, God inaugurated truly significant periods of history by political strife and wars. A provocative sermon title gave Ide's theme away: "Great Eras Marked by Great Judgments." He called attention to the nexus of events that surrounded previous advances, each of which had been accompanied by bloodshed. For example, the Hebrew nation could not enter upon its divinely commissioned vocation until the hosts of Pharaoh were slaughtered; and Jesus's advent, hardening the Jews, led to their political destruction by the legions of Vespasian. Ide concluded: "When individuals or communities have become so sunk in degeneracy, or so wedded and sold to enormous vices, as to be insensible to every motive derived from His goodness; and, especially, when from wicked laws, institutions or governments, obstacles stand in the way of His purposes which ordinary appliances fail to remove—then it is that He makes bare His arm for judgment; then it is that 'by terrible things in

29. Ibid., p. 689.
30. Ibid., pp. 698, 715.

righteousness,' He answers prayer, and annihilates the barriers that oppose the going forth of His salvation."[31] Within Ide's remarks lay the outlines of a dialectical view of divine activity within history, for God wielded alternately the suasion of the Gospel and the hammer of violence.

According to Protestant spokesmen, this dialectic was intrinsic to Christianity's claim of authority over the profane as well as over the sacred. As the Reverend James L. Corning of Milwaukee said bluntly, "Christianity is not, I think, like our natural sun, which lights one hemisphere while the other is left in darkness. Contrariwise, it was sent into the world to touch *all* of life remedially, life individual, life social, life civil and political, life of every kind which contains an atmosphere, healthy or malarious, where immortal souls live and breathe."[32] The Gospel, in a word, broached issues that made inevitable collision with the world's entrenched powers. By raising the moral consciousness of society, the Christian message eventually threatened vested interests, which, fearing the diminution of their empire, resorted to violence. The Reverend Sherman Canfield of Syracuse, New York, explained: "On its way towards the millennium the Kingdom of Christ occasions strifes and conflicts by causing a portion of a world lying in wickedness to differ from the rest. The very goodness, frankness, and courage which it produces in its subjects, renders them odious to evil-doers."[33] The "precious seed" of progress, said William Goodrich of Cleveland, was indeed sown by the proclamation of the church, but the fruits of that labor could be harvested only on the battlefield. "You will mark it as a fact of general history, that in the establishment of great rights, and the overthrow of great wrongs, there has always come a point where the issue must be fought out in battle. Rooted wrong and ancient despotism never yield that last point, till they are confronted with force greater than their own. Selfish power, even when deserted by its old advocates, and disowned by the surrounding world, will always make one last stand, and will yield only when conquered and abased."[34] Thus the alternating rhythm

31. Ide, *Battle Echoes,* pp. 64–65.
32. James L. Corning, *Religion and Politics!* pp. 6–7.
33. Sherman Canfield, *The American Crisis,* "A Discourse Delivered on the Day of National Thanksgiving, November 24th, 1864," p. 11.
34. William H. Goodrich, *A Sermon on the Christian Necessity of War,* p. 10.

of Gospel preaching and violent strife would drum out the onward march of the Lord's hosts until at last the vision of a restored earth was realized. Then the Christian ideal incarnate in history, the poles of the dialectic would disappear as the kingdoms of this world became the Kingdom of God.

As one of the upheavals necessary to this consummation, the Civil War could be intelligible only within the framework of world history. Indeed the logic of millennialism prohibits that any event be merely parochial, for history is not the random eruption of economic struggles, dynastic rivalries, or chauvinistic vendettas; it is essentially one struggle between two opposing forces. God and Satan—Christ and Antichrist—are the only real contestants; all others are mere epiphenomena. The Reverend William Gaylord translated this dualism into political terms: "There are but two fundamental principles in human government, and these are directly and widely antagonistic. There may be many modifications of each of these, to suit different circumstances and grades of human society, but the underlying principle is either monarchical or republican. It is either irresponsible, centralized power vested in one, or power derived from and amenable to the people. Wherever these opposing principles come in contact, there always has been and always must be a conflict of moral and physical forces. This is the struggle that has raged with varying aspects throughout the Old World for centuries past. It [the Civil War] is now the old conflict reenacted of Despotism against Freedom."[35] In similar language the New School Presbyterian Assembly declared in 1862 that the present slaveholders' rebellion had a direct lineage to "the first two great rebellions—that which assailed the throne of heaven directly, and that which peopled our world with miserable apostates."[36]

If every event was part of one struggle, the most minute historical occurrence was never lost. A civilization in each success bequeathed a valuable legacy to its successors or in each failure a moral warning. All fit perfectly into the plan of the Kingdom. "With infinite wisdom and sovereign authority," explained the Reverend Daniel March of Philadelphia, "He [God] assigns to nations their periods

35. Gaylord, *The Soldier God's Minister*, p. 13.
36. *Minutes of the General Assembly of the Presbyterian Church in the United States of America, New School* (1862), 13: 23.

of trial and of conflict, of prosperity and of repose, in such order as best to secure the ultimate triumph of righteousness and truth. The great world-wide contest is ever-going on, not always with the sword, but always with resources of vast extent and with weapons of mightly power." Although the United States had hoped to avoid writing "another page of the bloodstained annals of war," such innocence had been denied. "But the active conflict which the powers of darkness are ever waging for the possession of this world, has at last rolled toward that quarter of the field where the Divine Commander has assigned us our station. And we must take our turn in resisting the attack, considering what we do and suffer in this contest is not for ourselves alone, but for the ages and generations of the human family in all the future."[37] The American war had global significance because it was the current theater of operations in a much larger struggle; and in such universal strife whatever happens in one arena, even if removed by thousands of miles, affects every other sphere of hostilities. It was therefore axiomatic to Protestants that the Civil War was fraught with incalculable consequences, and the *Christian Advocate and Journal* echoed March: "There is not an island in the sea, nor a hamlet on the broad continents, that has not a stake in the issue."[38]

The significance of the war was further heightened by the fact that America occupied a unique place within this struggle. With the country reposed the inheritance of all previous human success. President Barnas Sears of Brown University, discussing "The Religious and Moral Value of our National Union," said that the moral and cultural wealth of the past had been lavished upon America. The best of classical antiquity had been fused with the pure Christianity of the Reformation, which in turn was brought into providential conjunction with the sturdy Anglo-Saxon race. God then transplanted His precious hybrid to a virgin land where the last "aristocratical remains of earlier feudal times" could be cast aside. There prospered by physical abundance and strenghtened by the engrafting of immigrant peoples onto the basic Teutonic stock, the

37. Daniel March, *Steadfastness and Preparation in the Day of Adversity,* "A Sermon Preached in the Clinton Street Presbyterian Church, Philadelphia, September 14th, 1862," pp. 8–9.
38. *Christian Advocate and Journal,* May 16, 1861, p. 156.

American nation would "inaugurate a new phase of society" in which Christianity and political freedom were exemplified.[39] Tracing the rise of American nationality from Greco-Roman times, the Reverend C. L. Goodell of New Britain, Connecticut, expounded the same theme: "Our civilization is a golden braid, each age furnishing its test strand, and all together combining what is best and excluding what is worst, in the experience of man." The culmination of the past and the earnest of the future, America was the destined type of the new humanity that would ultimately people the earth. America, said Goodell, was the "pledge of those principles which are dearest to the heart of man."[40]

Their conception of history converted the Civil War into a crusade for Protestants. If the chosen light should fail, how great would be the darkness! The collapse of the model republic would sink the aspirations of freedom-loving people everywhere, and thus the contest had to be pressed with unceasing vigor. In the first Presbyterian Church of Pittsburgh W. W. Eells affirmed: "We hold up the banner of terror to tyrants, the banner of hope to oppressed millions. And justly do we contend to the utmost, lest in our failure, gloomy darkness spread its pall over all lands, and it be held as proven, that man is not worthy to be free."[41] Methodists in New Haven, Connecticut, heard an even more somber warning from their pastor, B. H. Nadal: "If this rebellion could succeed, the civilized world would experience the beginning of a second deluge, which would leave the broken remnants of human rights clutched in the hands of a few Neroes and Napoleons. . . . The world would be subverted, and stand on its head, the spheres of reason and conscience, and science, would be eclipsed, and it would be proved that all our notions and hopes in regard to a personal and righteous God had been a dream."[42]

39. B. Sears, "The Moral and Religious Value of our National Union," *Bibliotheca Sacra* 20 (January 1863): 124–52.

40. C. L. Goodell, *Thanksgiving Sermon,* "Preached at the Union Service of the First and South Congregational Churches, New Britain, Conn., November 26, 1863," pp. 5, 13.

41. W. W. Eells, *How and Why We Give Thanks,* "A Thanksgiving Sermon Preached in the First Presbyterian Church, Pittsburgh, on Thursday November 26th, 1863," p. 15.

42. B. H. Nadal, *The War in the Light of Divine Providence,* p. 19.

Yet the same sense of high mission that summoned the nation to heroic sacrifice ensured eventual victory. The dialectic of history always advanced. The trumpet of God, in Julia Ward Howe's memorable phrase, "shall never call retreat."[43] "Revolutions," said the *Christian Review*, "when produced by the pressure of moral causes, never go backward; the world moves, moves forward, for this is the line [along] which these forces act, and the direction of God's providence and purpose."[44] Protestants remained fundamentally incredulous, moreover, that the world's appointed example would fail at the moment that European upheavals indicated that the peoples of the world were turning to the light. "The latter day glory is already dawning," Henry Ward Beecher predicted. "God is calling to the nations. The long-oppressed are arousing. The despotic thrones are growing feeble. It is an age of liberty. The trumpet is sounding in all the world, and one nation after another is moving to the joyful sound, and God is mustering the great army of liberty under his banners! In this day, shall America be found laggard?"[45] The notion seemed patently absurd, and Cyrus D. Foss of the Hanson Place Methodist Church in Brooklyn noted sarcastically: "I would almost as soon expect the chariot of Immanuel to retrace its course to Bethlehem, and thence ascend from this orphaned world to heaven." "This nation will never perish," he concluded.[46]

### THE CIVIL WAR IN WORLD HISTORY

Victory for the Union would undeniably conclude another of those periodic upheavals by which the progress of the Kingdom was traced, but triumph might well mean even more. The unique position of America in history suggested that the current conflict might well be part of the final battle. The Reverend Joel Bingham asked a Buffalo audience to consider the future of the Republic after the guns fell silent. Could it be otherwise than that America would offer "such a home of liberty, such a scene of peaceful order and

43. From "Battle Hymn of the Republic." See Ninde, *Story of the American Hymn*, p. 251.
44. "The Vital Forces of the Age," *Christian Review* 26 (October 1861): 574.
45. Henry Ward Beecher, *Patriotic Addresses*, p. 245.
46. Cyrus D. Foss, *Songs in the Night*, pp. 16–17.

contented industry, . . . such a land of right and virtue and religion as would well answer to the figure of millennial glory and the reign of the Redeemer of men upon earth?"[47]

By the time of the Civil War, Protestants had been introduced to schemes purporting to draw from the Scriptures, verse by verse, a time-specific scenario for the millennium. William Miller, whose prediction of the end of the world in 1844 created national attention, was merely the best known of the "watchers for the Second Coming."[48] From the British Isles emanated a more literate variety of prophetic speculation. After 1840 the works of such English authors as John Nelson Darby, George S. Faber, and John Cumming were widely disseminated in America, and in 1859–60, Michael Baxter, a Church of England missionary, had toured the United States preaching a message encapsulated in the title of his later published work, *The Coming Battle and the Appalling National Convulsion Foreshadowed in Prophecy Immediately to Occur During the Period 1861–1867*. *Prophetic Times,* a Philadelphia-based interdenominational publication, was established in 1863 to promote careful study of the prophecies; and in the same year the *Christian Intelligencer,* the organ of the Dutch Reformed Church, attracted widespread attention with a spirited debate about the millennial timetable. Most Protestants scoffed at these theories. The Millerite fiasco had severely discredited efforts to predict the Second Coming, and, in any event, these prophetic schedules usually operated upon premises rejected by most clergy. Such schemes tended to be, almost without exception, premillennial, and they claimed a greater foreknowledge than Protestants generally thought attainable.[49] Nevertheless, the war did induce a few people to seek scriptural evidence that the details of the current crisis had been predicted.

An obscure Methodist preacher, L. S. Weed of Brooklyn, provides

47. Joel F. Bingham, *The Hour of Patriotism,* "A Discourse Delivered at the United Service of the First, Lafayette Street, North, and Westminster Presbyterian Churches, Buffalo, Nov. 27, 1862," pp. 23–24.

48. Brown, "Watchers for the Second Coming."

49. For a discussion of efforts to fix precisely the prophetic timetable, consult Sandeen, *Roots of Fundamentalism,* esp. pp. 81–102. Sandeen notes on p. 97 that such commentators generally made little effort to relate their scenarios to the Civil War.

a representative guide into these exotic realms. Weed surveyed the contemporary scene rife with "debates in Congress, and Parliament, and Chambers; insurrections in the Ottoman Empire and Greece; the upheaval of society in Russia; the Italian difficulties; the discontent of Hungary and Poland; the dissensions of Germany; the unrest of France and Spain; the tramp of foreign mercenaries in Mexico, and the rage of civil conflict and the boom of cannon on our shores." Turmoil on such a global scale, he concluded, could be only the "ascending dust of the world's gathering squadrons for the decisive conflict."[50]

Weed was confident that the specifics of this apocalyptic drama could be learned from the Scriptures. In particular he turned to the dream of Nebuchadnezzar in the second chapter of Daniel—a book that has frequently inspired millennial speculation—to find a clue to the present world situation. In this dream, the Chaldean king sees a human image whose body is divided into four sections composed of different substances. A stone cut without human hands smashes the image and becomes a great mountain filling the entire earth. Daniel interprets the human figure as a symbolic representation of the future succession of earthly empires, the head signifying Nebuchadnezzar's own kingdom and the remaining portions of the body three political powers to arise later. The great stone indicates a fifth empire that will destroy every trace of the preceding ones and will establish a permanent dominion throughout the earth. Following a standard interpretation, Weed suggested that the political units foreshadowed by the image had virtually passed away, although remnants of the fourth empire—the Roman—persisted in the modern nations of Europe. Since Europe's turmoil indicated it was in decline, the hour of the fifth and universal empire was at hand. "Our country," suggested Weed with no false modesty, "is the exact fulfillment" of this prophecy.[51]

Weed found explicit prediction of the Civil War and its outcome in the twelfth chapter of the Apocalypse, which recounts a celestial conflict between the Archangel Michael and the dragon. After stubborn resistance, this satanic rebellion collapses, and the dragon's

50. *Christian Advocate and Journal,* November 20, 1862, p. 370.
51. Ibid.

hosts are cast from heaven—a symbolic representation, according to Weed, of the certain defeat of the Confederacy. This expulsion proved to Weed's satisfaction that tyranny would henceforth be confined to Europe, whose tottering aristocracies would attempt a final abortive alliance against the Union. Near the end of the secession struggle, the United States and these corrupt powers would confront one another, probably on the field of battle; and as prophesied in the thirty-eighth and thirty-ninth chapters of Ezekiel, this coalition against the American Israel would be "entirely overthrown." Then revolutions would reverberate around the globe, and all nations would submit to the Gospel and to democracy as exemplified by the United States. As Weed described this era, "The genius of this government is to sweep the world. Universal suffrage, constitutional guarantees, and the separation of Church and State, opens the way for the universal spread of the Gospel, and the sublime realization of self-government among all people. . . . That long cycle of ages called the millennium will then be ushered in." Stripped to its essential features, Weed's exegesis represented a vigorous affirmation that the Civil War would prove the pivot of world history. Through the present suffering, the United States' moral character would achieve "vindication for all coming time," and America would stride onto the world stage to democratize and evangelize the nations. Weed summed up: the Civil War is the "first great conflict to precede the millennium."[52]

The Reverend Hollis Read, a sometime missionary to India and agent for the American Tract Society, read the same portents in contemporary events. In *The Coming Crisis of the World, or the Great Battle and the Golden Age* (1861), he disclosed his conviction that the millennium would begin within approximately five years. He reached this conclusion from a study of the seven vials that, according to the sixteenth chapter of Revelation, shall be poured out before the end of time. Prophetic investigation had long focused upon the fifth of these: "And the fifth angel poured out his vial upon the seat of the beast; and his Kingdom was full of darkness." With virtually every other Protestant commentator, Read agreed that the seat of the beast lay in papal Rome and that his kingdom

52. Ibid., November 27, 1862, p. 378.

was Catholic Europe. The "hopeless confusion" betokened by the 1848 revolutions, the collapse of the papal states, and the Crimean conflict indicated to Read that the contents of this vial were currently being emptied. Europe trembled, he said, "over a volcano. Its internal fires are boiling and ere long we shall hear the explosion."[53] If the libation of the fifth vial were in process, the sixth— which would dry up the Euphrates River—was in readiness and could not long be delayed. Since that river flowed through the heartland of Islam, Read concluded that the demise of Muslim power was here prophesied, and the prediction appeared timely. Under the impact of European encroachment, the Turkish empire had declined to its nadir. The disintegration of Near Eastern strength augured the region's early "glorious emancipation," an awakening that would correspond to the drying up of the Euphrates. Thus the eschatological timetable hastened toward the seventh and final vial, which would announce the final cataclysm. In the political intrigues and military preparations of the great powers, Read saw clear evidence that the Lord would soon "stir up the kings of the earth to the last great conflict—to the battle of the great day of God Almighty . . . the battle of Armageddon."[54]

Other predictions from the Bible added weight to the former missionary's belief that the millennium must be close. The mysterious Man of Sin, whose advent Paul designated as a precursor of the end, was appearing in the "condition of unparalleled lawlessness and impiety" manifest in the modern world. The "fast maturing germs of the last great antichrist" were rapidly reproducing in the "Owenism, the Non-Resistance, the Fourierism, Transcendentalism, and Come-Outerism of our country"—heterodox persuasions revealing the dangerous infidelity of "large classes of men [who] tread with vandal steps on the long-tried institutions of their fathers and trample down the long ago venerated structures of wisdom and experience."[55] Simultaneously the prophecy of Joel was remarkably fulfilled, this last generation enjoying a widespread outpouring of the Holy Spirit. The ambassadors of the Gospel successfully used

53. Hollis Read, *The Coming Crisis of the World, or the Great Battle and the Golden Age,* pp. 6–63.
54. Ibid., pp. 117–18.
55. Ibid., pp. 70–75, 140.

the scientific inventions of modern civilization—the telegraph, the steamship, and the press—to spread the good news around the earth. There dawned "a day of unparalleled light, and light is increasing in a more rapid ratio than ever before." The prayer meeting revivals that had begun in New York City in 1858 had been marked by "extraordinary influences of the spirit" and had inaugurated a "Pentecostal season" whose first fruits promised the final ingathering.[56]

Ironically modern history witnessed the development of two contradictory forces as infidelity and Christianity gained ground simultaneously. Movement was at once forward and retrograde because the earth was dividing into two hostile camps, each mustering its army at full strength for a decisive test. The hour of that conflict had come.

> God makes no vain preparations. The great Captain is not thus so greatly recruiting his army, and collecting the munitions of war—storing his arsenals—preparing the weapons of war— and appropriating to his service the silver and gold—the time, talents and various services of all sorts of laborers, if he is not about to arise and enter on the warfare with renewed vigor and carry it to the strongholds of the enemy. . . . We may then very legitimately infer, from the greatly increased numbers of men enlisted and the vast amount of resources engaged that our Lord and great Captain is about to push the warfare to a final victory.[57]

"The great centre of the conflict," Read argued, "is for the present transferred to America." On the eve of the millennium the United States was summoned to purge the rot of slavery and "to stand up before the nations of the earth as a model nation, to exhibit to them the beauty and glory of free institutions." The certain renovation attained, America would truly be God's "modern Israel," would vindicate for all time the viability of republican government, and would proclaim throughout the world a "year of Jubilee to all that still are bound." Viewed from the perspective of God's foreordained plan, the Civil War could be none other than the preparation for the millennium. The war, he said, "is one of the last mighty strides of

56. Ibid., pp. 273–75.
57. Ibid., p. 188.

Providence towards the goal of humanity's final and high destiny. A few more such strides, a few more terrific struggles and travail pains among the nations; a few more such convulsions and revolutions, that shall break to pieces and destroy what remains of the inveterate and time-honored systems and confederations of sin and Satan, and the friends of freedom may then lift up their heads and rejoice, for their redemption draweth nigh."[58]

Most Protestants, especially the theologically sophisticated, maintained a healthy skepticism toward efforts to achieve a precise calibration of particular prophecies with the events of the Civil War. In January 1861 the *Princeton Review* denounced the view that the Bible projected a detailed scenario of the historical process. Prophecy adopts "a more comprehensive view by condensing the whole [of God's plan] into a single picture." It depicts the divine purpose in a fashion comparable to a landscape painting whose "principle features can be discerned" but whose specific details are frequently blurred into broad contours. As the *Review* summed up its argument, the Bible presents a "foreshadowing of God's great designs," but it does not "write a history beforehand."[59]

A similar critique appeared in the *American Presbyterian and Theological Review.* Doctor E. F. Hatfield argued that Old Testament predictions could not be forced into a coordinate system with the Book of Revelation. All prophecies within the Jewish canon point either to the life of Israel or to the earthly ministry of Jesus— that is, to his first, not his second, coming. Thus on principle no modern nation could answer to the figure of the stone kingdom in Daniel 2. Furthermore Hatfield insisted that New Testament prophecies, in particular the Revelation of John, depict the church's hope amid the Neronic persecution of the first century and bear upon the last things only insofar as the ultimate triumph of God's purpose in history is affirmed. Hatfield averred the relevance of prophecy to the contemporary situation, but his was a millennialism that rested upon  the general motifs of biblical eschatology rather than upon a tenuous collection of proof texts, each of which supposedly foretold a specific contemporary event. Of commen-

58. Ibid., pp. 221, 227–28, 237, 242.
59. "The Fulfillment of Prophecy," *Biblical Repertory and Princeton Review* 33 (January 1861): 84–122.

tators who attempted more, he remarked acidly: "Those who watch for the fall of the Beast require a perpetual succession of new works, as those who speculate in stocks require a daily newspaper."[60]

The popular religious press sounded the same warning as did the quarterlies. A month after the shelling of Sumter, the *Presbyterian* admitted that elaborate predictions of the end of time "may be nearer right" than heretofore supposed, but it warned against efforts to fit current events into a "Procrustean bed" of prophetic interpretation.[61] Similarly the *Independent* dealt circumspectly with "several communications whose object it is to trace in the present war the fulfillment of certain prophecies in the Revelation of John." Although the editor commended these students for their willingness to view secular events in the light of God's word, he warned against the "wild enthusiasm" that confidently asserted that this battle or that defeat had been charted out, chapter by chapter, in the Scriptures. In every age the paper recalled, "The people of God have been wont to seize upon and apply to their own times the predictions that seem so applicable to our own." The failure of so many cunningly devised schemes was a reminder to Christians that prophecy is "fulfilled anew from age to age" as God's Kingdom advances to its culmination "in all these great events that baffle human foresight."[62]

Yet if the majority of Protestants rejected the interpretive method of an L. S. Weed, they did not oppose his substantive affirmations about the meaning of the war. They accepted the apocalyptic character of the struggle and described it in language suggestive of the ultimate crisis in world history. Although the *Independent,* for example, denied that the Bible foretold the present in detail, the paper did not hesitate to assert that the final destiny of the world hinged upon the successful mastery of the secession crisis.

60. Edwin F. Hatfield, "The Messiah's Second Advent," *American Presbyterian and Theological Review,* n.s. 2 and 3 (April 1864): 197–223, (July 1864): 411–40, and (April 1865): 195–227. See especially Hatfield's summation in the April 1865 issue, pp. 225–27. Similar arguments can be found in Heman Lincoln, "The Millennium of the Bible," *Christian Review* 28 (January 1863): 131–44, and Henry M. Harmon, "The Apocalypse and Its Exposition," *Methodist Quarterly Review* 47 (April 1865): 230–53.

61. *Presbyterian,* May 18, 1861, p. 78.

62. *Independent,* December 19, 1861, p. 4.

"This third American generation . . . [is] the warrior in the deadly breach of the great siege of the ages. If it falters all is lost. . . . We shall stand in history as the most beneficent or maleficent of human generations, and as the most faithful or the most false in the eye of God."[63] Shortly after the battle of Antietam, Theodore Tilton, one of the leading editorial voices of the paper, wrote a hymn that expressed his hope for the war's outcome:

> By, the great sign, foretold, of Thy Appearing,
>   Coming in clouds, while mortal men stand fearing,
> Show us, amid this smoke of battle, clearing,
>   Thy chariot nearing![64]

Throughout the Protestant denominations, people whose works indicated little affinity to the making of prophetic timetables echoed the sentiments of Tilton. William B. Sprague, the sober Old School Presbyterian editor of *Annals of the American Pulpit*, predicted that the war would end in "a flood of millenial [*sic*] glory" and would introduce "the great Thanksgiving Day of the World."[65] Daniel C. Eddy assured a Baptist gathering in Philadelphia that once the rebellion had been crushed there would dawn "such a day as Washington and Hancock and Adams pictured and dreamed about, and prayed for. It will come with blessings, and be greeted with Hallelujahs, it will be the Millennium of political glory, the Sabbath of Liberty, the Jubilee of Humanity."[66] Brief remarks in the *Christian Advocate and Journal* summarized the prevailing opinion: "We live in the world's crisis. God is doing in the earth just what he has promised to do before his kingdom can come. Prophecy is marching with stately tread into the vestibule of glorious fulfillment."[67] Their differences over the vagaries of biblical interpretation did not

63. Ibid., May 21, 1863, p. 4.
64. Ibid., October 1, 1862, p. 4.
65. William B. Sprague, *Glorifying God in the Fires,* "A Discourse Delivered in the Second Presbyterian Church, Albany, November 28, 1861," p. 58.
66. Daniel C. Eddy, *The Union, The Constitution and the Laws,* "A Discourse Delivered in the Tabernacle Church, Philadelphia, before the First and Tabernacle Baptist Congregations, on the National Fast Day, April 30th, 1863," p. 35.
67. *Christian Advocate and Journal,* August 13, 1863, p. 258.

prevent Protestants from uttering a nearly unanimous affirmation that on the fields of Shiloh, Gettysburg, and the Wilderness a decisive eschatological struggle was being enacted.

## THE MORAL REBIRTH OF AMERICA

As the crux of history, the Civil War was expunging the sins of the nation and preparing for the American people a victory that would fundamentally alter their relationship to other nations. The Reverend Daniel March of Philadelphia foresaw an unparalleled moral renaissance that would transform America into that for which it had been originally created—"a mountain of holiness for the dissemination of light and purity to all the nations."[68] The *Christian Advocate and Journal* suggested: "God shall melt the moral granite of the nation, and raise up through the sediments and fossils of successive stages of iniquity a new Mt. Sinai from the Gulf to the St. Lawrence, thundering from its top right, and truth, and justice, and liberty through the centuries and the milleniums and the aeons and out into eternity."[69]

The moral victory of the ages seemed well begun in the charitable organizations formed to aid the war effort. Of these various endeavors, the United States Christian Commission was by far the most intimately connected with American Protestantism. In the summer of 1861, leaders of the New York Young Men's Christian Association circulated an appeal to similar organizations to join in the establishment of a ministry to soldiers. A conference in New York City on 14 and 15 November 1861 formed the commission and elected as its president George H. Stuart, a Presbyterian lay leader and evangelical philanthropist. By the war's end the organization had become a vast interdenominational fellowship virtually absorbing the YMCA into itself and including in its ranks the representatives of the major communions. Although its fundamental motivation was religious, the commission never forgot, in the words of Stuart, that "there is a good deal of religion in a warm shirt and a good beefsteak."[70] The nearly 5,000 unpaid delegates sent to the army presided at revival meetings, distributed tracts, and offered

68. March, *Steadfastness and Preparation*, p. 13.
69. *Christian Advocate and Journal*, February 12, 1863, p. 52.
70. Robert Ellis Thompson, ed., *The Life of George H. Stuart*, p. 129.

spiritual counsel to the distressed; they also wrote letters for the wounded, nursed the sick, operated lending libraries, and ran soup kitchens supplementing the regular fare of the soldiers. In conjunction with women's auxiliaries, the organization received and disbursed over $6 million in cash, goods, and services.[71] This benevolent outpouring from all the churches made the commission the fullest institutional expression of the antebellum dream of an evangelical united front—Christians of every Protestant denomination working together to hasten the Kingdom.

The other great voluntary agency created in response to the conflict was the United States Sanitary Commission formed in June 1861 under the leadership of Henry W. Bellows, a prominent Unitarian minister in New York City. If the Christian Commission realized the ideal of interdenominational benevolence, its counterpart advanced the cause of systematic or scientific charity. The United States Sanitary Commission, with the aid of the separate Western Sanitary Commission, dispatched medical inspectors to the front. Initially the unwanted guests of the military, these workers lobbied and criticized until they had secured a much needed streamlining of sanitary practices in the armed forces. Ultimately the War Department accepted the commission as an adjunct for maintaining the depots and transportation facilities necessary to the distribution of medical supplies, clothes, and food. This systematized benevolence may be justly cited as one of the progenitors of the American Red Cross.[72]

Narrower in function and less explicitly religious, Bellows's organization also shunned the personalized involvement with individual soldiers that marked the work of the Christian Commission. Differences in philosophy occasioned some mutual suspicion, the Sanitary leaders expressing misgivings about the structural looseness of the Christian Commission and the delegates of the latter resenting the

71. Lemuel Moss, *Annals of the United States Christian Commission*, p. 729 and passim. See also Thompson, *Life of George H. Stuart*, esp. pp. 129–70. A brief useful account is in Hopkins, *History of the Y.M.C.A. in North America*, pp. 84–98.
72. See Robert H. Bremner, *American Philanthropy*, pp. 80–84, and William Quentin Maxwell, *Lincoln's Fifth Wheel: The Political History of the United States Sanitary Commission*.

superior financial resources and the paid "hirelings" of the Sanitary Commission.[73] Nevertheless the two organizations cooperated with one another, and their endeavors were indissolubly linked in the popular mind as expressions of one benevolent impulse. Although Protestant clergy were more concerned with the Christian Commission, they did not neglect the claims of the other. The Sanitary Fairs held throughout the nation to raise money and goods for the commission received their warm endorsement and participation.[74]

The two great charitable establishments were only the leading examples of an eager philanthropic spirit that found numerous institutional expressions. Scarcely a town or hamlet did not have a Soldier's Aid Society, usually staffed by women volunteers who sewed garments, collected packages, and ran fairs to obtain money for the work among the troops. In New York City the Woman's Central Relief Association, which had provided the germ of the idea for the Sanitary Commission, served as a central collecting agency for the local societies.[75]

Every major population center also had its freedmen's relief association. In addition to supplying materiel, schools, and teachers for the impoverished ex-slaves who came within the Union lines, these bodies maintained an especially intimate and crucial relationship with the federal government's slowly evolving Negro policy. When the Lincoln administration agreed to create under the Treasury Department a pilot project for the education of freed blacks on the Sea Islands off South Carolina, these private groups provided workers and paid their salaries. From Freedmen's Relief Committees

73. Maxwell, *Lincoln's Fifth Wheel*, pp. 191–93, 222–23.

74. For numerous examples, see Charles Brandon Boynton, *History of the Great Western Sanitary Fair*, passim.

75. Their wartime activities probably furthered the social emancipation of women. Linus P. Brockett and Mary C. Vaughn wrote in 1867: "Thousands of women learned in this work to despise frivolity, gossip, fashion, and idleness; learned to think soberly and without prejudice of the capacities of their own sex; and thus, did more to advance the rights of woman by proving her gifts and her fitness for public duties, than a whole library of arguments and protests." See Brockett and Vaughn, *Woman's Work in the Civil War: A Record of Heroism, Patriotism and Patience*, p. 59. For a corroborating judgment, consult William L. O'Neill, ed., *The Woman Movement: Feminism in the United States*, p. 23.

came the stream of requests that led ultimately to the creation of the Freedmen's Bureau in March 1865 under the leadership of Major General Oliver O. Howard.[76] These, of course, were not the only organizations engaged in relieving the wants of ex-slaves. A particularly honorable place accrues to the American Missionary Association. The AMA entered the field early, and by the end of the war had over 250 preachers and teachers dispersed throughout the Confederacy. This figure represented approximately a quarter of the more than 900 teachers of all the secular and religious aid societies.[77]

Finally, the war reinvigorated traditional channels of benevolent endeavor. The Bible and Tract societies expended thousands of dollars in the dissemination of reading material to the soldiers, and individual denominations followed suit through their own colportage and domestic missions boards. Although the churches lagged far behind such independent agencies as the AMA in work with the freedmen, by April 1865 all of the major communions had formed their own freedmen's societies.[78]

Linus Brockett estimated early in 1864 that over $212 million had been given by the American people to various war-related charities. This staggering sum surely justified Brockett's boast that "neither in ancient nor modern times, has there been so vast an outpouring of a nation's wealth for the care, the comfort, and the physical and moral welfare of those who have fought the nation's battles or been the sufferers from its condition of war."[79] Such statistics form the empirical base of the widespread conviction that an unprecedented moral awakening was occurring within America. Although he spoke specifically of the Christian Commis-

76. James M. McPherson, *The Struggle for Equality: Abolitionists and the Negro in the Civil War and Reconstruction,* pp. 154–91. See also Julius M. Parmelee, "Freedmen's Aid Societies in the South, 1861–1871," in *Negro Education: A Study of the Private and Higher Schools for Colored People in the United States,* 1: 269–80.

77. "Anniversary at Boston," *American Missionary,* 2d ser., 9 (July 1865): 146.

78. Linus P. Brockett, *The Philanthropic Results of the War in America,* pp. 104–09, and Parmelee, "Freedmen's Aid Societies," pp. 280–82. For further information on the churches and blacks, see chapters 3 and 5 of this book.

79. Brockett, *Philanthropic Results of the War,* pp. 150, 160.

sion, Henry Boynton Smith might well have included the entire philanthropic enterprise when he said of that organization: it "stands out alone in the records of civilization and Christianity. More thoroughly than any other institution it has carried the spirit and principle of Christianity to the battle-field. . . . It is a new chapter in Church History."[80] Echoing this appraisal, Senator J. R. Doolittle told a gathering of the friends of the commission that its work "demonstrates that at this hour Christian prayer and influence upon earth is greater, more potent, more beneficent, than at any other period since the Saviour appeared."[81] Similarly when the *Independent* surveyed the overwhelming public response to the Sanitary Commission fairs, it could discover no analogous event since the tongues of flame had descended upon the church apostolic. "It has been a sort of pentecostal gathering," the editor said of a recent fair in Brooklyn, "wherein Catholics, Jews, Presbyterians, Methodists, Unitarians, Swedenborgians, Baptists, Congregationalists, Quakers, and Moravians forgot all their differences, and poured into one common reservoir their thank offerings, from the rich gifts of the opulent merchants of the Hights to the widow's mites of the alleys and byways. No lovelier, soul-satisfying spectacle was ever witnessed on this earth."[82]

Religious excitement provided another token of moral renewal. The delegates who went among the troops from Virginia to Mississippi reported revivals and conversions virtually without number. Accounts of the soldier won to Christ on his deathbed or by the pleading letter of a pious mother came from the pen of practically every member of the commission, and reports of successful prayer meetings were ubiquitous. As Sherman's army prepared for the historic march that would make Georgia howl, a lay delegate recounted a series of revival services that indicate the depth and character of religious life in the army.

> We made arrangements for holding two daily meetings, at one and seven o'clock, P.M. At the night meeting the church was crowded to overflowing—not a foot of standing room unoccu-

80. Moss, *Annals of the United States Christian Commission,* pp. 60–61.
81. Ibid., p. 266.
82. *Independent,* March 3, 1864, p. 4.

pied. The doors and windows were filled, and the crowds extended out into the street, straining their ears to catch the words of Jesus. Sometimes hundreds of persons would go away unable to get within hearing distance. Day after day the interest deepened, and large numbers came forward nightly for prayer. Scores of men long hardened in sin cried out, "What shall we do?" A number of the converts had never been baptized, and as they expressed a desire to remember this command of Christ, we invited all candidates for baptism to meet at the church on Sabbath afternoon, April 10th. Forty-four presented themselves. . . . We marched in solemn procession to the tune and hymn—"There is a fountain filled with blood"—down to the Chickamauga Creek. The soldiers stood on the banks, joining hands and continuing the hymn, while their comrades went down into the water—some for immersion, some for sprinkling, and others for pouring, but all for baptism in the name of the Father, and of the Son, and of the Holy Ghost. After administering the ordinance we returned to the church, singing—"Jesus, I my cross have taken"—and then sat down, about four hundred in number, at the table of our common Lord. Commissary bread, currant wine, tin plates and tin cups—these were the circumstances of the Lord's supper in the army.[83]

How many men were actually converted in the camp can never be accurately determined; the best contemporary estimates oscillate considerably between one hundred thousand and two hundred thousand.[84] One must also allow due consideration to the promotional character of the literature emanating from the front; stories of success surely recruited more support than did accounts of failure. Yet if the army never became the vast chapel of prayer that reports indicated, the sheer bulk of testimony partly validates the assessment of the anonymous delegate who wrote in the spring of 1864: "Probably no army, in any age, has ever witnessed such outpourings of the Spirit of God as our own armies have experienced."[85]

83. Edward P. Smith, *Incidents of the United States Christian Commission*, pp. 277–78.
84. Ahlstrom, *Religious History of the American People*, p. 677.
85. *Presbyterian*, April 23, 1864, p. 66.

Signs of grace in the army were duplicated in the churches, and by midwar the hope of an extended and universal shower of spiritual mercies filled the land. When Methodists gathered for their quadrennial General Conference in 1864, the sense of expectancy was high. Bishop Thomas A. Morris confidently summoned the denomination to "its grand mission, to spread Scriptural holiness over these and all lands. . . . We shall have such a revival of the work of God as the world has never seen. We have the dawning of this glorious day already; and we believe the sun will soon rise in full splendor, and from every hill and valley go up the shout, 'Halleluiah.' the Lord omnipotent reigneth."[86] The 1863 Presbyterian General Assembly (Old School) received so many reports of revivals in the midst of its congregations that it concluded joyfully: "The proof is unmistakable, that he whose coming is as noiseless as the wind has descended."[87] A "great national baptism," explained the Reverend William Patton, was beginning. "God will so pour out his spirit upon the army, the navy, and churches that millions of immortal beings will be converted, and the nation stand redeemed and sanctified."[88]

Henry Clay Fish, pastor of the First Baptist Church in Newark, New Jersey, saw in the war the fulfillment of the hope he had expressed in *Primitive Piety Revived* in 1855. There he urged the necessity of a "general and powerful revival of religion" if the nation's future were to be secured.[89] By Thanksgiving Day 1863 he was confident that a spiritually reborn United States was indeed emerging from the conflict. He described in extravagant detail an idyllic, if not utopian, vision of the new America:

Happy day of the Nation's renovation! O fellow-workers, I congratulate you upon its coming in our time! I see it! I see it! The war successfully ended; the bondman everywhere a freeman; the degraded white man everywhere educated and ennobled; the diverse elements in the national composition fused and welded inseparably together; local jealousies and animosities at an end; treason and traitors expelled from the

86. Marlay, *Life of Thomas A. Morris*, p. 356.
87. *Minutes of the General Assembly of the Presbyterian Church in the United States of America, Old School* (1863), 17: 77.
88. *Independent*, February 18, 1864, p. 2.
89. Fish, *Primitive Piety Revived*, pp. 231–49.

country; the heresy of state sovereignty and secession killed; loyalty and patriotism a life in the heart's core of every inhabitant; the extremities of the country drawn into a closer relationship; its physical resources developed; a school-house and church in every district; the people taking the highest type of civilization—intelligent, God-fearing, liberty-loving, self-governed, and bound together in one tender and beautiful brotherhood.[90]

This exhilarating doctrine was reiterated in many pulpits, and its central affirmations were everywhere the same: a new and perfected America, whose preeminent status in the world would be "recognized of God, mankind, and posterity," was being born.[91] No one could foretell the glories of this "spectacle that angels will delight to behold."[92] Raised to the "front rank among the Great Powers," the United States would stand forth "the best merely human government the world ever saw," "the wonder and envy of nations."[93]

### THE FUTURE MISSION OF THE UNITED STATES

God did not rescue America for its own benefit alone; an exalted mission awaited it once the guns fell silent. The United States was to be consecrated "to Jehovah as a national Israel and servant of the Lord, fit for her Master's use."[94] "A new career," observed Doctor H. M. Johnson in a letter to the *Christian Advocate and Journal,* "then opens to us; a divine commission is given us which imposes responsibilities of appalling magnitude. We stand the nearest representatives of God's government on earth; we are made the chief

90. Henry Clay Fish, *The Valley of Achor a Door of Hope: or, the Grand Issues of the War,* "A Discourse Delivered on Thanksgiving Day, November 26, 1863," p. 22.
91. Joel Bingham, *Great Providences Toward the Loyal Part of This Nation,* "A Discourse Delivered at a United Service of the Seven Presbyterian Congregations of Buffalo, November 24, 1864," p. 16.
92. Henry Darling, *Chastened, but Not Killed,* "A Discourse Delivered on the Day of the National Fast, August 4th, 1864," p. 37.
93. Elisha P. Cleaveland, *Our Duty in Regard to the Rebellion,* "A Fast Day Sermon, Preached in the Third Congregational Church, New Haven, April 3, 1863," p. 13.
94. Nathaniel West, Jr., *Establishment in National Righteousness,* "A Sermon Preached in the Second Presbyterian Church, Brooklyn, N.Y.," p. 37.

leader in the great work of establishing the kingdom of righteousness among men."[95] The *Independent* reminded its readers that the nation as God's new Israel would be constrained to validate its election by a vigorous Christian witness to the world. "All this national power and greatness, which God has so marvellously produced for us out of our great calamity, is the property of the Lord Jesus Christ and is to be employed under his direction for the advancement of his Kingdom in this world. This nation is solemnly bound to exist for the glory of God. It is a covenant obligation, that no power can repeal."[96]

Once America was reborn, its mission of moral suasion, so long hampered by the nation's internal inconsistencies, could properly be undertaken for the first time. A candid world would perceive that democratic government was no longer a tenuous experiment but the wave of the future and would, in imitation, shake loose the ancient bonds of despotism. Before the Union armies had fought a major battle, the Reverend William Goodrich already foresaw the result: "If the Revolution which gave this land its birth, sent forth a wave of influence which rocked the thrones of the old world, and whose vibrations still tremble in the hearts of nations, so the issues of this contest are to be felt with swifter impulse in every land that knows the American name."[97] With more expansive rhetoric, J. W. Hough of Williston, Vermont, predicted that after the war had perfected the nation, "its voice will be heard around the world; it will stir the peoples of Italy and Germany and Hungary; it will echo from the Ural heights to the Chinese Wall; it will penetrate even the jungles of Africa, proclaiming everywhere 'liberty to the captives, and the opening of prison to them that are bound.'" An inseparable aspect of the American witness would be a renascent Protestantism, which was being prepared for the aggressive evangelization of all peoples. "Then shall the church have power in the land and in the world. Then shall the Christian Republic, gathering its wealth from Southern plain and Western prairies and still more Western mountains of gold; opening with its commerce the gates of every sea; stimulating mind by its very freedom to the highest research, culti-

95. *Christian Advocate and Journal*, June 23, 1864, p. 193.
96. *Independent*, April 28, 1864, p. 4.
97. Goodrich, *Sermon on the Christian Necessity of War*, p. 12.

vating society by giving the highest culture to individual man; bring its gold and its commerce, its wealth of learning and its social wealth, and lay them down at the foot of the cross." Beyond all other nations, concluded Hough, the United States would be consecrated the "missionary land" par excellence. Democracy and the blessings of civilization in service to the Gospel that gave them birth—these were the aspects of the mission to which American Protestants looked forward once the Union was restored. Hough found new meaning and relevance in the lines of Bishop Arthur C. Coxe:

> We are living, we are dwelling,
> In a grand and awful time
> In an age on ages telling,
> To be living is sublime.[98]

The exemplary character of the United States was scarcely a new element in Protestant patriotism, but the experience of the early 1860s had given the churches' usually pacific concept of mission a new hardness and belligerence. Millennial imagery, of course, depicts marching armies and sanguinary battles, and thus the struggle of the saints, even if spiritualized, is potentially separated from more carnal warfare by a thin line only. After fighting their apocalyptic contest with saber and rifle, Northern churchmen were in danger of losing sight of that boundary altogether. Henceforth, predicted the *Christian Watchman and Reflector* in 1862, no country "will dare hazard the issue of a contest with a people who, in a single year, can ex-

---

98. J. W. Hough, *Our Country's Mission, or the Present Suffering of the Nation Justified by Its Future Glory,* "A Discourse Preached at Williston, Vermont, on the Day of the National Fast, August 4th, 1864," pp. 18, 20–22. Arthur Coxe (1818–96) wrote this hymn, "Watch-words: A Hymn for the Times," in 1842. A vigorous affirmation of millennial expectancy, the hymn has suffered the expurgation of its more explicit references to apocalyptic Scripture. Included in the original was this stanza drawn from the imagery of Ezekiel 38–39 and Revelation 20:

> Hark! The waking up of nations,
> Gog and Magog to the fray;
> Hark! What soundeth is creation's
> Groaning for the latter day.

See Ninde, *Story of the American Hymn,* p. 322.

temporize an army and a navy unsurpassed in history."[99] From the necessity of taking up arms, the Reverend Samuel T. Spear augured "a new career for the nation." Because the United States had acquired "that military experience, and those military preparations, which secure respect among the nations of the earth," Americans could defiantly unfurl their flag as the emblem of a "first class nation, whose ability to defend its rights will protect it against injury." In the future none of the corrupt regimes of Europe—especially an "ineffably mean" England whose coolness to the Union cause rankled Spear—would dare "to trample on our rights with impunity." Soon the commonly held belief that a republican government "cannot be a great military and naval power" would be happily dead.[100]

The tested arms of the nation might require further use abroad if America's mission were to be achieved. In April 1864 Gilbert Haven deduced that possibility from the fact that the present conflict was part of a larger "World War" between aristocracy and democracy. Failure to perceive this global interdependence, particularly at a time when "all peoples are fast becoming one," had previously cost the forces of freedom dearly. The collapse of the French Revolution into Napoleonic Caesarism, the destruction of Kossuth's revolt in Hungary, and the failure of the Irish to win home rule—these reverses befell democracy in part because the United States had abdicated its responsibility to support liberty everywhere. This tragic negligence in turn drew upon America a bitter retribution, for its apathy left intact the corrupt thrones of France and England permitting them to grant the Confederacy a quasi-recognition. But Haven believed that his countrymen had been rescued from somnolence and were now ready to assume their global responsibilities. "To save ourselves, we may be compelled to save others. We shall then be the inspiring and molding nation that they have long needed. As England molded and inspired all Europe for a quarter of a century to resist and overthrow Republicanism in Europe that she might preserve her own aristocratic institutions intact, so America, her grander daughter, may have to guide those peoples in a

99. *Christian Watchman and Reflector,* August 21, 1862.
100. Samuel T. Spear, *The Nation's Blessing in Trial,* "A Sermon Preached in the South Presbyterian Church of Brooklyn," p. 36.

conflict for republicanism, however long, however costly, however bloody. We are the only great nation that represents the sovereignty of the people. We may be compelled to maintain that sovereignty everywhere with the sword." As once the Concert of Europe tried to stabilize the old order, the United States would now lead an alliance of free peoples. A pax Americana would descend upon the earth and merge with that great and final era of peace. The United States, prophesied Haven, was now prepared to "renew and unite the world. The nations that have so long sat in darkness, and have now seen the great light, will come to that light, and kings to the brightness of its rising. Thus and then will wars cease to the end of the earth, the millennial glory rest upon the world-republic and universal liberty, equality, and brotherhood bring universal peace."[101]

A collection of essays, *Christ in the Army,* published by the Ladies' Christian Commission in 1865 adduced a similar national destiny as a result of the war. One author acknowledged that the United States had stumbled into military power against the received wisdom of the "fathers of the republic," but he insisted that a providential design had thrust this unwanted greatness upon America. Reflective minds perceived that there could be no retreat from global responsibility—"we cannot sell or give away" the country's armed forces or return to an "isolated, private situation among the nations of the world." Even if no United States' soldier ever fired a gun again, the country's armed might had been convincingly demonstrated and would hereafter enter into the calculus of international diplomacy. Only one real question remained: for what purpose had God bestowed power upon the United States and how should it be employed? The pamphlet answered resoundingly that the Lord intended American military force to play a decisive role in the advent of his Kingdom.

> The Lord is mustering the nations to the last great struggle between freedom and slavery, truth and error, and wish it as we may, He does not design that we bury the power He has forced on us. We are not being thus trained for idleness. We are entering, fellow-citizens, upon a period foretold by prophets of

101. Haven, *National Sermons,* pp. 448–71.

old—looked for and longed for by lovers of their country in past generations—which kings and prophets waited to see, and have not seen—a period of the overthrow of despotism, and the downfall of Anti-Christ; and it is evidently the design of Almighty God that the United States of America should be found prepared for taking their part, whatever it may be, in that great struggle. In that struggle the army and navy of the United States will doubtless find some appropriate work to perform, not with the design of subjugation or territorial extension, but in brotherly defence of right and truth, beside the European defenders of the rights of God and man. The arbitrament of the world's destiny, the fate of the liberty of mankind, depends upon the American army and navy.[102]

In one sense, these pretensions cannot be taken at face value. Inflated rhetoric in the midst of civil war scarcely constituted the churches' last word on national policy. As yet no one was proposing that the army be dispatched to any specific wars. Apart from dark mutterings against the French-supported regime of Mexican Emperor Maximilian, there was a splendid vagueness in the jingoistic assertions of American power.[103] Yet having allowed proper discount for bombast, these strident assertions were of major importance. Little more than four calendar years separated *Christ in the Army* from Walter Clarke's sermon before the Foreign Missionary Society, but ideologically the time span might have been a century. "The people of God have no need to assail the nations; they have no use for arms, and no license for invasion," Clarke had said. By war's end, the message had changed: "The arbitrament of the world's destiny, the fate of the liberty of mankind, depends upon the American army and navy."

### THE HOLY HISTORY OF THE REPUBLIC

This transformation of the Protestant sense of national purpose cannot be easily categorized. Heightened preoccupation with rifles and politics betokened, in a limited sense, a secularization of reli-

102. *Christ in the Army: A Selection of Sketches of the Work of the U.S. Christian Commission,* pp. 137–40.
103. See, for example, *Independent,* April 23, 1863, p. 4.

gious concern; and it may be that the churches' stress upon the profane served ultimately to displace the spiritual from a central position in American life.[104] That result, however, was only an indirect outcome of the war and was utterly contrary to the wishes of Protestants. They interpreted the conflict as the sanctification of American life; or as an anonymous pamphleteer said, paraphrasing the Book of Revelation, "'And the seventh angel sounded; and there were great voices in heaven,'—in the Free States,—'saying: The kingdoms of this world are become the kingdoms of our Lord and of his Christ.'"[105] Henceforth the history of the Republic would itself by a holy history, and the voice of God could now be heard as surely in American politics and power as in the various benevolent enterprises that antebellum Protestants greeted as harbingers of the millennium. As the Reverend Israel Dwinnell of Salem, Massachusetts, observed: "God has no need now after all the discipline of his providence, and all his preparations, to continue the circuitous process [of evangelization and moral influence] but can make political changes direct steps in the advancement of his Kingdom."[106]

No creeds were formally altered, but the Protestant community had recognized another source of religious authority that coexisted with formal assertions of a faith formed sola scriptura. Just as Israel experienced the direct leading of God in the Exodus, America was learning the divine will from the events of the Civil War. At Dartmouth in 1861, the Reverend S. P. Leeds suggested: "We are under God's leading, we would trust, like the Israelites in the wilderness. Let us not seek presumptuously to anticipate His time; but watching 'the cloudy, fiery pillar,' move on to do His will—and our faith shall

104. See William A. Clebsch, *From Sacred to Profane America: The Role of Religion in American History*. Clebsch offers a subtle analysis of the way in which religious concerns have been transmuted into secular ones in the American context. He argues that the churches have launched different crusades to mold society; but in each instance success is claimed by the secular order as its own peculiar property, and victory thus becomes failure for the churches. The great merit of Clebsch's thesis is that it rejects any simple discontinuity between the sacred and the profane in American life. See also Martin E. Marty, *The Modern Schism: Three Paths to the Secular*.

105. *The Bible on the Present Crisis*, p. 82.

106. Israel Dwinnell, *Hope for Our Country*, "A Sermon Preached in the South Church, Salem, October 19, 1862, p. 6.

not be disappointed."[107] When he pondered how his fellow citizens might learn the "Divine pleasure" without a supernatural miracle, George Ide concluded that "we are in possession of other means, by which the same end may be secured in a manner not less convincing—His will is declared to us by the out-flashing of events on the bosom of Time, which is God's priest."[108] Henry Ward Beecher stated the same doctrine in bolder language:

> What then, I ask in conclusion is infidelity in our day? It is refusing to hear God's voice, and to believe God's testimony in his providence. There are plenty of men who believe in Genesis, and Chronicles, and the Psalms, and Isaiah, and Daniel, and Ezekiel, and Matthew, and the other evangelists, and the rest of the New Testament, clear down to the Apocalypse. There are plenty of men who believe everything that God said four thousand years ago, but the Lord God Almighty is walking forth at this time in clouds and thunder such as never rocked Sinai. His voice is in all the earth, and those men who refuse to hear God in his [sic] own time, and in the language of the events that are taking place are infidels.[109]

Julia Ward Howe's "Battle Hymn of the Republic" is the most enduring expression of the wartime conviction that religious fulfillment was appearing in secular phenomena. On the hot summer evening when she imagined the coming of the Lord, the portents of his advent were the "burnished rows of steel" and the "watchfires" of the Union army. One of the earliest performances of this hymn occurred in Richmond's Libby Prison during the early hours of 4 July 1863. On the evening of July third, the dispirited Northern prisoners retired under the impression that Gettysburg had been a Union rout. Awakened the next morning by the correct report that the Confederates had suffered a disastrous reverse in Pennsylvania, the inmates jubilantly unveiled a hidden Union flag. Chaplain Charles McCabe, afterward a Methodist bishop, began singing the

107. S. P. Leeds, *Thy Kingdom Come: Thy Will Be Done,* "A Discourse Delivered on the National Fast, Sept. 26, 1861, in the Congregational Church at Dartmouth College," p. 27.
108. Ide, *Battle Echoes,* p. 15.
109. Beecher, *Patriotic Addresses,* p. 326.

"Battle Hymn," and five hundred prisoners joined in the chorus.[110] This piece of Civil War memorabilia evokes the churches' patriotic faith in classic form—the North's greatest victory of arms heralded on the national birthday as the fulfillment of God's promise to establish his kingdom.

The crusading millennialism of the Civil War was neither a simple continuation of previous faith nor a rejection of it. William Clebsch has recently described the American churches as "traducers of tradition"—traducers in the dual sense that they have transmitted their heritage but in so doing have altered its character.[111] Clebsch's thesis provides an appropriate description of the Protestant sense of national purpose in the decade of the rebellion. On one hand, ecclesiastical attitudes obeyed the inner logic of antebellum hopes. Evangelicals had long awaited the time when the Christian faith would permeate society so completely that the church would be the world and the profane the incarnation of the sacred. In this sense, the investiture of the Republic with the holiest trappings perpetuated a trend long underway. Nevertheless, something did change after the bombardment of Sumter. In spite of their awareness that the Apocalypse foretold wars, calamity, and judgment, the previous generation had usually spoken of a spiritual process—at least in America—by which the saeculum would be claimed for God: tract and Bible distribution, voluntary reform associations, and missionaries would evangelize the world until the millennium dawned. These activities remained, of course, crucial instruments in the building of the Kingdom; but after the federal war effort become a battle at Armageddon, the weapons of the saints were hopelessly confounded with the military power of the nation. Christians sang within one breath: "May we be freedom's soldiers true, nor less true soldiers of the cross."[112] Furthermore, the war generation believed that national life was being regenerated in one decisive test. Once the war

110. For an account of this incident, see Smith, *Incidents of the United States Christian Commission*, pp. 395–99. Julia Ward Howe cited the notoriety of this event as an important factor in the popularization of her hymn. Cf. Julia Ward Howe, *Reminiscences, 1819–1899*, p. 276.

111. William A. Clebsch, "American Churches as Traducers of Tradition," *Anglican Theological Review* 52 (January 1971): 21–34.

112. Moss, *Annals of the Christian Commission*, p. 179.

ended, the United States would have passed the crisis of its history, and thereafter, said Gilbert Haven, "the transfigured face of Christ" would shine from America.[113]

As the war drew to a close, Protestants experienced heightened confidence that God had vindicated his elect, indeed that he had made the Republic his indispensable tool for world renovation. It was ominous, however, that the clergy had identified this mission so closely with America's military power and achievement. Certainly no one would deny that some American churchmen had seen earlier wars as contests for the Kingdom of God; neither would one wish to claim that religious attitudes produced bellicose nationalism. But what happened in the 1860s did constitute a crucial moment of truth for the United States and its churches. With an unrivaled unamimity and fervor, Northern Protestants presented the struggle for the Union as a decisive religious battle. In the context of the country's first approximation of modern, total warfare, this inauspicious fact disclosed with peculiar force a dangerous substrate in the idealistic conception of American destiny: spiritual struggle particularly as expressed in those dark and ambiguous millennial symbols of warring hosts and final battles could be easily transformed into more earthly crusading. Thus the Northern response to the crisis of the Union was in part a premonition of later efforts in 1898 to export by gunboat the blessings of Christian civilization or to make the world safe for democracy in 1917; and in more recent memory, Americans have witnessed the mischief of the doctrine that "the fate of the liberty of mankind . . . depends upon the American army and navy."

In terms of short-range implications, the apocalyptic mentality was equally unfortunate. What could follow Armageddon? Expectations had been inflated to unreasonable proportions, and within several years the stubbornness of events belied the hope of total victory and demonstrated the unpreparedness of the churches for peace.

113. Haven, *National Sermons*, p. 359.

# 3

## Slavery and the Kingdom

After the Union disaster at Bull Run in the summer of 1861, President Lincoln set aside 26 September as a fast day on which citizens should humble themselves before God and seek out the meaning of the national reverse. At the State Street Congregational Church in Portland, Maine, the Reverend George L. Walker suggested that the debacle revealed God's intention to scourge the Union with military defeat until the North vowed to end slavery. "This [emancipation] is not what is proposed," Walker acknowledged. "No party represents such a purpose. No administration cherishes such a design. No caucus admits it in a platform. It is chargeable as the object of no section or leading man of the times. It is the logic of *events* which points to this issue. It is the shadow cast before the approaching Providence which indicates it."[1]

Walker gave voice to the conviction that God had taken the slavery question unto himself, and no doubt many like him were relieved to surrender custody of that dilemma which more than any other had tried their faith. Protestants had discovered that their attempts to advance the Kingdom by teaching the moral government of God did not yield anything close to an unequivocal answer to the slavery issue; and by 1860 consensus had long since dissolved into conflicting opinions. The almost joyous abandon with which the churches had thrown themselves into the business of war was in part an escape from ambiguities that had become too burdensome to sustain, and the apocalyptic trumpet sounded the glad promise that these uncertainties would be forever eliminated when God shortly made perfect his model republic. From this cathartic surge

1. George Leon Walker, *The Offered National Regeneration*, "A Sermon Preached in the State Street Church, Portland, on the Occasion of the National Fast, September 26, 1861," p. 12.

82

of emotion, the nation reaped considerable benefit. The slaves were emancipated, and three constitutional amendments guaranteeing civil liberties rode the crest of popular fervor to enactment. A heavy price, however, was exacted for these gains. Faith in cataclysmic answers, coupled with other simplistic assessments of slavery, did not bode well for the future. When America's perennial dilemma returned in a new guise, Protestants would be poorly equipped to deal with an enemy that refused to die on schedule.

## ANTEBELLUM LEGACIES

To understand Protestant attitudes toward slavery, one must begin by noting that opposition to human bondage is almost entirely a modern movement and lacks unqualified support from the older Western moral tradition. Following the legacy of classical antiquity, most theologians or ethical theorists before 1700 viewed slavery as a legitimate part of the natural order, and they recalled that in the Old Testament the Hebrews owned servants, and the New Testament enjoined obedience upon those in bondage. The Judeo-Christian heritage did contain, to be sure, certain motifs latently hostile to slavery—for example, the Exodus story and the spiritual equality of all persons in Christ—but it was difficult to demonstrate that the Bible required emancipation. Although the decline of slavery within the Roman Empire was coterminous with the rise of Christianity, undue significance should not be attached to this fact. Changing economic patterns were laying waste the foundations of the institution, and church teaching was far from an abolitionist spirit. The Christian community did praise manumission as a good work, and many received their freedom from pious owners; but a recent student of the period concludes: "Yet there is no sign of anything in the nature of a propaganda for the wholesale liberation of slaves." The church fathers, he notes, were "more concerned to ennoble the existing relation between master and slave than to reconstruct the social order."[2] During the Middle Ages slavery had largely expired, but Christian moralists continued to argue that it was a legitimate

2. F. Van der Meer, *Augustine the Bishop: Church and Society at the Dawn of the Middle Ages,* pp. 136–37. See also David Brion Davis, *The Problem of Slavery in Western Culture,* pp. 62–90.

form of social organization in a fallen world.[3] Thus when the European expansion into the New World revived human bondage on a large scale, there existed no coherent antislavery rationale within the Western tradition.

That possibility was not realized until a number of social and intellectual forces changed the Weltanschauung of the Atlantic community. Weary of the religious fanaticism that had characterized the English Civil War, an influential segment of British Protestantism in the late 1600s opted for a tolerant orthodoxy, stressing the rationality of faith and the moral capacity of humanity. The latitudinarian position, as it was called, relaxed the bonds of dogma, affirmed the hopeful possibilities of life on earth, and opened the way for various eighteenth-century speculations subversive of the traditional defenses of slavery. In the eighteenth century a number of theorists—including writers of the Scottish Enlightenment destined to be of seminal influence in antislavery circles—argued that man by nature possessed a feeling of benevolence or, alternately, that he discerned intuitively self-evident laws of morality written into the order of things. These notions, in combination with popular literary trends glorifying the noble savage or extolling the sentiment of compassion, cast the slave in a new light: he became potentially an object of pity, a prototype of natural innocence, or a supplicant for rights wrongly denied. Economic theorists, such as Adam Smith in *The Wealth of Nations* (1776), supplied another devastating criticism that later became common: the supposed economic inefficiency of the slave system.

The Age of Reason, however, was also an age of piety, and the international evangelical awakenings of the mid-1700s also contributed to the sources of antislavery conviction. These revivals summoned Christians to a more ardent warfare against sin and convinced many that it was possible to attain a more complete sanctification. Opposition to slavery was not the necessary outcome of this perfectionism, but the demand for radical conversion or demonstrable holiness—in a time when former justifications for slavery

3. Davis, *Problem of Slavery in Western Culture,* pp. 91–121, and Ernst Troeltsch, *The Social Teachings of the Christian Churches,* 1: 326–27, 430–31.

were eroding—psychologically prepared believers to oppose this institution with the same zeal that they directed against other vices.[4]

These trends cannot be subsumed under a single grand theme, but they lead to a cautious generalization: together they represented a heightened confidence in the potential of temporal existence. The medieval notion of the earth as a tear-filled anteroom gave way to the hope that life in this world could bring significant human fulfillment, whether that goal was defined as distinterested benevolence, economic utility, natural rights, or perfect sanctification. In this atmosphere the traditional contention that slavery was a necessary institution in a fallen world lost much of its force. Abolitionism was not, of course, the inevitable corollary of these sanguine views; indeed optimism sometimes worked to smother protest under a blanket of complacency. Moreover, widespread sentiment for manumission or for outlawing the slave trade did not take root until certain economic weaknesses in the existing slave system became apparent. But at very least the sense of a new day coming made involuntary servitude appear an anachronism.

Contemporary Americans viewed their Revolution as the chief demonstration that history indeed moved in a progressive direction and that in fact a new world order had been inaugurated. This order was founded upon the inalienable rights of all men, and yet slavery persisted in its midst. More than any other factor, the perception of inconsistency between the ideals of the new era and the harsh reality of the present transformed the lonely pre-Revolutionary antislavery witness of such Quakers as John Woolman and Anthony Benezet into a widespread revulsion against the system. By 1804 this moral awakening had secured what Arthur Zilversmit calls the "first emancipation"—the passage of manumission laws or the achievement of abolition by judicial decision in the Northern states.[5]

4. Davis, *Problem of Slavery in Western Culture*, pp. 333–45. For a splendid brief summary of these issues, consult also C. Duncan Rice, *The Rise and Fall of Black Slavery*, pp. 153–85.

5. Arthur Zilversmit, *The First Emancipation: The Abolition of Slavery in the North.* Zilversmit lays heavy stress upon the ideological roots of "the first emancipation" and minimizes economic factors. For a wider perspective on this period, see David Brion Davis, *The Problem of Slavery in the Age of Revolution, 1770–1823.*

The churches shared the conviction that slavery was a relic inconsistent with the new day. The Methodist Church, organized in America as a separate body in 1784, incorporated John Wesley's strictures against slavery into its discipline, and the highest judicatory of the Presbyterian Church expressed its hope in 1787 and in 1818 for a speedy end to human bondage.[6] Although they lacked a national organ to voice their sentiments, many local Baptist and Congregational associations expressed a similar faith during the generation following the close of the Revolutionary War.[7] Some Protestants drew an explicit connection between opposition to slavery and the common conviction that the millennial age was drawing nigh. The Reverend Samuel Hopkins, a noted disciple of Jonathan Edwards, wrote of black slavery:

> Thanks be to God! He has assured us that all these works of the devil shall be destroyed, and that the time is hastening on, when all the people shall be righteous and benevolent, and there shall be none to destroy or hurt in all the earth, . . . and there is reason to conclude that this light and conviction, and these exertions, will continue and increase till the slave traders shall be utterly destroyed. . . . And the gospel shall be preached to all nations; good shall be brought out of all the evil which takes place, and all men shall be united in one family and Kingdom under Christ the Savior; and the meek shall inherit the earth, and delight themselves in the abundance of peace. In the prospect of this we may rejoice in the midst of the darkness and evils which now surround us, and think ourselves happy if we may be, in any way, the active instruments of hastening on this desirable event.[8]

In a word, slavery was dying because the Kingdom was hastening among men.

6. Mathews, *Slavery and Methodism,* pp. 3–29; Andrew E. Murray, *Presbyterians and the Negro—A History,* pp. 3–28; and Lester B. Scherer, *Slavery and the Churches in Early America, 1619–1819,* pp. 126–52.

7. Conrad James Engelder, "The Churches and Slavery: A Study of the Attitudes Toward Slavery of the Major Protestant Denominations" (Ph.D. diss., University of Michigan, 1964), pp. 56–62, 95–98.

8. Samuel Hopkins, *The Works of Samuel Hopkins,* 2: 605, 609.

Too much should not be claimed for the antislavery spirit of the first emancipation. It was essentially a conservative movement, cautious of the rights of property and seldom willing to assault the institution directly. The manumission laws it secured were exceedingly gradual in application, and in states like New York and New Jersey where bondsmen constituted a significant economic interest, the financial loss of slaveholders was minimized by a de facto compensation.[9] Furthermore, those who wished to free slaves looked forward to colonizing them in Africa—an ambition that found institutional expression in the creation in 1816 of the American Society for Colonizing the Free People of Color in the United States. The Colonization Society dominated virtually all Protestant antislavery thought before the 1830s and a significant portion of it thereafter. Complex and often contradictory, the colonization impulse tapped optimism that slavery was moribund and pessimism that blacks were incapable of being integrated into American civilization. Seeking the broadest possible support, the society placed its faith in voluntary manumission, avoided any semblance of attack against the property rights of slaveholders, and offered a solution compatible with virulent racism.[10]

The churches, most of which endorsed colonization, agreed with the gradualist approach and eschewed controversial positions. For example, the Methodist Church by 1800 began to remand all infractions of the constitutional prohibition against slave trading and ownership to lower judicatories, which invariably chose to ignore them.[11] The Presbyterian Assembly's famous 1818 deliverance, although it branded slavery as "totally irreconcilable with the spirit and principles of the Gospel of Christ," also warned against immediate emancipation or censorious attacks against slaveholders. In a related action, the assembly sustained the deposition from the ministry of the Reverend George Bourne whose strident denunciation of human bondage had roused the ire of Virginia's Lexington Presbytery.[12] Faced with the prospect of schism, the churches

9. Zilversmit, *First Emancipation,* esp. pp. 175–200.
10. P. J. Staudenraus, *The African Colonization Movement, 1816–1865,* esp. pp. 1–22.
11. Mathews, *Slavery and Methodism,* pp. 2–29.
12. Murray, *Presbyterians and the Negro,* pp. 20–28.

decided that their mission was to engage in the nondisruptive propagation of the Gospel and thereby to ameliorate slavery gradually. Leonard Bacon, minister to New Haven's First Church and a leading Congregational proponent of colonization, wrote a classic defense of the gradualist philosophy in a series of articles published in the 1830s and 1840s. Bacon condemned those "extra zealous abolitionists" who would disturb the "peaceful and prosperous union of these states" in the quixotic search for immediate emancipation. Such fanatics only hardened Southern intransigence and demonstrated that they did not understand how social abuses were to be reformed. The Gospel did not directly influence the world by "way of interference with politics and legislation." "It simply proposes to make *men* better—individual men—by inspiring them with new ideas and new principles of action . . . and it leaves these new ideals and principles to work out their own effects upon the structure of society." In so doing, Christianity opened the true "path of revolution . . . the breaking of every aristocracy and every throne." Temporary setbacks, such as the momentary hostility of Southerners to abolition, could not forever impede the progress of the millennium. Already Bacon saw signs that a "benignant providence" was overriding the evils of slavery and that soon "it will be found that the cause of truth, of freedom, of happiness, while suffering temporary disaster, has been imperceptibly approaching the hour of final triumph."[13]

Bacon articulated an optimistic doctrine of history, which gave coherence to the gradualist approach to slavery. Since the Gospel enunciated principles to be slowly unfolded over time, the churches should not cavalierly issue utopian programs incapable of present realization. In a celebrated editorial debate, Francis Wayland conceded this point to his proslavery opponent Richard Fuller, a Baptist clergyman of Beaufort, South Carolina. Although Wayland insisted that slavery was always at variance with the "immutable relations which God has established between his moral creatures," he nevertheless admitted that the measure of personal guilt accruing to participants in the system depended upon historical context. Culpability had to be gauged by the available "light, knowledge of duty,

13. Leonard Bacon, *Slavery Discussed in Occasional Essays, from 1833 to 1846*, pp. 35, 36, 98, 177, 178.

means of obtaining information on the subject, and may be different in different persons at different times." If wrong be "established by law," as was slavery, wisdom required an oblique effort to elevate public opinion by the preaching of the Gospel—a tactic that would wither the roots of the evil without a direct attack on it. In the interim, it was legitimate for slaveholders to maintain their bondsmen in a state of paternal tutelage preparatory to eventual freedom. That the extirpation of slavery would soon follow the preaching of the Gospel, Wayland did not doubt; and he spoke for most churchmen.[14] Even the *Princeton Review,* which asserted vigorously the biblical legitimacy of human servitude, suggested on occasion that a thorough permeation of the South by Christian principles would yield "a peaceable and speedy extinction of slavery."[15] At bottom, evangelical moderates and conservatives rested their case for benign neglect upon the assurance that the tide of the Kingdom was cresting with such moral force that evils would be automatically swept away if the churches sustained a quiet adherence to irenic Christian principle.

A more ancient interpretation of millennialism's import for slavery was possible. According to the Synoptic Gospels, Jesus announced God's imminent reign with a call for immediate and thoroughgoing reformation: "Repent for the Kingdom of God is at hand." After 1830 growing numbers of Protestants came to view the peculiar institution from a similarly urgent perspective, and the demand for immediate emancipation was raised. Immediatism does not lend itself to an easy definition. The term might indicate a personal decision, analogous to conversion, to disentangle oneself from association with slavery; yet others might consider themselves immediatists if they adopted a policy of gradual emancipation immediately begun.[16] These ambiguities suggest that immediatism was more a state of mind than a particular program, and it arose

14. Richard Fuller and Francis Wayland, *Domestic Slavery Considered as a Scriptural Institution,* pp. 25, 32–33, 41, 43, 105, 108. The letters initially appeared in the *Christian Reflector* in 1844.

15. "Slavery," *The Biblical Repertory and Princeton Review* 8 (April 1836): 304.

16. With regard to the problem of defining immediatism, see David Brion Davis, "The Emergence of Immediatism in British and American Anti-slavery Thought," *Mississippi Valley Historical Review* 49 (September 1962): 204–30.

from a changed perception of the process by which progress toward universal freedom would occur. After 1835 the House of Representatives passed a gag rule tabling all abolition petitions, Southerners ransacked the mails to destroy antislavery material, and the Jackson administration quietly supported this violation of the postal service. Abolitionists were hounded from lecture halls, dragged through the streets, and occasionally killed. The annexation of Texas suggested that the South was determined to perpetuate, if not extend, the system of domestic servitude. In this environment, it was difficult to maintain that slavery was an anachronism gradually succumbing to the influences of an enlightened age. Although this sorry record did not make radical abolitionists of most Protestants, it did convince a swelling number that immediate, uncompromising steps had to be taken to prevent further encroachments by the slavocracy. In this sense, the immediatist spirit extended far beyond the abolitionist vanguard to influence those who worked for the nonextension of slavery through such political instruments as the Liberty, Free Soil, and Republican parties.[17]

Edward Beecher, the president of Illinois College, epitomized this awakening of conscience. His father Lyman had supported colonization and opposed the "he-goat men" who demanded immediate emancipation—a stand that gave the elder Beecher the dubious honor of presiding over the secession of Lane Seminary's abolitionist student body.[18] Until 1835 Edward was the true son of his father, but thereafter he became convinced that the "great current of human destiny" had brought the question of slavery to the point where a clear, unequivocal decision had to be made.[19] Beecher denounced the argument that the Gospel had to be disseminated into all hearts and its principles allowed to unravel the problem quietly. That response misread the hour to which the Kingdom had

17. See, for example, Filler, *Crusade Against Slavery*, pp. 48–159. On the nature of antiabolition mobs, consult Leonard L. Richards, *"Gentlemen of Property and Standing": Anti-Abolition Mobs in Jacksonian America.*

18. Lyman Beecher, *The Autobiography of Lyman Beecher*, ed. by Barbara M. Cross, 2: 260.

19. Edward Beecher, *Narrative of Riots at Alton in Connection with the Death of Rev. Elijah P. Lovejoy*, p. 17. Further information about Beecher can be found in Robert Meredith, *The Politics of the Universe: Edward Beecher, Abolition and Orthodoxy.*

come: the present was the appointed season in which the full meaning of Christianity should be unashamedly proclaimed.

It is vain here to say, that this age of the world needs nothing but the preaching of the gospel. Most fully do I admit that nothing is needed but fully to unfold the principles of the gospel, and to apply them to every department of life. But the great question of the age is: What do the principles of Christianity say on this subject? Do they tolerate slavery; or do they cut it up root and branch? Indeed until this question is decided no man can tell what the gospel is. If, indeed, the gospel authorizes, or does not condemn, and call for the immediate abandonment of a system which fundamentally subverts every principle of right, the infidel wishes to know it; for he needs no better reason to scorn its pretensions to be a message from God. But if it rebukes this with divine authority, as it does all other sins, and requires its immediate abandonment, then it is time for the church to know it, and fully to declare all the counsel of God.[20]

For Beecher this sense of urgency was confirmed by the death of his friend Elijah P. Lovejoy, the abolitionist editor who perished in 1837 at the hands of an angry mob in Alton, Illinois. The unwillingness of that community to protect Lovejoy's civil rights suggested to Beecher the imminent collapse of American law unless the country immediately addressed the decision before it. "On this subject as a nation," he warned, "we must act or suffer. If in this season we learn and do our duty, we shall escape the judgment of God. If not, the hour of retribution is hastening on."[21]

By the 1850s, the war with Mexico, the Fugitive Slave Act, the Kansas-Nebraska Act, and the Dred Scott decision had roused from somnolent optimism large numbers of the clergy; and Chester A. Dunham rightly observes that this decade witnessed a "rising tide of social action" against slavery.[22] The apocalyptic urgency of the crusade against human bondage revealed the failure of "benignant providence" to undo "imperceptibly" the shackles of the oppressed

20. Beecher, *Narrative of Riots at Alton,* pp. 156–57.
21. Ibid., p. 17.
22. Dunham, *Attitude of the Northern Clergy Toward the South,* pp. 35–80.

whose chains, if anything, appeared more firmly riveted in place than ever. The 1856 General Conference of the Methodist Church voted 122 to 96 to require discipline of lay slaveholders within the denomination, but the measure failed to receive the two-thirds majority necessary for constitutional change. The spirit that impelled many to this position was conveyed eloquently by the Reverend Israel Chamberlayne of the Genesee Conference: "You must have noticed, sir, that our contestants for apostolic slavery apologize for it on the ground that being underlaid with the principles of equity and love, it was expected that those principles would soon obliterate it by obliterating the distinction between the master and the slave. . . . Supposing much of this assumption to be true as regards the idea that the principles of the Gospel were expected by the apostles to operate the gradual, if not the speedy, extirpation of slavery, I shall only express our common regret that . . . the apostles' expectation has never yet been realized."[23] Gradualism had simply not worked, and it was operating perniciously to blind men to the need for direct confrontation with the evil. "For he must be a dull interpreter of history and the signs of the times," concluded Chamberlayne, "who does not see that if freedom does not extirpate slavery, slavery will extirpate freedom."[24]

The impression should not be inferred that the gradualists were routed by the 1850s. That almost 45 percent of the delegates to the 1856 Methodist General Conference voted against the change in the church's constitution illustrates the tenacious hold of the "benignant providence" theory upon the churches. In spite of the presence of abolitionist agitation, the New School Presbyterians consistently avoided disciplining slaveholding communicants and rested content with relatively mild antislavery statements that would not unduly upset the church's approximately ten thousand Southern members. The Old School Assembly, although subjected to occasional grumbling from midwestern churches, refused to speak against human servitude until 1864.[25] Interdenominational agencies

23. Lucius Matlack, *Antislavery Struggle and Triumph in the Methodist Episcopal Church*, p. 242.

24. Ibid., p. 245.

25. Victor B. Howard, "The Anti-Slavery Movement in the Presbyterian Church, 1835–1861" (Ph.D. diss., Ohio State University, 1961), passim; Marsden, *Evangelical Mind and the New School Presbyterian Experience*, pp. 88–103.

such as the Tract Society and American Board for Foreign Missions similarly continued, against heavy pressure, to search desperately for a position above the slavery struggle. Local Congregational and Baptist associations frequently issued more strident denunciations, perhaps because they were not hindered by the connectional polity of the Presbyterians or Methodists, and thus an association in an abolitionist stronghold was freer to give vent to its sentiments.[26] Uncertainties were multiplied by the absence of a clear program to end the evil. Many cheered John Brown as a martyr or at least accorded him the accolade bestowed by Henry Boynton Smith—"a conscientious monomaniac"—but virtually no one was prepared to launch an army into the South or to foment slave insurrection.[27] Nor were legislative proposals suggested to loosen the chains of the oppressed. The evangelical attack against slavery was directed primarily to setting one's own house in order by renouncing personal complicity with the evil, by resisting the advance of the institution into free territory, and by refusing to obey such iniquitous statutes as the Fugitive Slave Act. Once the war had begun, Henry Ward Beecher recalled that Northern Protestants had been willing to let the South have its peculiar institution if only they were not compelled to play slave catcher.[28] His description was an appropriate, if inadvertent, statement of the limits of prewar antislavery conviction.

Horace Bushnell explained the rationale for this attitude. After the passage of the Kansas-Nebraska Act, he urged Northerners to stand firm against further concessions to the slavocracy—compromises that, he said, were changing the North into "a continent of dough."[29] As late as 29 November 1860, Bushnell was still insisting, however, that the firmness he advocated was merely resistance to the territorial expansion of slavery; more was not demanded. "Why should I be contriving the abolition of slavery," he asked, "when the Almighty Himself has a silent campaign of inevitable doom against it, marching on the awful census tramp of South and North to push it away forever." Bushnell heard the "census tramp" in the 1860 figures, which proved to his satisfaction that slavery was an

26. Engelder, "Churches and Slavery," pp. 53–54, 97.

27. Lewis F. Stearns, *Henry Boynton Smith*, p. 224.

28. Beecher, *Patriotic Addresses*, p. 236.

29. Horace Bushnell, *The Northern Iron*, "A Discourse Delivered in the North Church, Hartford, on the Annual State Fast, April 14, 1854," p. 27.

unprofitable, decaying institution destined to be floated away by an influx of Northern free labor.[30]

As an economically ruinous system, slavery was expected to die rapidly unless it continually acquired new domains to cover its losses. At the election of James Buchanan—"the national midnight," wailed Gilbert Haven—the Methodist clergyman argued that slavery "is a bankrupt swindler, who will have to abandon his show of wealth, unless he can extend his villainies. . . . They [the planters] must grow. Land, land, they must have to be rifled of its virgin sweets and then abandonned."[31] The corollary was plain: resist the monster slave power, and the economic as well as moral laws of nature will suffocate the beast. The profitability of slavery continues, of course, to provoke lively debate down to the most recent work by Fogel and Engerman; and the question does not yet appear conclusively settled.[32] Yet even if research were to prove beyond dispute that slavery was a devastating drain upon the resources of the South—a very unlikely prospect—it would not follow that the system was destined to fall apart within a generation or so. As a method for controlling a racially divided society, slavery represented an interest incalculable solely in terms of productivity tables or financial return; and it is therefore unlikely that the peculiar institution would have obeyed the invisible hand of Adam Smith and gone quietly to its grave. The various surrogates for legal servitude developed after 1865 suggest the illusoriness of this hope.

30. Bushnell, *Census and Slavery*, p. 16.
31. Haven, *National Sermons*, p. 105.
32. Relatively few, if any, contemporary historians accept the view of Ulrich B. Phillips, *American Negro Slavery: A Survey of the Supply, Employment and Control of Negro Labor as Determined by the Plantation Regime,* that slavery was slowly perishing because it was economically ruinous. However, the exact nature of the slave economy remains a hotly contested subject. Did investments in slaves, for example, compare favorably to investments in manufacturing? Was slave labor sometimes more efficient than free labor or the plantations more productive than the free farms of the North? By use of quantitative techniques, Robert W. Fogel and Stanley L. Engerman in *Time on the Cross: The Economics of American Negro Slavery* offer affirmative answers to these questions. Widely praised and attacked, Fogel and Engerman have encountered their most thorough critic in Herbert G. Gutman whose *Slavery and the Numbers Game: A Critique of Time on the Cross* denies the accuracy of their statistical analysis and the adequacy of their interpretive method.

By 1860 Protestants faced conflicting alternatives, neither of which was fully adequate to the complexity of slavery. Whether given a socially quiescent or radical twist, the moral government of God in the hearts of men described an ideal social order that Donald H. Meyer has rightly called "a hypothetical, frictionless universe" in which the interests of all people were automatically meshed.[33] Thus according to the Protestant conception, a social evil might be ignored as a mere epiphenomenon that would vanish if enough citizens were imbued with the spirit of Christianity; or it might be attacked as an external enemy, a demon, which if condemned and resisted would necessarily collapse, leaving God's natural order. If the former was being discredited by the intransigence of Southerners, the latter was also a problematic solution to the American dilemma. From the perspective of Protestant attitudes toward history, the conflict had become ideologically necessary, if not irrepressible.[34] God's American elect, bedeviled

33. D. H. Meyer, *The Instructed Conscience: The Shaping of the American National Ethic*, p. 116.
34. For a good account of the scholarly debate over the irrepressibility of the war, see Pressly, *Americans Interpret Their Civil War.* Those who contend that the strife was inevitable have pointed to supposedly irreconcilable regional attitudes toward slavery, or they have portrayed war as the necessary outcome of Northern capitalism's fight against the agrarian economy of the South. On the other hand, opponents have sometimes argued that the war was a needless crusade against a dying institution, that sectional differences were inflamed by irresponsible extremists, particularly the abolitionists, or that inept politicians blundered the nation into a conflict that sober statesmanship might have avoided. Though subject to numerous criticisms, Allan Nevins's four-volume *The Ordeal of the Union* remains one of the best efforts to synthesize the opposing views, and the final work of David M. Potter, *The Impending Crisis, 1848–1861,* provides an especially thorough and balanced account of this and other issues.
  I make no pretension to resolve this complex question, but candor requires an admission of my bias toward a modified irrepressibility thesis. It appears to be the unspoken assumption of the "repressibility" advocates that passion and prejudice will readily yield to self-interest and rational compromise. Even if one grants that people can dispassionately apprise their true self-interest— the criteria of definition are by no means transparent—it is scarcely certain that they are completely free to act in accord with these perceptions. As the Dutch historian Pieter Geyl has written of the problem of the war's inevitability: "In the sequence of cause and effect, of which the human mind will never have complete command, the category of the imponderabilia, passion and emotion, conviction, prejudice, misunderstanding, have their organic

by inadequate and uncertain notions about the means of the Kingdom's coming, had exhausted the received wisdom. It is little wonder that a holy war and its attendant emancipation came as a profound relief from the vexing question that apparently had no answer. Awakened from his earlier confidence in the automatic progress of the Kingdom, Francis Wayland strenuously opposed the Kansas-Nebraska bill, and when it passed, he concluded forlornly: "I can only look to God to overrule it for the cause of righteousness."[35] Protestant America waited with Dr. Wayland.

## PROVIDENCE AND EMANCIPATION

When Americans celebrated Thanksgiving in 1862, Lincoln's preliminary emancipation proclamation was already two months old, and in its issuance Christians saw evidence that God had at last taken unto himself the conundrum of slavery. In the Twenty-third Street Presbyterian Church of New York City, the Reverend Frederick G. Clark recounted gratefully: "God has taken this great question out of the hands of statesmen, and states, and politicians. . . . He is holding everything in suspense until all the world shall pause to give attention. What we hear is only the rumbling of earth's great clock, before it strikes the hour of God's full time."[36] Elsewhere in the city Joseph P. Thompson saw in Lincoln's announcement the same portents: "The Proclamation of Emancipation has challenged all the powers of darkness to defeat it. Unclean spirits, like frogs, seem to swarm out of the mouth of the dragon, and out of the mouth of the beast and the false prophet. But we

---

function." See his "The American Civil War and the Problem of Inevitability," *New England Quarterly* 24 (June 1951): 168. Few, North or South, wanted war in 1860 or supposed that their self-interest dictated such; but the conflicting emotions, ideals and commitments of the two sections propelled them into a path that neither had sought. This is not to suggest that history is predetermined by irrational fears or ideology but rather that these impose their own inevitable constraints upon freedom of action and set in motion forces beyond reasoned self-interest.

35. Francis Wayland and H. L. Wayland, *A Memoir of the Life and Labors of Francis Wayland, D.D., LL.D.,* 2: 136.

36. Frederick G. Clark, *Gold in the Fire: Our National Position,* "A Sermon Preached in the West Twenty-Third Street Presbyterian Church, City of New York, on Thanksgiving Day, Nov. 27th, 1862," pp. 14–15.

cannot be dismayed. We will still march on with the psalter in our hand; for soon the seventh angel shall 'pour out his vial into the air, and there shall come a great voice out of the temple of heaven, from the throne, saying, IT IS DONE.'"[37] The years of anguished waiting were about to be rewarded with fulfillment.

At the outset of the war, it was far from certain whether or how emancipation would occur. Some abolitionists saw immediately a God-given opportunity to destroy slavery, and Lewis Tappan rushed into print in May 1861 a pamphlet urging the immediate freeing of all bondsmen. Recalling the suggestion of John Quincy Adams in 1842, Tappan averred that a state of war empowered the president as commander-in-chief to end forced servitude on the grounds of military necessity.[38] Ultimately abolition would be pushed through that loophole in the framework protecting slavery, but in 1861 such arguments still appeared of dubious legality. Although virtually everyone realized that chattel slavery lay at the base of the rebellion, the war was nonetheless being fought to preserve the Union; and it seemed an act of hypocrisy to fight the South in the name of the Constitution if the North were prepared to violate the guarantees of this sacred compact. "I know that slavery is the bitter root of all this trouble," lamented George Duffield, Jr., "and slavery for myself or any other member of the human race, I hate as much as I do its last and bitterest fruit, secession—but between the spirit and sentiments of Calhoun and his followers on the one extreme, and those of Garrison and his followers on the other, I see but little room to choose. The torch of disunion that would fire our national temple and reduce it to ashes, is just as hateful to me in the one hand as the other. The constitution as handed down to us by our fathers, the letter of it interpreted in its original spirit, is good enough for me, and I want no other, I want no better."[39] As Henry

37. Joseph P. Thompson, *The Psalter and the Sword,* "A Sermon Preached in the Broadway Tabernacle Church on Thanksgiving Day, November 27, 1862," p. 24.

38. Lewis Tappan, *The War: Its Cause and Remedy; Immediate Emancipation: The Only Wise and Safe Mode,* in Frank Freidel, ed., *Union Pamphlets of the Civil War,* 2: 102–17.

39. George Duffield, Jr., *The Great Rebellion Thus Far a Failure,* "A Thanksgiving Sermon Preached in the Presbyterian Church, Adrian, Michigan, November 28th, 1861," p. 19.

Ward Beecher summed up the mood of the hour, "The war must be carried on through our institutions, not over them."[40]

In spite of legal restraints against direct action, the churches sent their sons off to battle in the faith that God would somehow circumvent the barriers that limited the government and would in mysterious fashion turn the conflict against slavery. "Christian men at the North," said the *Christian Watchman and Reflector* during the first days of the war, "are beginning to feel that in the deadly conflict to which they have been driven, against their will by the madness of slavery, they see the handwriting of God on the wall, announcing the end of slavery. They have prayed long and earnestly that this national sin might be removed, and the answer has come in an unlooked for war, 'By terrible things in righteousness wilt Thou answer us, O God of our salvation.'"[41] As William Goodrich of Cleveland perceived the issue, a vigorous prosecution of the war for constitutional order would almost automatically be turned to the cause of liberty for the slaves. "We shall begin by vindicating our own freedom. But when we have thoroughly done that, we shall be apt to find that, unawares, we have shattered and cast down into the dust, the last power in Christendom, which dared to maintain the right to enslave a fellow-man."[42]

Some churchmen glimpsed the means by which the war for the Union would become an antislavery conflict. The *Christian Review,* for example, denied in July 1861 that the war was anything more than a battle for "legitimate Governmental organization," then added a warning: "But if slavery take the initiative and invoke the aid of the sword, if it place itself between us and the secure heritage of National liberty, we know nothing in it so sacred or beneficent that may shield it from the doom it has provoked."[43] In October the West and Central Baptist associations of New Jersey repeated the same threat. "If the rebels raise the issue between slavery and the constitution, . . . we will support the Government in sweeping from the country that infamous outrage on the rights of man."[44] The emerging line of argument was clear: if the cause of

40. Beecher, *Patriotic Addresses,* p. 333.
41. *Christian Watchman and Reflector,* April 25, 1861.
42. Goodrich, *Sermon on the Christian Necessity of War,* p. 13.
43. "The National Crisis," *Christian Review* 26 (July 1861): 516–17.
44. *Christian Watchman and Reflector,* October 24, 1861.

emancipation became entwined with the success of Union arms, then the providential signal to destroy slavery would have been given. The signal was not long in appearing. Except for successes in the Mississippi theater, the federal armies marched from defeat to disaster during the first two years of the war. The clergy decided that God had a controversy with his people and that persistent defeats constituted the divine warning that the Union would not be saved until the North committed itself to the eradication of slavery. In a typical jeremiad before the First Congregational Church of Sandwich, Massachusetts, the Reverend Henry Kimball suggested that the ship of state had fallen into a storm that would not abate until the crew threw overboard the "Jonah" for which God's wrath had been incurred: slavery. "It is preposterous for us to suppose that we can keep up long before a civilized world, and nourish the very cause of all our disasters. The venom of slavery is in the fang of treason; let us extract the poison, and the teeth of rebellion will be drawn."[45] Writing on 26 September 1861 to Walter and Phoebe Palmer, leaders with him in the Holiness wing of Methodism, Bishop Leonidas Hamline enunciated the fear that stared out of the ashes of defeat: "We feel that the North, under the present war regimen, has become responsible for slavery as never before, and must, under military rule, pronounce the slaves free, or God will not allow us to suppress this rebellion."[46]

On the day that Hamline posted his letter, the Reverend Starr H. Nichols noted gloomily that "it looks as if this generation were likely to grow old in the field, rather than the former state of things be restored." The inability of Union arms to achieve the expected swift victory suggested to Nichols that America stood before the Red Sea of its national experience and that God summoned the nation to choose whether it preferred to perish under the waves with the Egyptian chariots or to go forth unto the land of the promise. Did America side with Pharaoh or the Lord? "So long as the groans of millions of slaves rise to His ear, with the burden of their continued wrongs, so long will He punish this nation which oppresses

45. Henry Kimball, *The Ship of State Bound for Tarshish,* "A Sermon Preached in the First Congregational Church, Sandwich, November 21, 1861," p. 15.
46. Walter C. Palmer, *Life and Letters of Leonidas L. Hamline, D.D.,* p. 491.

them. His Providences say plainly, 'Let this people go'; now they
begin to thunder the command in our ears, like Mount Sinai, with
the noise of war waxing louder and louder; and if we do not this . . .
we shall be plagued as were those oldest of slaveholders the Egyp-
tians, and the war shall rage till there be not a house North or South,
where there is not one dead. There will be a passage of the Red Sea
for us also; a deep red sea of blood." If, however, the United States
recognized God's demand and took up its true "Manifest Destiny"
of proclaiming liberty to the captives, it would, like the children of
Israel, go through the water unscathed "towards a future more
brilliant than our splendid dawn . . . and the nation, washed of its
sin, shall learn war no more, but abide in peace to the latest generation."[47] At this contemporary Red Sea, the issue of slavery and
American nationality had been set forth as one question, and the
waters promised either destruction   or a baptismal regeneration.

The argument for emancipation was also pressed on the narrower
grounds of tactical necessity. Lewis Tappan's contention that military expediency required abolition moved well in advance of public
opinion, but churchmen began occupying the same ground when the
Confederacy failed to collapse after the first blows. Pondering the
failure of the federal drive up the Chickahominy toward Richmond
in 1862, Henry C. Fish asked his congregation how much longer
the government could prosecute a war until it seized every weapon
at its disposal. Fish contended that four million Southern slaves
were unwitting partisans of the Confederacy. "In growing the food,
digging the trenches, and doing nearly all the rude muscular work,"
these bondsmen permitted the white male population to go off to
war. "Can we afford to give them this mighty advantage?" he
asked. "This is supporting the rebellion. . . . Tenderness to slavery
is tenderness to the rebellion."[48] The editor of the *Christian Watchman and Reflector* echoed the common sentiment that a "decisive
policy" of "feeding our armies on rebel estates and setting free the
slaves of traitors" would supply the needed additional strength to
crush the rebellion.[49] Cautious Northerners were persuaded by this

47. Nichols, *Our Sins and Our Repentance*, pp. 11, 24–25.
48. Henry C. Fish, *The Duty of the Hour: or, Lessons from Our Reverses*,
p. 13.
49. *Christian Watchman and Reflector*, August 7, 1862.

rationale, for it appealed to patriotic motives in a way that abolitionism could not. It is, of course, debatable whether emancipation
weakened the Confederacy appreciably, since most "contraband"
slaves were not freed until Union armies had already smashed their
way into the Southern heartland. Still, the argument from military
expediency did have a basis in fact, especially with regard to the
larger strategic balance of power. Before emancipation converted
the conflict into a war for liberty, the governments of France and
Great Britain toyed with the prospect of recognizing the Confederacy.[50] After Lincoln's action, it was politically impossible for
either nation to undertake such a policy.

The case from necessity could be argued on a more profound
level of which the churches were partially cognizant. The use of federal coercion to subdue the seceded states had already irrevocably
destroyed the former superstructure of the Union; and a restoration according to the status quo ante bellum, though a useful rallying cry for Peace Democrats, was simply unrealistic. The *Independent*
went to the heart of the matter in an editorial that appeared one
month before the president's initial proclamation of freedom:

> It is simply impossible for the President to restore the Union as
> it was. The very first step toward it, Military Force, is a total
> change of the old status. He will appoint Military Governors.
> Where in the past is there anything like that? He will appoint
> courts and their officers, and maintain their authority by the
> sword. . . . This is not Restoration. It is Reconstruction. . . .
> Since, then, the old Union is *de facto* ceased, and all the local
> rights lapsed by rebellion to the hands of the Government, and
> it is to Reconstruct the Union, would it be a stretch of authority
> in the Government so to reconstruct it as to insure its perpetuity
> by purging out all possible cause of future discord?[51]

Contained here in embryo was the doctrine of "state suicide" that
Radical Republicans would employ in several years to justify the
treatment of the defunct Confederacy as a conquered province.

50. For example, Erastus O. Haven, "The American Crisis," *Methodist
Quarterly Review* 44 (October 1862): 663. See the first two essays in Harold
Hyman, ed., *Heard Round the World*, pp. 3–144.
51. *Independent*, August 28, 1862, p. 4.

Whatever the legal merit of the theory, it correctly perceived that the old Union had died beyond hope of resurrection and with it the basis of slavery.

The advance of the federal armies also disrupted the institution of slavery in another way. "The masters desert the plantations," said one Baptist clergyman, "and there are no claimants for the service of the blacks. They are practically raised to freedom without any liberating act, and when, once in the employ of the government, they have learned the luxury of self-ownership and of recompensed labor, they will never again be contented bondmen. The government cannot hold them as slaves, or return them to masters guilty of treason, and the march of our army must, of necessity carry freedom with it."[52] The writer was alluding to the capture by federal forces of the Sea Islands off the coast of South Carolina in the winter of 1861. When the islands were seized, plantation owners fled, leaving their slaves behind. Recent scholarship belies the assertions that these contrabands were truly "raised to freedom" or that they had already attained the "luxury of self-ownership and of recompensed labor"; but the chief contention—that the former relationship of master to slave had been irreversibly changed, even without formal emancipation—is substantially correct.[53]

Similarly the revulsion of public opinion destroyed what little moral credibility slavery still possessed within the North, and this tide of abhorrence surely imposed its own necessity that the institution be ended. "Its respectability will be gone," predicted the Methodist *Western Advocate and Journal.* "The remembrance that it has been the fruitful parent of treason, the direct and responsible cause of the most wicked rebellion that ever existed—a rebellion that has cost the country thousands of millions of dollars, a hundred thousand valuable lives, and brought mourning and anguish to almost every heart in the nation, must forever associate the institution of slavery with crime and infamy."[54] This loss of respectability stemmed primarily from the damage slavery had inflicted upon the

52. *Christian Watchman and Reflector,* January 23, 1862.
53. For further information on the work with freedmen on the Sea Islands, consult Willie Lee Rose, *Rehearsal for Reconstruction: The Port Royal Experiment.*
54. Quoted in *Christian Advocate and Journal,* June 19, 1862, p. 196.

nation and its white majority. It is significant that the *Western Advocate* did not include among the reasons for slavery's universal disfavor its effect upon blacks. But in spite of its limitations, this awakened conscience had so thoroughly stripped the last vestiges of moral legitimacy from human bondage that its legal framework could not long endure.

Thus a series of interconnected forces appeared to conspire to force the nation toward emancipation. When the slaves in rebel territory were at last freed by presidential fiat, the churches saw clear evidence that God had taken the issue from human hands to administer the coup de grace. "Our blunders, our disgraces, everything, He has adopted to His plans," said J. E. Rankin in Lowell, Massachusetts, in August 1863, "and converted to His own wise purposes. All our base alloy of purpose, all our failure of achievement, introduced into his counsels, has been transmuted into pure gold. He made the proclamation of freedom to the oppressed a military, as it was in the nature of things, a moral necessity."[55] On Thanksgiving Day 1863, W. W. Eells echoed the same gratitude from the pulpit of the First Presbyterian Church in Pittsburgh: "He [God] interposed, through disaster to our army, through treachery and imbecility, it may be, among the trusted leaders, until his own purpose should be seen as inevitably interwoven with that of the Government, and all thoughtful men should know assuredly that true peace in this land should be built upon the foundation of universal emancipation."[56] In the October 1862 issue of the *Christian Review* appeared an article almost certainly written before Lincoln's preliminary proclamation. The author admitted that slavery was not explicitly condemned in the Scriptures, but he appealed to another court—the "subjective revelation" of the purpose of God in the events of secular history. Slavery, he said, would be condemned "by the majesty and power of God's onward-marching providence."[57] By the time his article came from the press, the author no doubt felt amply justified.

55. J. E. Rankin, *The Battle Not Man's, But God's,* "A Discourse Delivered Before the United Congregational Churches in Lowell on the Day of National Thanksgiving, August 6th, 1863," pp. 19–20.
56. Eells, *How and Why We Give Thanks,* p. 14.
57. "Does the Bible Sustain Slavery?" *Christian Review* 27 (October 1862): 585.

It would be misleading, of course, to suggest that the conversion of public opinion to this position went forward at a uniform rate. Some publications, judicatories, and individual churchmen began chiding the administration as early as the fall of 1861 for its failure to liberate the slaves; and others, most notably the Old School Presbyterian Assembly, were many steps behind the president.[58] Nevertheless, this conviction, whether reached early or late, was accompanied by the overwhelming joy that God had resolved the dilemma of slavery and that a magnificent future now lay before the country. Emancipation meant that the final vial of the Apocalypse was almost poured out and that shortly the voice would sound from heaven: "IT IS DONE." Or in the Old Testament motifs frequently used, the way to the promised land had been graciously opened by God. Commenting upon the first proclamation of the president, the *Christian Advocate and Journal* rejoiced: "Twice forty years we as a nation have wandered in the wilderness; now we have come to the Jordan. . . . [Let] the priests . . . lead the people to the stream, and bear the ark into the waters."[59] At the quadrennial General Conference two years later, the only such meeting during the war, one Methodist said of the destruction of slavery that America "had passed through the Red Sea, and it was well to sing psalms, and take the timbrel and go forward." At that same meeting, Daniel Curry tore away the biblical allusions to state the meaning of freedom plainly: "We have now reached a position of which our fathers did not dream. The whole world is before us."[60]

### COLONIZATION DURING THE WAR

The same doctrine of providence that helped the churches to accept emancipation might be turned to uses less congenial to resolution of America's racial dilemma, and the project of sending freed blacks abroad provided a crucial example. Although the colonization movement had been disowned by many abolitionists and had suffered acute embarrassment in its colonial ventures in

58. See, for example, *Christian Advocate and Journal,* October 17, 1861, p. 332; *Independent,* January 8, 1862, p. 4; *Presbyterian,* July 30, 1864, p. 4.
59. *Christian Advocate and Journal,* October 9, 1862, p. 324.
60. Ibid., May 12, 1864, p. 149.

Liberia, the idea of black removal continued to beguile white America. After Liberian independence in 1848 removed this financial albatross, the Colonization Society achieved a new prosperity during the 1850s. In the same decade, numerous public figures—including Daniel Webster, Edward Everett, Henry Clay, Stephen Douglas, Millard Fillmore, and Harriet Beecher Stowe—endorsed black colonization. In the first part of the war, President Lincoln toyed with several abortive emigration schemes, and colonization was not thoroughly eclipsed until wholesale emancipation and the conferring of citizenship on ex-slaves made the proposal anachronistic.[61]

Colonization fed upon blatantly racist assertions that blacks are "not fit for citizenship in such a Republic as ours." "One might as well harness the cart-horse with the full blooded racer" as mix Africans and Anglo-Saxons, snorted one advocate of removal.[62] Emigration also appealed to what George Fredrickson has called "romantic racialism"—the belief that each people possesses a distinct genius or character.[63] Stress on the particularity of race did not necessarily imply a derogatory view of blacks, but it lent itself easily to an argument for separation so that heterogeneity might be preserved.

This ploy for maintaining a lily-white America found support in one version of millennial interpretation. The Psalmist had predicted: "Ethiopia shall stretch forth her hands unto God."[64] Or as many Protestants understood the promise, the African continent would experience a spiritual renaissance in the latter days. By carrying

61. Staudenraus, *African Colonization Movement,* pp. 246–48. See also Robert H. Zoellner, "Negro Colonization: The Climate of Opinion Surrounding Lincoln, 1860–1865" *Mid-America* 42 (July 1960): 131–50, and V. Jacque Voegeli, *Free But Not Equal: The Midwest and the Negro During the Civil War,* passim.

62. "Address of Lewis H. Wheeler, Esq.," *African Repository* 40 (March 1864): 83.

63. George M. Fredrickson, *The Black Image in the White Mind: The Debate on Afro-American Character and Destiny, 1817–1914,* pp. 97–121. For the genesis of American racial attitudes, see the already classic Winthrop D. Jordan, *White over Black: American Attitudes Toward the Negro, 1550–1812.* Also helpful is Carl N. Degler, *Neither Black Nor White: Slavery and Race Relations in Brazil and the United States.*

64. Psalms 68:31.

thither the preparatory lessons in civilization and Christianity learned in America, ex-slaves were expected to fulfill that prophecy. Before an enthusiastic gathering of the Maine Colonization Society in June 1862, the Reverend E. W. Blyden of Liberia painted the standard picture of Africa's coming glory.

> I look for the day when black men in this country, roused to the sense of their condition here, and of their duty to Africa, will rush to those shores to bless that benighted continent. Soon shall those beautiful valleys, now lying in mournful loneliness, be peopled by a happy and thriving population. Soon shall those charming hilltops all over the land, now untrodden by the foot of man, be crowned with temples to the Most High. Soon shall science again establish her sway in Africa. The vast wilderness and the solitary places, yielding to the hand of culture, shall blossom as the rose. Genius, and learning, and skill shall revolutionize the land. Ethiopia, in all her length and breadth, shall be filled with the knowledge of the Lord, as the waters cover the sea. For the mouth of the Lord has spoken it.[65]

The most systematic argument for colonization came from the clergyman who had also written the most extensive millennial interpretation of the war. The etching on the frontispiece to Hollis Read's *The Negro Problem Solved* bears testimony to the extent to which the coming Kingdom informed his argument for emigration. On a palm-lined African shore, a black man, hands prayerfully uplifted, receives a Bible descending from the heavens. At his side repose a lion and a lamb, and a discarded spear lies unused in the dust. These pictorial representations of Isaiah's vision are buttressed by a catalog of prophecies which supposedly adduce that Africa has been reserved for the development at the end of time of a "higher order of civilization and a better type of Christianity than has yet been known."[66]

By sending blacks to Africa in fulfillment of prophecy, Americans would add another piece of confirmatory evidence that their coun-

65. "Rev. E. W. Blyden's Address at the Annual Meeting of the Maine Colonization Society, June, 1862," *African Repository* 38 (September 1862): 278.
66. Hollis Read, *The Negro Problem Solved,* frontispiece and p. 25.

try was indeed the redeemer nation, for the freed slaves would export the blessings of Christian civilization patterned according to the model of the United States. Liberia, said Read, would prove "a reproduction of New England—destined to do for that continent what Plymouth colony has done for North America."[67] His picture of "Africa as She Shall Be" was a transplanted version of a Northern village and industrial center in one—a landscape dotted with one-room schools, the steeples of austere New England meeting houses, and factories belching smoke into the air.[68]

A similar brief for colonization was filed by the *Princeton Review* in October 1862. The author, probably Princeton Seminary's A. T. McGill, saw at the completion of the war the advance from the United States of a three-pronged missionary campaign to subdue the world for Christ. Latin America by its very nearness would speedily succumb to the example of its northern neighbor. Simultaneously Yankee merchants would carry the good news to Asia, and the return to Africa of freed blacks would complete the grand outflowing of spiritual power from the United States. Colonization, in short, constituted one feature of a larger concatenation of events demonstrating "that the Anglo-Saxons of North America are to be the principle agents in the hands of God, in performing the works and in effecting the changes introductory to the Millennium."[69] From this perspective, the removal of the freedmen would be for America an act of self-definition as God's elect.

This rationale for colonization covered the racial prejudices of Caucasian Americans with a patina of respectability. If it were God's intention that blacks should return to Africa, then an oppressive white racism was a providential inducement to emigration. As Hollis Read stated the argument:

> We have alluded to the insuperable disability which precludes the rise of the negro in this land. Call it prejudice against color; call it the tyrannical interdict of a wicked public opinion; call it what you will, it is a law which no legislation can repeal. . . .

67. Ibid., pp. 291–92.
68. Ibid., p. 371.
69. "African Colonization," *Biblical Repertory and Princeton Review* 34 (October 1862): 686–87.

By giving different constitutions and complexions to great branches of the human family, God evidently intended that they should be kept separate.[70]

To prolong the stay of ex-slaves in the hope of ameliorating white prejudice "is only cruelty to the colored man." Churchmen should rather surrender to the inevitable and recognize that God "by a series of most signal providences, [has] designated these United States as the habitation and theatre of action for the white man and as signally has he pointed out Africa as the home of the Black man."[71] In a similar endorsement of colonization, the editor of the *Christian Advocate and Journal* argued that racial prejudice was God's natural encouragement to maintain the separate destinies he had assigned to the peoples of the earth. "God writes his laws in nature as well as in the Bible," suggested the *Advocate,* "and the course of his providence sometimes indicates his will as clearly as the decalogue"—and if the war had taught Protestants anything, it was surely that providence must be obeyed reverently.[72]

The significance of colonization goes beyond the number of its adherents. Among the clergy, these appear to have dwindled during the war, although churchmen frequently argued that the South itself or some designated portion of it would become a separate homeland for the freedman. In no event did Protestants envision an influx of blacks into the North, and many suggested precisely the reverse—that Northern Negroes would be drawn off to the South.[73] Colonization thus expressed in extreme form the inability of the religious community to deal with slavery, its horrors, or even the continued presence of blacks as problems integral to the American experience. Colonization bewitched churchmen with the notion that the "Negro problem" was essentially an excrescence upon American life and could, like a tumor, be excised by a swift surgical stroke. Even though most churchmen did not accept the drastic formula of emigration, they generally shared the view that slavery

70. Read, *Negro Problem Solved,* p. 332.

71. Ibid., pp. 310–11.

72. *Christian Advocate and Journal,* September 4, 1862, p. 284.

73. Samuel Spear, "Radicalism and the National Crisis," *National Preacher,* 3d ser. 1 (November 1862): 329–38; *Independent,* October 9, 1862, p. 4; "Editor's Repository," *Ladies' Repository* 22 (December 1862): 757.

was an isolated, aberrant growth; and this attitude was encouraged by the interpretation of the war as an apocalyptic contest where Christ was polarized against Antichrist and evil was an external enemy.

## SLAVERY AS ANTICHRIST

Freedom and slavery were not principles intermingled in all human action; they were ideas hypostasized—made material—in the North and the South. The conflict, said the Reverend T. H. Archibald to the Vermont Baptist Convention in October 1861, "is the collision of two opposing, and mutually destructive principles, which have been incorporated into the whole administration of the Republic. We have witnessed the attempt to mingle, in harmonious union, the freest institutions which were ever known among men, with the most vile and oppressive system of despotism upon which the sun ever gazed. That attempt was clearly an effort to perform an absolute impossibility."[74] M. L. P. Thompson of the Second Presbyterian Church in Cincinnati agreed with this assessment. "Freedom and slavery," he said, "cannot live peaceably together in the same house. Their natures are diverse; and as oil and water cannot be mingled, these two cannot be harmonized."[75] The slave system, in short, was the incarnation of a principle alien to American life; and the war was a cataclysmic ejection from the body politic of that which had always been extrinsic to its nature.

From the retrospect of the war, Protestants interpreted previous American history as the maturing struggle between irreconcilable Yankee and Cavalier mentalities. The Reverend Nathaniel Eggleston told his congregation in Stockbridge, Massachusetts, that the existence of slavery in the South was traceable to the different religious commitments of the original Northern and Southern colonists. The former were Puritans whose life was directed toward disciplined liberty, whereas the latter were spiritually formed—or rather misformed—by the remnants of a superstitious feudal culture that valued only luxury and material gain.[76] When Frederick Clark, a

74. *Christian Watchman and Reflector*, October 24, 1861.
75. Thompson, *Discourses*, p. 14.
76. Eggleston, *Reasons for Thanksgiving*, pp. 8–13.

Presbyterian pastor in New York City, surveyed the national chronicles, he reached a similar conclusion. "All our troubles," he insisted, "are the legacy of British rule in America." England "overbore the consciences of the colonists by sheer force" to plant in the Southern portions of this Protestant country a pre-Reformation despotism.[77] The *Christian Advocate and Journal* traced the ideological origins of the warfare between Yankee and Cavalier as far back as the Battle of Hastings. There a libertarian Anglo-Saxon culture collided with the tyrannical Norman character. Throughout the centuries, these opposed systems struggled for mastery, and at the moment when the Norman curse was "exhausted in England by the triumph of Anglo-Saxon ideas"—that is, by Puritanism—it "was transferred" to the Southern portion of America.[78]

Wherever they located the beginning of the struggle, Protestants saw the outlines of two distinct civilizations, embodying opposing ideological commitments. In a more refined form, this thesis offers fruitful insights. Some historians still suggest that fundamental aspects of sectionalism may be traced to a prior intellectual cleavage—an industrious North disciplined in the Protestant ethic set against a "lazy South" unfamiliar with institutionalized Puritan nurture.[79] The extent to which this theory can be sustained is a question for further research, but it is safe to warn that any simplistic portrayal of the North and South as opposed ideological entities runs aground on the hard fact that the two regions shared a similar heritage of evangelical religion and political rhetoric. Indeed, the Confederate clergy drew upon many of the same motifs as the North to justify their cause. Southerners, too, believed their nation to be the new Israel, "the pillar of cloud by day and of fire by night" guiding the Army of Northern Virginia no less than the Army of the Potomac.[80] The problem of slavery and sectionalism was too diverse, and com-

77. Clark, *Gold in the Fire,* pp. 9–12.

78. *Christian Advocate and Journal,* June 6, 1861, p. 180.

79. See David Bertelson, *The Lazy South.* For a classic description of the rise of sectional self-images, consult William R. Taylor, *Cavalier and Yankee: The Old South and American National Character.*

80. For views opposing Bertelson's, see Edmund S. Morgan, "The Puritan Ethic and the American Revolution," *William and Mary Quarterly,* 3d ser. 24 (January 1967): 3–43, and C. Van Woodward, "The Southern Ethic in a Puritan World," *William and Mary Quarterly,* 3d ser. 25 (July 1968): 343–70.

mon intellectual commitments too many, to permit the explanation
that reified ideas were at war.

An alternative means of externalizing the problem of slavery
reversed the previous argument. If human bondage were the result
of evil lurking in the Cavalier mentality, it might also be portrayed as
the unique cause of the South's woeful condition. As a violation of
the right order God had ordained, slavery spun out immorality,
ignorance, and the poverty of the masses. "This institution," said
Sherman Canfield, "changes and peculiarizes a people, generating
interests and characteristics antagonistic to the interests and characteristics of a free society. It associates labor with servitude and thus
puts a stigma upon it. It brings the land into the possession of a few
who generally reside so far apart from each other that churches are
rare and public schools impossible; and thus it takes away the key
of knowledge, the means of spiritual culture, and independence from
the mass even of the whites. It produces an aristocracy proud,
sensitive, irritable, accustomed to rule and prone to violent ways.
Especially does it beget in the dominant class an inordinate feeling
of local importance."[81] Writing from the occupied South, Chaplain
Alonzo H. Quint summed up the indictment: slavery was the root of
societal evil, for "it perverts the conscience, warps the intellect and
brutalizes the heart."[82]

An argument making slavery at once the cause and effect of
personal immorality might have yielded insight into the subtle
complexity of the institution; but in practice, Protestant social
analysis was ambiguous, even muddled, rather than profound.
Corporate evil was conceived as either the manifestation of personal
immorality or as the result of an external barrier to natural harmony. The median term uniting these conceptions was the idea of
the frictionless society—a perfect, immutable structure that would
run amok only if malevolent persons abused it or if an extraneous
element were introduced. This was the same brittle, undiscriminating
analytic tool that had broken in the years before Sumter, but in
the midst of war it appeared to function once again. It worked
because the American Apocalypse had localized immorality in the
Cavalier civilization of the South, had fully identified that region's

81. Canfield, *American Crisis,* p. 24.
82. *Christian Watchman and Reflector,* April 10, 1862.

peculiar institution as the arbitrary element disrupting the native soundness of American life, and had made both physically incarnate in the armies of the rebellion. Slavery was now an external enemy, waiting at Armageddon for the hosts of righteousness to march out and put him to final rout.

### HOPES FOR RECONSTRUCTION

On Thanksgiving Day 1863, Chaplain James Marshall preached to wounded soldiers in a hospital near Fortress Monroe, Virginia, and enumerated the blessings that should impel the loyal citizen to gratitude. Chief among the divine mercies was the Emancipation Proclamation, the symbol of the total defeat of slavery. A reborn nation might now go forward confidently in the knowledge that the moral forces of the age would soon sweep it into a cloudless future. "The First Day of January 1863," he predicted, "will be a new starting point in our national career. . . . These victories . . . are the mightiest moral ones of the century. For men to attempt to stay the onward march of such growing moral energies would be as futile as to try to dam up the waters of the Niagara."[83]

Although some problems still awaited solution, Protestants were generally convinced that the successful conclusion to the "Negro problem" was now a virtual fait accompli. Veteran abolitionist James Thome expressed this hope in a pamphlet asserting the early fulfillment of millennial prophecies concerning black destiny. Unlike colonizationists, he believed that "Ethiopia shall soon stretch out her hands unto God"—in the United States. "What will not the civilizing forces of the country do for these apt, imitative, observant learners?" he asked. "What will not the laboring classes do when, dismissing their ungenerous antipathies, they admit the freedman to the competition of honest industry and set them on a footing of self-support. . . . Limits can scarcely be assigned to the improvement of a capable race who, leaping forward at the echo of their falling shackles, commence the onward march under the lead of a free Christian people. The sympathies and enthusiasms inherent in the American heart, employing the rich resources of the land, will work

83. James Marshall, *The Nation's Changes*, "A Discourse Delivered in the Chesapeake General Hospital, near Fort Monroe, Va., on the Day of the National Thanksgiving, Nov. 26th, 1863," pp. 20, 22.

all but miracles in so humane a cause as the elevation of down-
trodden millions."[84]

Since black destiny in the United States would be inextricably
united to that of the larger white community in the South, churchmen foresaw a concomitant early regeneration of the entire region.
"The Old South," predicted Dr. George Ide, "impenitent, incorrigi-
ble, will be swallowed up by the billows of the bloody sea into
which she has cast herself. The new South, transformed by the
awful baptism, will emerge to a fresh life and a magnificent destiny."[85] Unitarian Nathaniel Hall, turning from the grim view of
an ignorant poverty-stricken South, caught the glimmer "of the
day when, beneath the orb of Liberty, those hills and valleys should
be clothed with the prosperity and gifts that spring but at its genial
shining." The South, he concluded, would shortly "come to a new
birth and a glorious transfiguration."[86]

This confidence reflected the assumption that once slavery was
torn away, God's natural order would stand intact amid the rubble.
The American Missionary Association provided a classic example of
the extent to which organizations committed to work among the
freedmen were unprepared to sustain a long campaign of Reconstruction. Although the association warned somberly that the effort
among former slaves would require an outpouring of "consistent,
generous, and universal offerings such as the world has never witnessed," the call for teachers, ministers, and money was softened
with the assurance that "this is not to be a permanent demand. In
a few years the freed slaves will be able and willing in a great measure to support their own institutions."[87] The inability of the AMA
to envision a protracted struggle for equality was rooted in the
belief that slavery was essentially an arbitrary interference with
the natural order: remove the hand tampering with the machine,

84. James Thome, *The Future of the Freed People,* pp. 15, 41, 42.
85. Ide, *Battle Echoes,* p. 97.
86. Nathaniel Hall, *The Moral Significance of the Contrasts Between Slavery
and Freedom,* "A Discourse Preached in the First Church, Dorchester, May 10,
1864," pp. 14-15.
87. "Appeal for the Freedmen," *American Missionary,* 2d ser. 7 (January
1863): 14; "Raising the Freedmen," *American Missionary,* 2d ser. 8 (May
1864): 123.

and it will function properly. To have stressed too unequivocally the need for an indefinite Northern philanthropy would have been to call into question this theory—the very one from which the attack against slavery had been launched. We hear the echoes of this logic in the approving citation by the *American Missionary* of the remarks of a Northern observer.

> In slavery, one can hardly imagine a more shiftless, indolent being than a Missouri negro. But the change from slavery to freedom effects an instantaneous and complete revolution in his character. With the consciousness of liberty comes the necessity for exertion; and effort is born of necessity. The slave who worked carelessly felt that he had no interest in the result of his labor; no amount of industry would benefit him, and he naturally did as little as he could consistently with safety. But when he is a free man, he rises equal to the emergency. This has been the case wherever my experience has extended. There is not a man who has been liberated by this brigade but is abundantly able and willing to take care of himself. In every case we have found the slave fit for freedom.[88]

Similar sentiments came from that dedicated band of workers who toiled among the freedmen in the South. Married to a leading figure among the Protestant missionaries in the Port Royal area, Austa M. French typified the best evangelical tradition of compassionate, unflagging benevolence. Yet she, too, shared the confidence that the single act of emancipation would cause an early elevation of the black community to prosperous equal citizenship. After describing the terrible condition of slaves in terms so bleak that amelioration seemed impossible, she rejoiced in the certain reversal of this situation. "But here comes the remedy, free labor! free labor!" "The Colored in freedom," she predicted will not hoard, but spend money. They will dress and ride in good style. . . . Imagine the trade set in motion once they get wages. What brisk market for everything conceivable."[89] French was not, of course, alone. After 1862 virtually every issue of the *American Missionary* contained letters

88. "Colored Refugees," *American Missionary,* 2d ser. 6 (February 1862): 29–30.

89. Austa M. French, *Slavery in South Carolina,* p. 300.

from teachers and clergymen who extolled the eagerness of black children to learn Northern teaching, their rising prosperity under the aegis of freedom, and their near accession to the equal status so devoutly wished. Willie Lee Rose has shown that this veneer of confidence sometimes hid, especially as their labors dragged into years, a private disillusionment with the failure of the freedmen to rise to their appointed destiny in the free market.[90] The missionaries scarcely dared admit doubts to themselves, however, for in so doing they subverted the basic convictions that had brought them to the front line of the war against slavery.

Emancipation was also expected to eliminate the source of evils in white society. Austa French, for example, concluded that the Southern family structure was deformed because the master's arbitrary power over servants encouraged him to play the tyrant with his wife or children and because his easy access to slave women tempted him to adultery. From the major premise, the rest of the argument followed ineluctably: eliminate slavery, and the Southern family will become, as if by magic, the paragon of domestic felicity. "That man," said French, "were noble, were a husband, a father, without the vice of oppression, which maketh a man mad! Wrest slavery from him, and he will soon be reasonable. He will return to bless his household. He will bless you in heaven!"[91]

From the cessation of slavery, one might also prophesy the smashing of the planter aristocracy and the rise of a large white middle class. This new bourgeoisie, aided by Northern immigrants, would accept libertarian, free labor concepts as essential to their own material well-being and intellectual advancement. Into this growing homogeneity of belief and interest, sectional antagonisms of earlier years would vanish. "Our peace would flow as a river," Lewis Tappan predicted in May 1861, "the people of North and South would grasp each other's hands in mutual friendship; commerce, agriculture, and manufactures would receive a new impulse; the burdens of the people would be lightened; and, under the benignant smiles of a kind Providence, the civilized world would exclaim: 'Behold, how good and how pleasant it is for brethren to dwell together in uni-

90. Rose, *Rehearsal for Reconstruction,* passim.
91. French, *Slavery in South Carolina,* p. 196.

ty!"[92] More than a year later, the *Christian Watchman and Reflector* foresaw the same results when Lincoln announced his intention to free the slaves in rebel territory. "A new race of leaders will spring up; new aims will animate the people, and as the social condition of Europe was changed by the influx of new men and new methods after the wasting of the Crusades, so must it be in the Southern states. If slavery perishes, the antagonism between the North and South goes with it, and the old, fretting sores must soon be healed."[93]

When he reflected on the glories of a reconstructed South, Samuel T. Spear enunciated in classic form the reason for the hope that "the present ruling class" would soon lose power to an invigorated bourgeoisie. "New ideas, new men, new institutions, and new modes of industry will take possession of the South" because of a fundamental law in God's universe: "All political societies, however violent their passions for the moment, at last yield to their interest and their necessities; this is their history, and I do not anticipate that the South either will or can be an exception to this rule." Let the cataclysm, in other words, tear down the artificial wall imposed by slavery, and God's natural order would assert itself through the interplay of free agents. Throwing the slaves onto the marketplace of free labor would give them "a chance to do something for their humanity" and would simultaneously convince "the non-slaveholding whites that their interests lie with the Union and the principles of a free democracy." If slavery were killed without mercy, Spear insisted, "at no distant period a reconstructed Union will be the result, resting, as I believe, on a much firmer base than ever before." Spear's uncomplicated program for a swift reconstruction had one further precautionary element: in case black and white Southerners were slow to understand their true self-interest, Yankees must be prepared to instruct them and to "send into the South a powerful current of Northern emigration" as a model for emulation.[94]

The demand for an exemplary "powerful current of Northern emigration" represented the other half of the Protestant prescription for corporate ills. If such maladies were the result of interference

92. Tappan, *The War,* 1: 105.
93. *Christian Watchman and Reflector,* October 2, 1862.
94. Spear, *Nation's Blessing in Trial,* p. 35.

with the natural equilibrium of society, they also stemmed from a want of enlightened virtue in individuals. It was therefore axiomatic that the abolition of slavery had to be complemented by a vast missionary effort to uproot the Cavalier mentality and to teach freedmen Christian self-discipline. "The whole South," insisted the Reverend Moses Smith in Plainville, Connecticut, "must be supplied with the Bible—the unmitigated Bible. The Colporteur must hasten with his treasures of life. The preacher must gather the scattered sheep, and the Churches and Sabbath schools must bless that land of darkness." Similar benefits should be extended to blacks so that they might "bear the standard of civilization to a loftier eminence."[95]

As larger areas of the Confederacy succumbed to federal arms, the colporteurs and their retinue indeed hastened to the land of darkness. In 1862 Secretary of War Edwin Stanton issued the first of a series of military directives placing captured Southern churches at the disposal of their denominational counterparts in the North. These "contraband churches" were gladly received—or more accurately, urgently sought—by the respective communions; and Unionist clergy were encouraged in their efforts to draw out from the apostate Southern churches the supposedly loyal masses. Although most wartime evangelistic and educational work among the slaves was carried out by the AMA and the interdenominational freedmen's aid societies, each of the major denominations had moved by 1865 to take up the work on separate bases.[96]

Any doubts about the difficulty of the job ahead were set awash in a sea of confidence that the North could speedily accomplish

95. Moses Smith, *God's Honor Man's Ultimate Success*, "A Sermon Preached on Sunday, September 27th, 1863," p. 11.

96. For a brief account of the spirit of this movement, see Ralph E. Morrow, *Northern Methodism and Reconstruction*, pp. 29–62. See also Vander Velde, *Presbyterian Churches and the Federal Union*, pp. 458–66, as well as Robert A. Barker, *Relations Between Northern and Southern Baptists*, passim. There were no Southern Congregational churches to "occupy," but an evangelization and church extension program for the region were among the motives prompting the formation of the National Council of Congregational Churches in 1865. See Williston Walker, *History of the Congregational Churches*, pp. 395–97. See also Beard, *Crusade of Brotherhood*, pp. 119*ff*, and Frank E. Jenkins, *Anglo-Saxon Congregationalism in the South*.

any task to which its energies were committed. The Reverend George Peck assured a Wesleyan conference: "This Society has a new field open for its cultivation in the Southern states. The way is open there for the reconstruction of Methodism in that desolated country. Rebellion has done its worst to desolate one of the fairest portions of our heritage, but allow the Yankees room to stand on and they will move the world."[97] Another Methodist looking South perceived "fields ripe for the harvest" and prophesied that "millions of white men there will soon learn to love our holy, benignant antislavery gospel."[98] To a generation that took as a first article of faith that rebellion was merely a "crafty plot" of Cavalier aristocrats, it was natural to believe that the deluded Southern masses, once freed of this immoral influence, could soon be roused from darkness to light.[99] Similarly a people that had learned from Harriet Beecher Stowe, as well as from Southern apologists themselves, that the Negro was particularly susceptible to the influence of religion, had little concern that missionary and educational efforts would be outstanding successes.[100]

In December 1864 the *Independent* summed up the dual thrust that would secure the regeneration of Southern people and the elevation of the slave:

> Looking at such an undertaking in the gross, it appears almost hopelessly formidable, so great has been the degradation of servitude. In effect the problem is simple, and its solution comparatively easy. The question of labor is settled at once by the excess demand over supply. The question of individual regeneration is determined by those familiar appliances which have raised the American character in the Free States to its present altitude. The common-school system upon which we depend for the sanity and safety of the Republic will, if extended to classes hitherto shut out from it, produce the same beneficent results which are visible about us every day.[101]

97. George Peck, *The Life and Times of George Peck, D.D.,* p. 387.
98. Quoted in Morrow, *Northern Methodism and Reconstruction,* p. 96.
99. Mortimer Blake, *The Issues of the Rebellion,* "A Sermon Preached Before the Taunton and Raynham Volunteers," p. 4.
100. See, for example, French, *Slavery in South Carolina,* p. 176, and Read, *The Negro Problem Solved,* p. 323.
101. *Independent,* December 15, 1864, p. 4.

Free people, disciplined by Christian intellectual and spiritual nurture, would enter an economic market restored to its proper operation by the abolition of slavery; and these two conditions guaranteed the elevation of the freedmen. The implication of this program was that little more need be done for the slave. Beyond these measures, "God does not," said Henry Smith, "seem to call us at present to interfere in any special manner in behalf of the black man, except to protect him from violence."[102] C. L. Goodell in a Thanksgiving address in New Britain, Connecticut, underscored the point. If a people enjoy a widely diffused Christian education as well as the rights to civil liberty, free labor, and the ownership of property, no past degradation or present straitened circumstances can prevent them from rising to their proper place in society. He concluded: "Poverty excludes no man from respectability. There is no barrier to check the humblest child in all this vast republic."[103]

Unfortunately very real barriers did exist. Even if the former slave were diligent in industry, the right to self-ownership afforded little advancement unless it were sustained by a viable economic base. In the South's agrarian society, this meant land—the bulk of which still remained in the hands of the planter aristocrats. An unregulated free market operating within the context of Southern society offered the freedman a sure formula for an indefinite economic vassalage. Furthermore slavery had willed to both blacks and whites a complex series of self-definitions, social roles, and deep-rooted fears that would not easily surrender to the North's gospel of freedom. Whether by reason of guile, psychological acceptance, or a measure of both, the slave was accustomed to adopt a deferential stance before the white ruling class. Northern logic might require a repudiation of this posture, but the needs of blacks adhered to their own rationale. Impoverished and faced with violent opposition, most ex-slaves as a matter of survival would ultimately have to sharecrop for their former masters and in other ways accommodate themselves to second-class citizenship. This adjustment would become necessary when another Northern truism failed to validate itself—namely, the conviction that the white masses of the South would soon cast their lot with blacks, emancipation, and

102. Smith, *God in the War*, p. 28.
103. Goodell, *Thanksgiving Sermon*, pp. 20–31.

political equality. Although some yeoman farmers had long dis-
trusted slavery, they hated the slave with equal vehemence, for he
was simultaneously a symbol of the power of the detested Bourbons,
a fearful reminder of a degradation to which the white farmer
himself might descend, and a useful figure whose loathesomeness
reassured the poorer white that he did possess some measure of
status because he was not black. To Protestants who believed that
moral enlightenment would harmonize individual self-interest and
the social good, this strangely logical irrationality remained forever
closed; and churchmen would never understand why many whites
who had never owned slaves would rather eat Jim Crow than the
satisfying meal of economic and political equality. When an ex-
slave was told by a Northerner that his race must improve itself by
moral and intellectual education, he asked: "Wat's de use ob niggers
pretendin' to larnin? Wat'll dey be but niggers wen dey gits through?"
This man grasped intuitively a hard fact invisible to most Northerners. Slavery was not merely the stultification of the ideal socioeconomic order nor the aggregation of personal immorality or
ignorance. Human bondage had become a nexus of institutional
restraints, customs, and fears that had assumed virtually independent
life. In face of this American dilemma, the prescription of emancipation cum moral education was indeed a facile, if well-intentioned,
illusion.[104]

104. The quotation is from Morrow, *Northern Methodism and Reconstruction*, p. 153.
    The effect of bondage upon the slave remains a source of scholarly infight-
ing. Stanley Elkins, *Slavery: A Problem in American Institutional and Intellectual Life*, has been justly criticized for the argument that blacks were
infantilized by bondage. Of the voluminous literature dealing with slave life,
several recent books are of special importance: John W. Blassingame, *The
Slave Community: Plantation Life in the Ante-Bellum South;* Fogel and
Engerman, *Time on the Cross;* Eugene D. Genovese, *Roll, Jordan, Roll: The
World the Slaves Made;* and Herbert G. Gutman, *The Black Family in Slavery
and Freedom, 1750-1925.* Although these authors are by no means in agreement on all significant issues, their works suggest that slaves, while making
necessary accommodations to oppression, maintained a high degree of cultural
and psychological autonomy.
    The persistence of racism, especially among whites who had never owned
slaves, marked one of the chief tragedies of the postwar period. How easily
Negrophobia could be espoused by those who had no vested interest in the

A glimmering awareness that something more might be required appeared in occasional calls for the confiscation of lands owned by rebels. In part, these suggestions were proffered more as a means of punishing traitors and crippling the rebellion than as a program for benefiting freedmen. The *Christian Watchman and Reflector* suggested: "Let the estates of civil and military officers under the Confederacy be confiscated, and their slaves be made free. Let all losses by bands of guerrillas be made good from the property of disloyal citizens. Let the rebels, disheartened by their defeats in the field, feel that their only safety from ruin lies in a prompt submission to the government and a return to loyalty."[105] A more positive rationale was advanced by the *Independent*:

> The soil of the South must be held by loyal citizens against all peradventure of a resurrection of rebellion or aristocracy. To that end, it must be parcelled out among a population thoroughly imbued with the democratic idea, and this population is to be partly indigenous, and partly introduced. The freedmen themselves, who are on the spot, will form the nucleus of the new society, and have by every just regard a natural claim upon the first provision. Next the soldiers, sailors, and laborers of our national forces, without distinction of color or race, are entitled to homesteads at the disposal of an appreciative country. Lastly, the field should be thrown open to the best stock of our Northern States, who will seek the South as a new Eldorado.[106]

The *Independent's* position is particularly illustrative of the Protestant difficulty of incorporating a plan of wholesale land reform

---

slave system or even opposed the institution may be gauged in the books of Hinton Rowan Helper, *The Impending Crisis of the South,* and *Nojoque: A Question for a Continent.* The long-term sources of racism—Northern and Southern—are treated in Fredrickson, *Black Image in the White Mind* and more extensively in Winthrop Jordan, *White over Black,* as well as in Degler, *Neither Black Nor White.* For information on the Southern churches' attitudes toward the Afro-American, consult Hilrie Shelton Smith, *In His Image, But . . . Racism in Southern Religion, 1780-1910.* A brief account of the triumph of racist policies in the postwar South is in C. Vann Woodward, *The Strange Career of Jim Crow,* 2d rev. ed. For a more detailed treatment, see Woodward, *Origins of the New South, 1877-1913.*

105. *Christian Watchman and Reflector,* June 12, 1862.

106. *Independent,* April 21, 1864, p. 4.

within the prevailing conception of society. The most politically radical of the major religious papers, the *Independent* from time to time issued similar calls for the imposition of land reform upon the South, only to relapse into bland assertions, without reference to confiscation, that the "familiar appliances" of the open market would solve the problem of reconstruction.

The inconsistency of land redistribution with the Protestant understanding of the social order was revealed in an address by Henry M. Dexter to the American Missionary Association shortly after the war ended. Dexter, later to achieve distinction as a noted church historian, argued the necessity of dividing rebel lands among former slaves. "Let the nation," he urged, "now divide this conquered confiscated territory among the freedmen, by gift or by sale of suitable terms, with due latitude of time of payment. Let it break up that old feudal, unrepublican monopoly of land in the hands of a few men of enormous wealth, and cut up the plantations into little farms, placing each able bodied freedman in possession of a spot which, under suitable restrictions, he can make his own home, and leave to his children after him. . . . A farm for every laborer, and every laborer for his own farm, is her [the nation's] millennial motto." Yet Dexter also insisted that questions "regarding social equality" lay beyond the scope of legitimate government action. He maintained that the economic and social position of the Negro should be determined solely by "the same social forces which carry along the white man." "If we can trust the grass to grow," he explained, "and the trees to blossom and bear fruit, under the bright urgency of the spring and summer sunshine, we can trust the great mass of emancipated negroes to become thrifty farmers and mechanics, and valuable members of the great industrial body, by natural promptings of opportunity and self-interest, in the propitious air of freedom"[107] Dexter failed to notice that large-scale confiscation would involve the use of means scarcely identical to the "same social forces" at work in northern society and would tacitly confess that the ideal frictionless social order—the open market of free competition—was not adequate to the realities of the Southern situa-

107. Henry Martyn Dexter, *What Ought to Be Done with the Freedmen and the Rebels?* "A Sermon Preached in the Berkeley Street Church, Boston, on Sunday, April 23, 1865," pp. 9–14.

tion. Either the Protestant doctrine of society and historical progress was insufficient, or confiscation could not be easily justified.

Others were quicker to perceive the dissonance and to act accordingly. Edward Norris Kirk, sometime revivalist and Boston's leading evangelical preacher, insisted that the North must "neither pet nor flatter" the former slave with extraordinary favors denied other groups. He must be assured a position "on a perfect level with every other before the law" and beyond that must work out his own destiny.[108] Writing to a missionary at Port Royal, Francis Wayland warned that special treatment of blacks would render them morally unfit to earn their own way in a society of free men. "To free the negroes," he said, "and pay them wages for their labor, will be hardly a blessing, unless you teach them the responsibilities of freedom. If they begin by having such wages as they never dreamed of, and besides this, have their *clothes* given to them, they will be ruined. They will expect it, and be idle, loafing beggars, without an atom of self-respect. I would not give away a rag except in cases of sickness."[109] And if a rag was too great a charity to bestow, how much more was land!

Limited by this conceptual framework, Protestants could scarcely rise beyond occasional vindictive calls to punish the South by confiscation; and the nation trained in this ethnic could do little more than dally ineffectually with such schemes, only to return at length to the starkly simple prescription of Henry Ward Beecher: "Educate men to take care of themselves, individually and in masses, then let the winds blow."[110]

This teaching implied that once formal emancipation were accomplished and a brief period of moral instruction had followed, blacks would be completely on their own with no one to blame but themselves if they failed to achieve equality. Frequently unspoken, this assumption was on occasion enunciated with frightening clarity. The *American Missionary* reported the address of a Northern officer to freedmen at Port Royal: "Supposing you fail down here; that will be an end of the whole matter. It is like attaching a cable to a

108. Edward Norris Kirk, *A Sermon Preached Before the American Missionary Association*, pp. 13, 14.
109. Wayland and Wayland, *Francis Wayland*, 2: 275–76.
110. Beecher, *Patriotic Addresses*, p. 347.

stranded vessel, and all the strength that can be mustered is put on this rope to haul her off. If this only rope breaks, the vessel is lost. . . . If you are idle, vicious, indolent and negligent you will fail and your last hope is gone."[111]

After the war when blacks did fall under a new and perhaps more odious form of slavery, there were other long-nourished attitudes that would reconcile Protestants to the apparent inevitability of the result. In stressing the innate docility and religiosity of the Negro, Harriet Beecher Stowe and others had prepared a powerful engine of assault against the slave system; but they also raised a lingering suspicion that these same amiable qualities ill equipped blacks for the rough competition of a free society. The Negro's feminized virtues implied that perhaps he, like idealized woman, belonged in a subservient role in the margins of society. In a pamphlet written for the American Tract Society, the Reverend Israel Tarbox argued the cohumanity of whites and blacks; but his picture of Negro destiny in America suggested images at variance with an equal status for the races. "In the wide and unoccupied spaces of our land there is room enough for them and us. We want them here . . . as laborers to till this vast domain. . . . We want their cheerful music to ring out amid our forests like songs in the night."[112] This language recalls Wilbur Cash's description of the stereotypical "banjo-plucking, heel-flinging, hi-yi-ing happy jacks"; and it is profoundly suggestive that Tarbox placed the black as a laborer happily singing away his nights in the forests of the Deep South—forests presumably uninhabited by whites.[113] Moreover, it was a short step from the docile, religious black to the image of the unfit "barbarian in the midst of civilization." With that appellation firmly attached to the Negro, the Reverend Julian Sturtevant, president of Illinois College, suggested that the "beneficent law" of free labor would shortly eliminate this incapable being from American life. After emancipation, Sturtevant predicted, "the negro, with his inferior civilization, would be crowded everywhere into the lower stratum of the social pyramid, and in

111. "General Mitchell's Speech to the Negroes," *American Missionary*, 2d ser. 6 (December 1862): 280.
112. Increase N. Tarbox, *The Curse; or, The Position in the World's History Occupied by the Race of Ham*, pp. 157–58.
113. Wilbur J. Cash, *The Mind of the South*, p. 95.

a few generations be seen no more." Free labor would award the
American black "a grave."[114]

It would be unfair to attribute this "racial Malthusianism," as
George Fredrickson has called it, to most Protestant clergy.[115]
Churchmen generally wished a better future for the Afro-American,
but their attitudes about society, slavery, and reform did not equip
them to face the complexity of the issues or to accept the unpalat-
able truth: the peculiar institution, far from being an aberration
from the essential goodness of the republic, was tragically enmeshed
in almost every aspect of the American experience, and this dark
legacy could not easily be dispersed in one decisive moment. Belief
to the contrary was comforting, but reassurance would be purchased in installments at terrible cost.

### CULTURE-PROTESTANTISM AND THE AMERICAN DILEMMA

But it was not an hour for somber musing. The Lord of history
had miraculously ended slavery and opened a bright future for the
United States. Americans could be confident that their times were
in God's hands and that the crisis had passed. Perhaps the most
subtly dangerous effect of this conviction was the complacence,
even passivity, that it sometimes bred. If God were revealing his
will through the national experience, it behooved Christians to
await his answer rather than to impose one. Events themselves
would be salvific, and to determine a specific political program in
advance was to demonstrate an appalling distrust of the guiding
hand that made all things work for good. As the Reverend George
L. Walker told his congregation in Portland, Maine: "It is our duty
reverently and expectantly to wait upon that Divine power whose
steps hitherto in this matter [slavery] have so transcended human
wisdom. 'Reverently' I say. By this I mean it is our duty not rashly
to inaugurate schemes for the accomplishment even of the holy
design of freeing our land from the crime of slavery. . . . It is rash
and wicked to go before the clear intimations of Providence. And
especially now when God so visibly walks in our land, and lifts

114. Julian M. Sturtevant, "The Destiny of the African Race in the United
States," *Continental Monthly* 3 (May 1863): 600–610.
115. Fredrickson, *Black Image in the White Mind*, p. 159.

upon us, almost daily, some new scene of the wondrous drama, it is criminal not reverently to subordinate our actions to the beckoning of His hand."[116] Or as the Reverend David Magie said in the Second Presbyterian Church in Elizabeth, New Jersey, as late as 6 August 1863: "God is working out in his own providential way a solution of the mighty problem, and our part is to stand still and see the salvation of God."[117]

Such conclusions were in part a logical outcome of viewing profane history as holy history. To an unprecedented extent, the war had broken down distinctions between the sacred and secular, endowing the arms and policies of the Union with religious significance. Therefore to know the will of God, the churches needed only to follow the forces and trends at work in the nation. Since God was providentially leading his people, Christians could safely trust their country's future to be itself the cloudy, fiery pillar guiding this new Israel unto its appointed destiny. What this could mean for slavery A. L. Stone made explicitly clear: "The stern logic of events will show emancipation actual, inevitable. Let that logic frame the declaration, and not our lips. Men may pick flaws in proclamations, and take sides, and question the right and wisdom, but what the progress of the onrolling war necessitates, that has unquestionable vindication. . . . Did the Israelites go blindly forward when they followed the pillar of cloud and fire?"[118] The exigencies of American history would be the salvation of America, and the task of the clergy was to follow events, not to lead them.

Many calls for immediate emancipation were, in fact, little more than retroactive endorsements of action already taken by the Lincoln administration. For example, in 1864 the Methodist General Conference was convinced by "the guidings of the divine Hand, whose power we reverently behold in the grand movements of our times," that abolition was desirable and that the discipline should be altered to bar slaveholders from communion.[119] By the close of hostilities, the amendment had been approved and incorporated in the constitution of the church. In later years Bishop Gilbert Haven

116. Walker, *The Offered National Regeneration*, pp. 22–23.
117. David Magie, *A Discourse Delivered in the Second Presbyterian Church*, pp. 16–17.
118. Stone, *Divineness of Human Government*, pp. 47–48.
119. *Christian Advocate and Journal*, May 26, 1864, p. 162.

wrote acidly of this decision: "When the war was over and not a slave remained in the country, the barren exploit of inserting the word 'slaveholding' into the rules was performed. . . . The battle is fought and the victory won. Why maintain a useless breastwork and the ashes of burnt powder?"[120] Haven rightly sensed that his church was following the national mood, not leading it. What he failed to comprehend was that the providential theory of nationalism, to which he fervently subscribed, was covertly furthering this result.

Henry J. Van Dyke, who represented that increasingly rare species of Northern minister—an unabashed Peace Democrat and apologist for slavery—perceived from his lonely position what Haven could not. Van Dyke was incensed that his own Old School Presbyterian Church had declared with virtual unanimity at its 1864 General Assembly: "The recent events of our history, and the present condition of our Church and country, furnish manifest tokens that the time has at length come, in the providence of God, when it is His will that every vestige of human slavery among us should be effaced, and that every Christian man should address himself with industry and earnestness to his appropriate part in the performance of this great duty."[121] This action represented a radical departure from the denomination's former insistence that it could issue moral guidance on public issues only in accordance with strict scriptural warrant. The Old School, too, had found irresistible the extracanonical revelation in the "events of our history."

Van Dyke argued that his denomination had erred in attempting to deduce the will of God from the course of American history. The assembly cited Lincoln's emancipation policy as evidence of the divine indictment of slavery, and Van Dyke asked sarcastically: "Ought they to take the declared policy of any civil magistrate or human government for a manifest token of His will, whose throne is surrounded with clouds and thick darkness?" With keen insight into the central issues at stake, Van Dyke rejected the notion that the war was an apocalyptic struggle. "I do not believe, but reject as blasphemous, the sentiment so often uttered even by Christian

120. Quoted in Charles Baumer Swaney, *Episcopal Methodism and Slavery: with Sidelights on Ecclesiastical Politics,* pp. 334–35.

121. *Minutes of the General Assembly of the Presbyterian Church in the United States of America, Old School* (1864), 17: 298.

ministers, that God cannot do without the United States, that the Church of Christ is in anywise identified with or dependent upon the national existence. According to my reading of God's covenant oath to his son, (in Psalm II), the kingdoms of this world are given to Zion's King, that he 'may break with a rod of iron, and dash them in pieces as a potter's vessel.' And whether it is his inscrutable purpose to dash this nation in pieces or not, the foundations of the Church are secure."[122] In repudiating America's supposed millennial role, Van Dyke had inadvertently diagnosed what was happening to the churches: they were sanctifying, in the name of providence, the policies of the nation.

Van Dyke and Haven discerned an American Culture-Protestantism that viewed the national order as a divinely perfected source of religious fulfillment and authority. In light of the interlocking series of attitudes Americans brought to the problem of slavery, this phenomenon raised ominous portents for the future of the Afro-American and a new South. The "clear intimations" of providence might thunder liberty for the captives during the war and perhaps during a brief, abortive attempt at radical reconstruction; but what would the churches do when the issues of the war blurred or when programs failed? If the voice of God no longer spoke clearly in history, a quiet resignation might be providence's only ascertainable orders.

The churches, however, never suspected this possible outcome. They believed that like a violent thunderstorm, the war would restore social equilibrium, and the nation would go forth to millennial splendor. Right order *had* to assert itself, the problem of slavery *had* to dissolve, the nation *had* to become the embodied Kingdom of God on earth. With such ideas, troops may be rallied for a season of bloody conflict, but protracted ill-defined combat will inevitably be lost. Yet to have questioned these assumptions would have been to admit that the Union was not waging an apocalyptic war and that America was not the redeemer nation.

122. Henry J. Van Dyke, *The Spirituality and Independence of the Church,* pp. 18, 22. Van Dyke was heavily influenced in his understanding of the spirituality of the church by James Henley Thornwell, a leading Southern Old School Presbyterian and formulator of the doctrine. For further information on this subject, see Benjamin M. Palmer, *The Life and Letters of James Henley Thornwell,* p. 436 and passim.

# 4

## The Crucible of Folk Loyalty

In an 1861 Fourth of July oration, the Reverend Samuel Harris of Bangor, Maine, stressed that the constitutive feature of American nationality was not shared geography, ethnicity, or historical origin, but an idea—the principle of universal justice and individual freedom.

> It is the embodiment of our great American idea into our institutions which constitutes us a nation. This is indeed the Saviour's teaching, loosely interpreted and applied, that a man is not a Jew because he is descended from Abraham, but only because, whatever his descent, he has the faith of Abraham. He who is not in sympathy with the American idea that breathes in our political institutions, is an alien, unworthy to bear the name of American citizen. But the Irishman, the Frenchman, every foreigner, who seeks the protection of our government, intelligently sympathizing with its idea and spirit, he is an American, a native 'to the manor born' by a new political birth, and entitled in due form of law to become a citizen.[1]

In one sense the mind creates every nationality, for as Hans Kohn has remarked, "The important element is a living and active corporate will . . . a state of mind inspiring a large majority of people and claiming to inspire all its members"; and yet the American sense of nationhood was a particularly abstract ideal.[2] By comparison with other peoples, Americans lacked a rich symbolism embodying their national unity. The Republic could not claim a monarch,

---

1. Samuel Harris, *Our Country's Claim,* "Oration at the Citizens' Celebration of the Eighty-fifth Anniversary of the Declaration of Independence," p. 10.
2. Hans Kohn, *Nationalism: Its Meaning and History,* p. 10.

centuries of blood intermingled with the sacred motherland, ancient folklore, or (at least officially) a racial self-designation. The Fourth of July oration was probably the most significant cultic rite of the civil religion and illustrated the relative abstractness of American nationality. Like the Protestant sermon, the Independence Day address was primarily an exposition of principle and might justly be called a political counterpart to the evangelical theology of the Word.[3] The difficulty of attaining a satisfactory ritual enactment of unity was further complicated by the fact that the national ideal, with its soaring affirmation of the individual's inalienable right to life, liberty, and the pursuit of happiness, was itself susceptible to a profoundly asocial, disintegrative interpretation. Harris knew these shortcomings, and he interrupted his praise of America's credal character to confess fear that the ideal had failed to develop a true national identity. "And yet we must own," he admitted, "that there has been some foundation for this charge of a lack of loyalty. So invisible is our government, so void of all symbols that set forth its presence and its majesty, so rarely have we come into contact with its civil and military officials, so silently fall its blessings like the noiseless sunbeams or the gentle dew, that we have not appreciated its beneficent agency, nor rendered it the affectionate loyalty which is its due."[4]

Although Protestants had long recognized the dangers inherent in democracy, they had relied upon the power of religion and morality to check divisive individualism. In the wake of several decades of political strife—and now civil war—the clergy were forced to admit that their countrymen had failed to learn the internal discipline befitting a free people. Beneath the moral carping of the jeremiads lay a fairly unified perception that a want of self-restraint had converted free society into a battleground for competing groups. The clerical community might denounce the citizenry for being a "jaunty, showy race," for surrendering to an "all absorbing party spirit," or for exhibiting an avarice that has "hardened and enervated us"; but one basic charge may always be read between the lines: "Man is taught to look upon himself as a unit, to consider

3. Gabriel, *Course of American Democratic Thought,* pp. 98–99.
4. Harris, *Our Country's Claim,* p. 8.

himself and his interests apart from society. . . . [Many] boast, that in this day man begins to feel his own individual importance, and must assert his own individual importance and must assert individual rights. Nothing can be more pernicious than such statements. The result is to dissociate society, to break it up into small companies and factions and insulate its members."[5]

Protestants foresaw a providential end to this condition as a result of the Civil War. If pulpit and school had failed to persuade men to loyalty, the lesson would be hammered into them by the rod of battle. As the *Christian Advocate and Journal* suggested in August 1864 during Grant's bloody offensive in Virginia:

> The first shock of war broke the enchantment to which the national heart was succumbing, and called the whole people to the unwonted task of doing and suffering something for the public good. And that which was at first only the impulse of the hour has grown into a living sentiment and the steady habit of many hearts. A more profound patriotism, a living spirit of unselfish devotion to country, now animates the breasts of our loyal masses, such as had not before been known since the fathers of the Revolution fell asleep. . . . Our patriotism has become more devout and God-fearing than at any former period, and the national character is rising under its chastisements to a more elevated patriotism.[6]

Through common suffering, Americans were being knit together as one people, strong in devotion to their country.

The clergy, to be sure, viewed the war as a fervent crusade for republican institutions—but for republicanism chastened and restrained. In particular they argued for an exalted conception of political power, one affirming that sovereignty is more than a creature of the popular will. Calling for a disciplined society, the

5. Eddy, *Our Country,* p. 28; William A. Niles, *Our Country's Peril and Hope,* "A Sermon Delivered on the Occasion of the National Fast, January 4th, 1861, in the Presbyterian Church, Corning, N.Y.," p. 14; James Marshall, *The Nation's Inquiry,* "A Discourse Delivered in the Chesapeake General Hospital," p. 18; and James P. Wilson, *Our National Fast,* "A Sermon Preached in the South Park Presbyterian Church, January 4th, 1861," p. 11.
6. *Christian Advocate and Journal,* August 11, 1864, p. 252.

churches utilized the classic scriptural argument that government is a divine ordinance; and they also took refuge in an organic theory of nationhood. This latter idea, which owed its modern inception largely to Romanticism, maintained that a nation is the living expression of a corporate identity or folk spirit transcending its individual parts. Although this romantic notion antedated the war and was not always tied to authoritarian sentiments, Protestants found here a useful rationale for the federal cause.[7] As the expression of America's folk spirit, the Union was a sacred reality that could not be set aside by momentary passion and to which every citizen was obligated by the fact of birth. To maintain and to perfect this holy bond of loyalty was for the churches a major goal of the war.

There was a profound irony in this search for an ordered society. At the same time that the clergy were demanding greater discipline and unity, they were also foretelling a speedy reconstruction premised upon socioeconomic individualism, minimal federal inter-

7. The 1860s did not, of course, create romantic nationalism in America. Antebellum writers such as George Bancroft, Ralph Waldo Emerson, and Walt Whitman had given expression to a widespread romantic vision of the nation and its destiny. Furthermore, the fact that these figures glorified individualism and the common man is a reminder that romanticism did not lead ineluctably to authoritarian views. Nor am I claiming that conservative political philosophy first arose in the United States as a result of the rebellion. Long before Sumter, the Federalist—and to a much lesser extent, the Whig—tradition had presented the case for strong government and for deference to a ruling elite. Political theorists such as Francis Lieber and John C. Hurd had begun to adumbrate these convictions into an explicitly organic notion of the state, and churchman John W. Nevin had expounded the theory with classic brilliance. In this chapter, I am contending merely that the Civil War gave new prominence and emphasis to authoritarian sentiments and that these were frequently expressed in romantic-organic categories. My argument is indebted to that of George Fredrickson, *The Inner Civil War: Northern Intellectuals and the Crisis of the Union*. See also Daniel Aaron, *The Unwritten War: American Writers and the Civil War,* and Robert M. Albrecht, "The Theological Response of the Transcendentalists to the Civil War," *New England Quarterly* 38 (March 1965): 21–34. On prewar political philosophy, see, for example, A. J. Beitzinger, *A History of American Political Thought,* pp. 247–66, 313–76; James Hastings Nichols, ed., *The Mercersburg Theology,* pp. 285–306; and Herbert W. Schneider, *A History of American Philosophy,* 2d ed., pp. 73–128, 143–77.

vention, and only modest reform. Most Protestants, however, were totally unaware of incongruity in their position. For them, the realization of corporate unity was not dependent so much upon institutional arrangements as it was upon the mind of America. A renovation of the spirit would bring order as citizens learned to venerate the common good. To that end, the war was a brutal but provisional tutor, teaching Americans the self-restraint that would enable free people to live as one organic folk. Yet if their praise of authority and the corporate ideal failed to produce a sustained or profound critique of laissez-faire policies, such rhetoric was not merely cosmetic. Draconian pronouncements revealed deepened suspicion of political dissent and discomfort with the more libertarian aspects of the United States' own revolutionary past. Protestants were glorifying the blind obedience of the soldier and strengthening the equation of nationalism with what Edmund Wilson appropriately called "patriotic gore."[8]

DEMOCRACY RECONSIDERED

During the war Protestants were at pains to elucidate the true theory of democracy and to dissociate it from an erroneous conception. The Reverend Truman M. Post, one of Congregationalism's foremost leaders outside New England, suggested to the students of Washington University in St. Louis that two interlocking principles lay at the base of free government: human rights and divine rights. Although God intended these to be complementary, men had perversely twisted them into opposites. Despotic powers, like the Roman Catholic Church, usurped the place of God and turned their energies to "crush and smother the rights of man"; or in reaction, the advocates of democracy, "finding the Heavens apparently banded with their oppressors," rejected all authority external to the people themselves. Thus history had lurched from the extreme of papal tyranny to the excess of the French Revolution. This tragic disjunction of mutually supportive principles found remedy in evangelical Christianity. This religion "weds human right to divine right." Protestant stress on the "exercise of private judgment" freed

8. Edmund Wilson, *Patriotic Gore: Studies in the Literature of the American Civil War*.

the individual person in things spiritual and, by implication, in the
political realm. Yet at the same time that Christianity assured human
rights, it also endowed civil government "with the authority of
heaven," enjoined obedience upon citizens, and thereby placed
liberty upon its only sure grounds. Without this restraint, a regime
based solely upon human rights "will at last run down" into ego-
tistic anarchy. Although Americans had forgotten this vital coun-
terbalance to liberty, the war was preparing the way for a right
conception of government as divinely ordained. The nation verged
on its "palingenesy"—a transliteration of the Greek word that Jesus
had used to indicate the new era, or universal regeneration, that
the Son of Man will inaugurate at the end of time. The eschatological implications of the American "palingenesy" did not escape Post.
"So built, our structure shall stand, guarded for ages, as never was
Eden by 'limitary cherub,' by the immortal forces of human soul
and the Christian faith; yea, o'erwatched perpetually by the Sab-
baoths of God, so constituted and guarded, it shall have no principle
of decay." A revitalized America, taught the divinity of government
by war, would be "in accord with eternal powers. It shall stand
through earth's better era. With God's favor it shall defy the corro-
sion of time. . . . And thus our political structure—the House of
Liberty and Law and Love—shall abide, till its glory of arch and spire
and dome shall blend with the amethyst and chrysolite and sapphire
of the New Jerusalem."[9]

Pulpits continually denounced the ideas of "spurious liberty" and
"false independence" that had degraded government into a malleable
instrument of popular passion.[10] John G. Atterbury told the First
Presbyterian Church in New Albany, Indiana, that parents had
greatly erred in teaching their children such slogans as "rulers are
responsible to the people" or "the people are self-governed." Atterbury concluded that "God has not conceded to man the right to rule
himself. So again magistrates, though constituted for the benefit of
the people and not their own advantage, are yet not the servants of
the people but God's servants. They are above the people, not below
them. Though designated for their trust by the people themselves,

9. Truman M. Post, *Palingenesy: National Regeneration,* pp. 9–12, 17.
10. West, *Establishment in National Righteousness,* p. 27.

they yet receive their commission from above."[11] Thus in exercising his office, the magistrate must not lower himself to be a mouthpiece for his constituents. He must rule according to his understanding of the divine will; and although they were the instruments of his elevation, the people have an irrevocable obligation to obey his injunctions. The Reverend James P. Wilson of Newark, New Jersey, mocked the current conception of democratic government as one in which the legislature "ought to sit in some immense magnetic telegraph office, and every man hold a wire in his hands to tell him what his constituents think on every question of importance that comes up for consideration." This vulgarized conception of democracy, charged Wilson, overturns social stability "in obedience to present opinion, present force, and present demagogueism." Instead the political order should be regarded as a "united family" or a "vast paternity" in which officials justly demand the people's obedience as surely as does the father in his smaller realm of authority.[12] The democratic process, in sum, was not popular rule but the instrument by which rulers were invested with their authority.

Thomas Jefferson in particular became the symbol of irresponsible democracy. His unorthodox religion and politics had made him controversial during his own lifetime, and in many quarters his memory had emerged only gradually from disrepute. With the coming of war, old charges against him were revived, and many damned his philosophy anew. As Merrill Peterson has shown, Jefferson's legacy was an ambiguous one. His thought wove enthusiasm for popular democracy, states' rights, and agrarian society into a complex tapestry, pieces of which could be claimed by both abolitionists and Southern fireaters. But to the Northern clergy, he epitomized primarily those errors which they believed had led to the disruption of the Union—belief that personal liberties are founded in abstract rights antecedent to the formation of society, that government is created by social contract and has no authority except by the consent of the governed, and that the sovereignty of individual states takes priority over federal power. There was considerable irony in the effort to fix on Jefferson the onus for the Confederate rebellion

11. John G. Atterbury, *God in Civil Government,* "A Discourse Preached in the First Presbyterian Church, New Albany, Nov. 27, 1862," p. 7.
12. Wilson, *Our National Fast,* pp. 8–10.

because its leaders were perhaps even less comfortable with the sage of Monticello than their Yankee counterparts. To be sure, his name had been a conjurer's word in Dixie; but theorists had chosen rather selectively from the Jeffersonian corpus. States' rights and the agrarian ideal suited their purposes well; his appeal to popular democracy was qualified, often ignored. By the eve of secession, many Southerners rejected his theories entirely as "powder-cask abstractions" and turned to social theories more rigorously organic and paternalistic than those advocated by Northern clergy. Yet Protestants hammered away at their bogeyman; and in Peterson's words, "The dark shadow of war fell across the Jefferson image like a great and furious Nemesis."[13]

According to A. L. Stone, the third president typified the frequent American error of regarding government as the "aggregate concessions of those who for the sake of dwelling together, strip themselves of a portion of their independence, and make over a common stock of delegated power to the community."[14] Opponents charged that this theory raised utopian expectations of government, and some of their criticisms were pointed. If, for example, the legitimation of civil authority required mutual consent among the members of society, this agreement would be subject to perpetual renegotiation as new citizens were born into the realm or as shifting majorities wished to change this or that feature of the compact. No nation could endure such an unceasing re-creation de novo and surrealistic attempts in this direction would reduce the state to chaos. George P. Fisher, Livingston Professor of Divinity at Yale College, summed up the Protestant attack against the compact theory:

> In whatever light you regard this theory, it will be seen untenable. If it is meant that the powers possessed by a government are actually conferred by those who at any given time actually live under it, it is manifestly false. We are born into civil society as we are born into the family. If it be meant that the unanimous

13. Merrill D. Peterson, *The Jefferson Image in the American Mind,* esp. pp. 17–111, 209–26. The expression "powder-cask abstractions" was that of George Fitzhugh, one of the South's leading proponents of an organic view of society.

14. Stone, *Divineness of Human Government,* pp. 16–17.

approval of the subjects of a government is requisite for its validity, it is manifestly absurd, as no government ever has such a sanction.  If it be meant that a majority of the adult males have a legal power to alter or abolish an existing system, we reply that no government, not the freest on earth, is so unstable but more than a numerical majority is necessary to effect an organic change.

Nothing could be clearer to Fisher than the fact that "society is not a compact to be dissolved at the caprice of the parties which are bound by it."[15]

Jefferson's advocacy of states' rights also drew angry criticism. After the spring of 1861, it was difficult to forget that this was a shibboleth by which the South justified its secession from the Union. Moreover Northerners had felt an acute sense of initial unpreparedness to subdue the rebellion. The standing army was poorly manned, the finances of the central treasury weak, and the memories of Buchanan's vacillation were strong. The president had refused to act, averring that the central government had no legitimate authority to coerce obedience by the states. These experiences suggested the deceptively simple explanation that Jeffersonian dogma, nurtured to its full growth, had spawned rebellion and had left the national government impotent. In 1864 Captain James F. Riesling, a Methodist layman, summarized this view of the rebellion as Jeffersonianism writ large. In the early days of the Republic, he argued, two parties had emerged. "The one, headed by Alexander Hamilton, held that the new government was really a *government*, established by the whole people, and endowed with all the functions and powers necessary for sovereignty and rule. The other led by that matchless leader Thomas Jefferson, claimed that the several states were still sovereign in a great degree, and that the federal government, having been derived from the states, was powerless except within certain limits expressly defined in the Constitution itself." In this Jeffersonian concept lay "doctrines that tended to a wild democracy," and the effects of this persuasion had

15. George P. Fisher, *Thoughts Proper to the Present Crisis,* "A Sermon Preached in the Chapel of Yale College, on Fast Day, January 4, 1861," pp. 7-8.

disclosed themselves as early as the Hartford Convention of 1814
and the nullification crisis of 1832. The inclusion of the Hartford
Convention entailed a forced oversight that this abortive venture
at secession had been launched by New England Federalists—the
enemies of Jefferson—who were disenchanted with "Mr. Madison's
War" against Great Britain. Riesling also forgot that Jefferson himself, in disregard of his own theory, had significantly enlarged the
effective power of the federal executive branch; nor did Riesling
try to fit within his two-party schema the efforts of Northern
Whigs and Republicans, scarcely the heirs of the Monticello Democrat, to nullify the proslavery laws of the 1850s. Although his
account offered an undiscriminating analysis of the past, Riesling
pressed confidently to a conclusion: "The rebellion under the form
of secession, is simply Jeffersonianism pushed to its logical results;
the war for the Union, waged under the form of coercion, is merely
the return of the government to the sound doctrines of Washington
and Hamilton. *They* fight for anarchy; *we* fight for government.
*They* fight for lawlessness; *we* fight for law."[16]

Riesling would have concurred with the judgment expressed by
Levi Paine in the Congregational Church at Farmington, Connecticut, in April 1862. Paine believed that Jefferson epitomized the
fundamental inability of Americans "to revere the name and authority of law, as issuing from a higher source than themselves and demanding their allegiance without regard to individual opinions and
prejudices." The democratic tradition as expounded by Jefferson
taught that the best government is the one that governs least and
made Americans "fearful of centralization, but never of license and
anarchy." Andrew Jackson's struggle against the second Bank
of the United States, as well as the Democratic party's opposition to the tariff or federally financed internal improvements,
represented the same truncated view of political sovereignty; and
the predominance of this belief had effectively forbidden the Union
"to strengthen itself and keep pace with the nation." Although he
did not question their patriotism, Paine insisted that Jefferson and

16. James F. Riesling, "The War for the Union," *Methodist Quarterly
Review* 46 (April 1864): 307–16.

Jackson had taught the nation attitudes that had produced the Civil War. "No other two I venture to say, have done half so much to bring the nation into its present condition."[17]

Horace Bushnell raised these issues with perhaps greater cogency than any other thinker. For him the war posed one central question: what had Americans accomplished on 4 July 1776? According to Jefferson's "glittering generalities" about the equality of all men and the derivation of political power from the consent of the governed, a nationality could be manufactured, "a machine could be got up," by the agreement of those in a state of natural equality. Thus Jefferson suggested that the Revolutionary generation had created by mutual compact a nationality where none had existed before. Bushnell found this conception totally unsatisfactory. For him the fundamental characteristic of a nation was its ability to oblige consent, but he did not believe with Jefferson "that man could somehow create authority over man." Unless obligation were given from above, from God, there could exist no moral constraint. "Nothing touches the conscience," he observed, "and becomes morally binding that is not from above the mere human level." Since a people could not be a nation without this higher imperative, the "fictions of theory" indulged by Jefferson could not establish true government. At most his system could yield "only a copartnership . . . [that] has no national authority, no obligation." Even if one were to grant the theoretical validity of the social compact theory, Bushnell added, it would be impossible to find a group of people who have in fact created a government by covenant:

> There never was in the first place, any such prior man, or body of men, to make a government. We are born into government as we are into the atmosphere, and when we assume to make a government or constitution, we only draw out one that was providentially in us before. We could not have a king, or nobility, for example, in this country; for there was no material given out of which to make either one or the other. The church life and order was democratic too. The whole English constitution also, was in us before. In these facts, prepared in history by

17. Paine, *Political Lessons of the Rebellion*, pp. 11–15.

God, our institutions lie. We did not make them. We only sketched them, and God put them in us to be sketched.[18]

"In these facts, prepared in history by God, our institutions lie": here in essence was Bushnell's alternative to the Jeffersonian understanding of the Revolution. God, not man, creates nationalities by a long temporal process, and this history is the imposition from above of moral obligation upon man. Bushnell believed that the Declaration of Independence only acknowledged formally the divine decree given through the American experience. The genesis of the United States could not be located at Philadelphia in 1776; the nation was contained in embryo among the first New England settlers. From the brotherhood of their churches sprang the notion of "political equality in the state," but this order was perceived as an obligation imposed on them from God, not as a creature of their own making. As Bushnell stated his case:

> They had nothing to do with some theoretic equality in man *before* government, in which as a first truth of nature, governments are grounded. They were born into government, and they even believed in a certain sacred equality under it, as their personal right. They had also elected their rulers, and so far they could agree to the right of a government by consent, but they never had assumed that men are *ipso facto* exempt from obligation who have not consented, or that an aristocratic and princely government is of necessity void and without "just power." Their "equality," their "Consent," were the divine right of their history, from the landing of the fathers downward, and before the French encyclopedists were born.[19]

The Civil War had revealed the coexistence of these two incompatible sets of ideas, and the purpose of the conflict was to disabuse Americans of the absurd Jeffersonian conception of a "copartnership." To this end, God was inflicting severe reverses and agony upon the nation. Americans had to learn to suffer unquestioningly

18. Horace Bushnell, *Reverses Needed*, "A Discourse Delivered on the Sunday after the Disaster of Bull Run, in the North Church, Hartford," pp. 11, 12, 16–17, 18.
19. Ibid., pp. 10, 12–13.

to acquire that higher loyalty without which a nation is only a fiction. "Without shedding of blood," Bushnell warned, "there is no such grace prepared. There must be reverses and losses, and times of deep concern. There must be tears in the houses, as well as blood in the fields; the fathers and mothers, the wives and dear children, coming into the woe, to fight in hard bewailings. Desolated fields, prostrations of trade, discouragements of all kinds, must be accepted with unfaltering, unsubduable patience."[20] Yet Bushnell remained confident that the outcome of this agony would be a reborn nation and a truly loyal citizenry. "We shall then have passed the ordeal of history. Our great battlefields will be hallowed by song. Our great leaders and patriots will be names consecrated by historic reverence. We shall no more be a compact, or a confederation, or a composition made up by the temporary surrender of powers, but a nation—God's own nation."[21]

On 27 January 1864 unofficial representatives of eleven Northern churches met in Allegheny City, Pennsylvania, to form the National Reform Association. This group wanted to give formal expression to the belief that the national government was the embodiment of divine sovereignty and wanted to strip from the Constitution any suggestion that "we the people" were the efficient cause or source of national authority. The convention petitioned the Congress to recommend an amendment of the preamble to read:

> We, the people of the United States, humbly acknowledging Almighty God as the source of all authority and power in civil government, the Lord Jesus Christ as the Ruler among the nations, his revealed will as the supreme law of the land, in order to constitute a Christian government, and in order to form a more perfect union. . . .[22]

Although the proposed amendment was never adopted, it received the endorsement of several denominations, including the Old School Presbyterian and the Methodist Episcopal; and the NRA continued

20. Ibid., pp. 18, 22.
21. Horace Bushnell, *Work and Play; or Literary Varieties*, p. 367.
22. *Presbyterian*, February 6, 1864, p. 22.

its work beyond the war.[23] In extreme form, this organization attested to a common Protestant conviction that the Union possessed a sacral status that should be given some form of public recognition. The stress upon the divine appointment of existing government, the exaltation of loyalty over inalienable rights—these were awkward sentiments on the lips of a people who owed their political existence to a rebellion against duly constituted authority. The question of slavery aside—and the North deliberately put slavery aside in the first portion of the war—the South could call venerable Revolutionary dogma to support its right to self-determination. In August 1861 George W. Bassett, a militant abolitionist and disaffected New School Presbyterian minister, placed this issue squarely upon the American conscience in *A Discourse on the Wickedness and Folly of the Present War*. Noting that the war was being waged to perpetuate the Union, not to free slaves, Bassett argued that this program repudiated the Declaration of Independence. To claim the right to political supremacy in the Southern states because they were at one time a portion of the Union was to assert the modern equivalent of "the divine right of kings." How, he asked, in the name of the "great natural and sacred right of self-government" could the North prevent a separate people from determining their own destiny? In attempting to destroy Southern independence, the Lincoln administration was adopting the high-handed policies of the English monarchs against whom the colonists had rebelled earlier:

> Already has a military despotism been inaugurated by our government, which puts the refined element of thought under the wardship of a rude soldiery, and incarcerates American citizens for the expression of sentiments which constituted the germ of our nationality, and which lie at the basis of all civil freedom. The language and sentiments of the American government are fast becoming those of James II and George III, and how soon her despotic acts will become equally sanguinary God only knows.[24]

23. *Christian Advocate and Journal*, June 2, 1864, p. 173; *Minutes of the General Assembly of the Presbyterian Church in the United States of America, Old School* (1864), 17: 315.

24. George W. Bassett, *A Discourse on the Wickedness and Folly of the Present War*, "Delivered in the Court House at Ottawa, Ill., on Sabbath, Aug. 11, 1861," pp. 4, 9.

Bassett wailed a lonely protest, easily dismissed as the ultimate demonstration of Jeffersonianism run wild; but theorists of the organic state failed to notice that their own arguments could also be employed in defense of the Confederacy. There was a disingenuous note in the contention that an existing government was to be obeyed, and therefore the seceded states should be coerced into obedience. By April 1861 the Confederacy had become the established law throughout the Deep South. In these areas, the Montgomery, later the Richmond, government was precisely that—a government, not a handful of outlaws or a disorganized guerrilla band. Those few who had opposed the Spring resolutions in the Old School Presbyterian Assembly in 1861 had, on one level, understood the issue better than had the majority who had urged support of the Union cause on the basis of the Romans 13 injunction that citizens should obey the powers that be. The minority rightly perceived that the issue was not really between government and no government or the powers that be versus anarchy, for there were now two established orders and two governments that had an effective de facto existence. In stating the case in this fashion, one does not offer a brief either for or against the Union war effort but rather clarifies the real alternatives that faced the North in 1861—whether to acquiesce in the existence of what had become for all practical purposes a separate nation or to destroy it by force.

Another ambiguity plagued Northern efforts to make peace with the spirit of the Revolution. By arguing that a rebellion acquired legitimacy only to the extent that it actualized the imperative of a people's history, Protestants intended to bar further upheavals not in accord with the logic of the American experience. Thus George Prentiss of Union Seminary argued that "ere it comes to its full birth, a people must have groaned and travailed together in pain for generations." Their nationality is woven from the "contingent and unconscious forces" of history; it cannot "be improvised." Prentiss believed that he had demolished the arbitrary Jeffersonian rationale that might vindicate Confederate rebellion and had proven the historical necessity of *one* nation, but he forgot that his argument cut two ways.[25] If the peculiar corporate life of a people provided the final legitimation of its right to independence, then

25. George L. Prentiss, *The Free Christian State and the Present Struggle,* "An Address Delivered Before the Alumni of Bowdoin College," pp. 7, 16.

endless pulpit declamations that the slave-whipping, man-stealing South constituted an alien civilization surely implied that the Southern states should have their own separate national existence. Before Sumter the *Independent* had declared: "Let the boundaries between them and the United States be defined by negotiation and peaceful agreement, if possible; and then let their destiny and ours be developed."[26] The *Independent,* of course, rescinded this suggestion once hostilities commenced; but the proposal continued to merit serious consideration if Protestants took their doctrine of revolution seriously. If the exigency of history had separated the colonies from the British crown, it had also, according to churchmen's own words, made Yankee and Cavalier two peoples. To paraphrase Bushnell, in these facts prepared in history by God, Southern institutions lay. Jefferson Davis and the Confederate authorities only sketched what providence had put in them to be sketched.

The difficulty of squaring the nation's revolutionary heritage with its war policy would have been largely obviated if from the first the struggle had been depicted primarily as a war of liberation on behalf of the slaves, but neither the government nor the majority of the churches so portrayed it. The clergy gladly accepted emancipation, but most agreed with the chief executive that saving the Union was the war's paramount goal. The Union, not antislavery, was the sacred trust imposed upon America.

One token of the status accorded the nation was the extent to which higher moral law became identified with obedience to government. In the 1850s, advocates of this apparently radical doctrine attacked the Fugitive Slave Act or the Dred Scott Decision and declared that these iniquities were not binding upon the conscience. In the hands of wartime expositors, the higher law became God's imposition of a binding obligation to obey civil authority. In part, this transmutation must be seen as an implication of regarding the war as Apocalypse. If the North, as Teddy Roosevelt would say years hence, stood at Armageddon and battled for the Lord, then its political system had been transformed into the sacred "ark of our civil and political covenant" never to be surrendered "into the hands of the Philistines"; and those who rebelled against its sover-

26. *Independent,* February 14, 1861, p. 4.

eignty had not only committed "treason against the United States" but were just as surely "rebels against the supremacy of God."[27] In a celebrated address before Abraham Lincoln in 1864, Methodist Bishop Matthew Simpson exposed the inner core of this doctrine. Simpson contended that the United States had come to epitomize the best products of the divine activity in history, and he concluded, amid waving handkerchiefs, wild applause, and tears in the President's eyes, "If the world is to be raised to its proper place, I would say it with all reverence, God cannot do without America."[28] The revolution had been achieved, its principles embodied in the new Israel. Henceforth the only legitimate revolutionary was he who loyally supported the American government.

The Civil War was a dual calamity to patriotic self-understanding. That the traditional right of rebellion was invoked to perpetuate human bondage was a shocking debasement of the American heritage; but the other tragedy—and just as damaging—was that the North and its religious community lost a lively awareness of the spirit that had pervaded the struggle for American independence. The beliefs that government is created by men, must acknowledge their legitimate rights, and requires their consent to attain legitimacy formed a beautiful, if somewhat airy, credo. To that high idealism may be contrasted the observation of Samuel T. Spear that no people should ever recognize the right of the governed to revolutionize the political order. To do so would be to admit "a principle of destruction" and to make "government nothing but a rope of sand." Revolution, said Spear, can be justified only after the fact— if it succeeds through bloody conflict. "If any portion of the people insist upon trying the question of force under the revolutionary right, then Government must insist upon trying the same question under the high, solemn, and majestic attributes of divine sovereignty."[29] Spear's contention that the providential victory of blood and iron in history affords the final test of political legitimacy was

27. N. S. Beman, *Thanksgiving in the Times of Civil War,* "A Discourse Preached in the First Presbyterian Church, Troy, New York, Nov. 28th, 1861," p. 45; and Dwight, *Nationality of a People,* pp. 27–28.
28. George R. Crooks, *The Life of Bishop Matthew Simpson,* p. 382. See also James E. Kirby, "Matthew Simpson and the Mission of America," *Church History* 36 (September 1967): 299–307.
29. Samuel T. Spear, *Two Sermons for the Times,* p. 15, 16.

perhaps evidence of a mature realism. Yet this hard-boiled language, redolent of vindication won by the sword and of consent enforced by the bayonet, indicated how far the Civil War generation had really departed from the belief in certain inalienable rights whose justice a candid world could readily perceive.

### LOYALTY AND THE LIMITS OF FREEDOM

Carl Becker has suggested that one who wants to understand a particular epoch must look for certain unobtrusive words that pervade its vernacular. Two such words that frequently recurred in the working lexicon of the Civil War clergy are *effeminacy* and *manliness.* With the former were connected the softness, love of ease, materialism, and selfishness of a degenerate citizenry. In the latter inhered those qualities of frugality, self-sacrificing simplicity, and heroic loyalty that befitted true patriots rightly esteeming the divinity of government. These virtues alone could ensure the success of the American experiment in freedom; but the sad lesson of history, Joel Bingham concluded in 1862, was that "no people as yet has conclusively proved itself equal" to them. The antebellum panacea to this dilemma had been the internal discipline of a widely disseminated evangelical religion. This lofty ideal had been comparable to the effort to run "a children's school without master," and the endeavor had failed.[30] Protestants had learned, in the words of the *Independent,* "that republicanized humanity can lie, cheat, steal, commit treason, stir up rebellion . . . and there is no wisdom nor power in man to save us."[31] Clearly the children's school required a headmaster; but the war, even as it disclosed the problem, prescribed the remedy. The God of battle would be the teacher, and his ferule would be the rod of enforced military discipline. Henry Boardman expressed the hope of the hour: "This war promises to arrest in a measure the extravagance and parade, the epicurism and effeminacy into which we were so fast running. It puts our young men upon a training which will nourish their manly virtues. It inculcates, as no moralist could, lessons of economy, of moderation, of patience, of self-control."[32]

30. Bingham, *Hour of Patriotism,* pp. 34–35.
31. *Independent,* September 26, 1861, p. 4.
32. Boardman, *Thanksgiving in War,* p. 17.

Boardman's reflections typified the clergy's fascination with war as a solution to the problem of creating a genuine patriotism. The American peace movement had been largely moribund in the 1850s, and, except for sectarian religious groups, the Civil War extinguished its remaining life. Initially a few people tried to salve their consciences by arguing that the nation was not in any proper sense engaged in war. Since the South did not represent a legitimate sovereign state, its forces were outlaw bands and the Union army a posse—a fiction that prefigured the twentieth-century euphemism *police action*.[33] Yet a posse of over a half-million men stretched the limits of credibility, and this incongruous notion had disappeared by the end of the war. Most churchmen readily accepted the salvific power of war as the inescapable corollary of an apocalyptic struggle. "Battlefields," said the *Christian Review,* "are the rallying points, not only of armies, but of principles as well; they are the jointings of history; nay more, they are the anvils on which God hammers the nations and shapes them to the end of his designs. By these rough smitings, he quickens the blood and wakens the energies of men; lays bare principles which get covered up, and inspires fresh loyalty to them; and so enlarges the life of nations, breaks the seals of prophecy, and opens new eras of the race."[34] In a volume explaining its work, the Sanitary Commission echoed these sentiments: "It is one of the great characteristics of the present age that the cause of humanity has become identified with the strength of armies."[35] George Ide summed up this faith in a striking aphorism: "Righteous wars are means of grace."[36]

If war opened a new channel of grace, the soldier dispensed the sacrament; and in death, he acquired the status of a Christian martyr. Horace Bushnell suggested:

We do not commonly speak of those who give up their lives on

33. For a good example of the "posse" theory, see Lavalette Perrin, *The Claims of Caesar,* "A Sermon Preached in the Center Church, New Britain, May 19, 1861," pp. 17–18. On the demise of pacifism, consult Peter Brock, *Radical Pacifists in Antebellum America,* pp. 221–63.

34. "The Vital Forces of the Age," *Christian Review* 26 (October 1861): 575.

35. *The Sanitary Commission of the United States Army: A Succinct Narrative of Its Works and Purposes,* p. iii.

36. Ide, *Battle Echoes,* p. 30.

the battle-fields of their country, as dying by martyrdom. And yet it is the martyrdom of loyalty unto which they freely gave their bodies, and knowingly consented to the sacrifice. The martyrs of religion scarcely make a sacrifice more real, or total, though they suffer in a way more trying to constancy. We believe too that there is a relation so deep between true loyalty and religion that the loyal man will be inclined toward religion by his public devotion, and the religious man raised in the temper of his loyalty to his country, by his religious devotion. The two fires will burn together and the one will kindle the other.[37]

The image of the soldier-martyr expressed more than casual or hyperbolic praise for military service. In yielding his life, the American warrior gave that "last full measure of devotion" to the cause in which the millennial hopes of the world resided, and thus Bushnell could juxtapose allegiance to the United States government with loyalty to religion because the holy war had conjoined the two. The soldier who died in battle also ranked among the martyrs, for his sacrifice, like theirs, would prove efficacious unto the redemption of the world. The *Independent* suggested that "the slain soldiers of our country . . . lay down their lives for the salvation, not of the land alone, but of justice, liberty, religion. . . . The objects for which they die are Union and Liberty—not for ourselves but for man, not for the present race and hour, but for all time and all generations. These are the highest calls to which earth can summon man: Union for the sake of Liberty, and Liberty for the sake of the world." The universal significance of their sacrifice distinguished the American war dead from the slain of other nations. Since the American soldier alone bore the future of mankind on his back, he only could offer the oblation that would effectively regenerate the world. "Not on Polish plains," concluded the editor, "or in Grecian glens, or in Parisian faubourgs, or upon English scaffolds, are the shrines of the truest martyrs for Man. For those fought and died chiefly for themselves—these [the American soldiers] for themselves and all the world. Upon these the ends of the world have come."[38]

37. Bushnell, *Work and Play*, p. 358.
38. *Independent*, August 4, 1864, p. 4.

In spite of their sacrificial offering upon the national altar, these Union soldiers would not, most of them, die in battle. Returning to their homes and occupations at the cessation of hostilities, these survivors were expected to exercise a beneficial influence upon the tone of American society. Bishop Janes of the Methodist Church believed that the "grandeur and solemnity" of their present suffering was preparatory to an even more significant work in peacetime. "When these armies shall be disbanded; when these men shall return home," he predicted, ". . . [they] will not be obscure persons. Everyone of them will have a history, and a name, and a story; and these returning soldiers are to have the ear of the boyhood of the nation for the next thirty years."[39] Clergy were in little doubt what lessons combat-tried warriors would teach their sons by the hearth. Chaplain James Marshall told the wounded in Virginia that they were "drilling in a severe school" by "skirmishes, hardships, and hairbreadth escapes, . . . the educators of the highest qualities" and that once returned to civil pursuits they would be models for emulation—"true men, genuine heroes, real iron-souled patriots."[40] From the rigors of camp life, said Baptist S. D. Phelps of New Haven, would emerge a "hardier and stronger [citizenry], both in physical endurance and in moral vigor." Although Americans had been "degenerating and becoming effeminate through luxury and ease," the returning soldiers would people the nation with "moral and Christian heroes," provide "stalwart influences," and ensure "a purer and more stable Republicanism."[41] These hymns to the salutary influence of war upon the soldier, and through him the nation, were ubiquitous; and the qualities to be disseminated by the veteran were usually described by the same adjectives we have just heard—heroic, iron souled, hardy, strong, stalwart. These so-called manly virtues sound an austere, even callous, note—the traits inspired by war are never gentle—but the churches were convinced that this militaristic sternness would inculcate that obedient patriotism which had been the missing element in American nationality.

39. *Presbyterian,* February 6, 1864, p. 22.
40. Marshall, *Nation's Changes,* p. 23.
41. S. D. Phelps, *National Symptoms,* "A Discourse Preached in the First Baptist Church, New Haven, on the Day of the Annual State Fast, April 18, 1862," p. 14.

Unfortunately war and the apotheosis of the soldier also inject into society an authoritarian note inimical to free institutions. Thus President Lincoln suspended the writ of habeas corpus, permitted the army to try civilians, and granted generals authority to bar the publication of disloyal newspapers. These policies created a *cause célèbre* when a military court imprisoned Clement L. Vallandigham, a prominent Ohio Democrat, for inflammatory speeches against the administration's war policy. Of course, Lincoln's common sense and respect for democracy restricted his use of arbitrary power; he commuted Vallandighams's sentence to deportation and frequently reversed or mitigated the worst excesses of his overzealous generals. There were, furthermore, none of the mass arrests, internments, or deportations that scar America's participation in the two world wars; and the unrelenting abuse with which the Democratic press vilified Lincoln belies any suggestion of a wholesale suppression of civil rights.[42] Yet a repressive mentality is still unmistakable. Proadministration spokesmen, including most of the ecclesiastical community, virtually identified dissent from the war policy with treason; and they voiced mounting concern that an effete humanitarianism not be permitted to stifle rigorous discipline of the civilian population.

The definition of disloyalty always poses a peculiar problem to a democracy in time of war. The American Constitution severely limits the meaning of a treasonable offense and the grounds for conviction of such a charge. Proof of culpability requires confession in open court or the testimony of at least two witnesses that an "overt act" was committed; and this act is alternately delineated as "levying war" against the United States or "in adhering to their enemies, giving them aid and comfort."[43] As James Madison declared in article 43 of *The Federalist Papers*, the intention of the writers was to oppose an effective barrier to the creation of "new-fangled and artificial treasons [which] have been the great engines by which violent factions, the natural offspring of free government, have usually wreaked their alternate malignity on each other."[44] The

42. An argument stressing that the basic constitutional structure was unaltered by the war can be found in Harold M. Hyman, *A More Perfect Union: The Impact of the Civil War and Reconstruction on the Constitution.*

43. Article II, sec. 3, 1.

44. Alexander Hamilton, James Madison, and John Jay, *The Federalist Papers,* introduced and indexed by Clinton Rossiter, p. 273.

constitutional proviso, as well as Madison's commentary, suggests that a citizen may strenuously oppose the war policies of a political faction currently in charge of the government, but he may not be held guilty of treason unless he actually makes war against the government or in some direct fashion aids the enemies of the nation. There is an implied distinction between dissent from those who happen to control the machinery of government and disloyalty to the nation itself. This theoretical differentiation establishes a vital safeguard to liberty, but in practice it may be profoundly ambiguous. At what point does public expression of dissent become an overt act of rendering aid and comfort to the enemy? This distinction and its practical ambivalence raised a difficult problem for the North in the 1860s. The Copperhead or Peace faction of the Democratic party claimed to be loyal to the Constitution "as it was" before the Lincoln administration allegedly subverted the compact to wage an illicit war. They proposed a negotiated peace with the Confederacy and the resuscitation of the old Union with all former constitutional guarantees intact—that is, slavery would be maintained. Their attacks against the administration and their anti-Negro propaganda did not, however, involve military support to the cause of the South, although certain verbal tirades might be construed as incitement to resist the draft law and other war measures. Choosing to put the darkest interpretation on this behavior, the Republican press loosely brandished the word *traitor* over the Copperheads and rejected their distinction between the government and the administration as disloyal sophistry. Historians vary widely in their assessment of the "Peace Democracy," but it seems difficult to sustain the polemical charges of Republican partisans.[45] The Copperheads' virulent racism was morally abhorrent, their hope for reunion by negotiation fatuously unrealistic, and their understanding of the executive's war power susceptible to serious challenge; but these appear dubious grounds—at least so far as the Constitution is concerned—on which to erect a charge of treason.

For the most part, the churches contributed to the blurring of lines between dissent and disloyalty. Ecclesiastical expressions varied

45. See, for example, Wood Gray, *The Hidden Civil War: The Story of the Copperheads,* and Frank L. Klement, *The Copperheads in the Middle West.* Also helpful is Voegeli, *Free But Not Equal.*

from relatively mild injunctions to avoid criticism of the administration to the outright stigmatization of Peace Democrats as traitors. Among instances of the former is the pronouncement of the Vermont Methodist Conference in April 1863, in which that body pledged

> That we will discountenance all attempts, direct or indirect, to distract or divide northern sentiment in respect to the justice of the present national struggle, or its management by the national government; and we will discountenance, in ourselves and others, all remarks tending to lessen confidence in those who administer the affairs of state, conscious that they rather need and deserve our sympathy and prayers in the present national crisis.

The resolution concluded with an expression of "perfect confidence" in a president whose cabinet would "challenge comparison with any administration which has ever existed in this or any other country."[46] In May of the following year, the New School Presbyterian Assembly echoed these thoughts in a call to "all Christians to refrain from weakening the authority of the Administration by ill-timed complaints and unnecessary criticisms, fully believing that, in such a crisis, all speech and action which tend to difference should be studiously avoided for the sake of the common weal."[47] The last phrase of the statement—"for the sake of the common weal"—aptly summarizes the conviction of the churches that dissent was inconsistent with the best interests of the nation.

Because they believed that united support of the war was essential to national security, Protestants frequently repudiated antiadministration criticism as virtually identical to treason. The New School Presbyterians who gently urged consensus in 1864 had spoken more bluntly the year before. Arguing that discrimination between constitutional government and an incumbent executive was largely fictitious, the 1863 Assembly asserted that the Lincoln administration had the right "to demand the entire, unqualified, and prompt obedience of all who are under its authority and resistance to such government is rebellion and treason." The statement amplified the

46. *Christian Advocate and Journal*, May 7, 1863, p. 148.
47. *Minutes of the General Assembly of the Presbyterian Church in the United States of America, New School* (1864), 13: 466.

definition of treason: "All attempts to resist, or set aside, the action
of the lawfully constituted authorities, in any way by speech or
action, to oppose, or embarrass the measures which it may adopt to
assert its lawful authority, except in accordance with the forms
prescribed by the Constitution, are to be regarded as treason against
the nation, as giving aid and comfort to its enemies, and as rebellion
against God."[48] This was a most curious pronouncement. It did not
actually label Copperheads as traitors—indeed no person or group
was explicitly named—and in theory the constitutional permission of
dissent was allowed. Yet the exposition of treason vastly broadened
its scope. The distinction between opposition to existing policies
and an assault against the nation itself was belittled into nonexis-
tence. Aiding and comforting the enemy included not only an
overt act of support for the foe but advocacy of efforts to change
("set aside") current programs and even endeavors to embarrass
them. In effect, this revised definition of treason brought a sweeping
indictment against every citizen who did not enthusiastically support
the war and President Lincoln. The inclusion of a formal bow to
the constitutional guarantees of free expression served only to
underscore the chief message of the resolution: even if Peace Democrats can technically escape legal guilt, they are nevertheless traitors
and should be so regarded.

The churches were suggesting the existence of a veiled treason,
which, though technically legal, was probably as dangerous as armed
rebellion. In 1863 the New York Annual Conference of the Methodist Church charged "covert treason" against those who used "the
pretext of discriminating between the administration and the government" to "throw themselves in the path of almost every warlike
measure." Such people, the conference noted contemptuously, have
"the malignity without the manliness of those who have arrayed
themselves in open hostility to our liberties."[49] Horace Bushnell
repeated the same accusation against this Northern traitor. "By
secret connivances, and factious words, and party cabals, he may
even serve the enemies of his country more than he could by the
open mustering of treason. . . . The meanest kind of disloyalty is
that which keeps just within the law and only dares not perpetrate

48. Ibid. (1863), 13: 242–43.
49. *Christian Advocate and Journal*, April 23, 1863, p. 133.

the treason it wants to have done; which takes on airs of patriotic concern for the Constitution when it really has none for all the wrong that can be done it by enemies openly fighting against it."[50] This enemy within had to be clearly identified, marked as the dangerous person he was, and effectively segregated from respectable society.

On the eve of the 1862 congressional elections, the Methodist women of America were urged to perform precisely this patriotic deed. In "An Appeal to Christian and Patriotic Women Upon Their Duties in Relation to the War," a writer in the *Ladies' Repository* urged loyal women to form local investigative teams to ferret out those who opposed the war. These persons were to be branded traitors, and public pressure was to be mobilized against them, hopefully with the result that they would be forced from the country.

> *Detect and expose the covert traitors in your neighborhood.*
> It is indeed mortifying to know that there are such all over the North. No city, nor village, or neighborhood is without them. It is hard to define the motives by which they are influenced. But whatever it may be, you may be assured that this sympathy with the cause of the rebels exists only where love of country has become extinct, or is subordinated to selfish or party ends. Do not be deceived by their professions of loyalty to the Union. Put those professions to the test. Ask them what kind of Union they would have—if it is not practically such a Union as would grant to the rebels all they demand; such as would restore the foulest traitor among them to place and power. See if that Shibboleth of Southern sympathizers—"the Union *as it was*"— does not hiss upon their lips. Ask them what they will do to destroy the rebels and to put down the rebellion; what to punish treason. You will not fail to find them weak, prevaricating, and false. . . . The hiss does not more certainly betray the

50. Bushnell, *Work and Play*, p. 362. Bushnell's remarks indicate the perplexity of the churches in the face of apparently disloyal behavior, which, however, was not technically a treasonable offense. Their quandary mirrored the difficulty of the Lincoln administration in finding ways of incarcerating extreme critics in a manner consistent with constitutional law. For further treatment of the problem, see Hyman, *A More Perfect Union*, esp. pp. 81–98.

presence and animus of the serpent. Do not spare this class of men. Hunt them out. Make the place, the society, the neighborhood too hot for them. Let them know that you have taken the precise gauge of their patriotism and honesty, and that it is about time for them to go and join the rebels. Tell them they are needed there but not here.[51]

Whether this injunction was obeyed is unknown, but Peace Democrats were in general made to feel that the churches were indeed "too hot for them." The overwhelming majority of Northern pulpits were loyal—according to the exacting connotation that term had acquired. The few pastors who openly avowed Copperhead sympathies often resigned their charges or were forced to leave by nonpayment of salary and other pressures from their congregations. Conversely Peace Democrats in the pew were cowed into silence; and if they refused to be silent, they had little choice except to bear the ostracism of their denomination or to secede outright. Particularly in the border states and in portions of the Midwest where Negrophobia and Southern sympathy were strong, a number of such withdrawals occurred.[52]

The Protestant conception of loyalty was most rigorously applied during the 1864 presidential campaign. The platforms of the major parties put before the electorate a clear choice of opposing philosophies. Abraham Lincoln's Union party—essentially a new name for the Republicans and a smattering of War Democrats—promised the abolition of slavery by constitutional amendment and continuation of the war until the South accepted the authority of the federal government. The Democratic convention denounced the war as a failure, called for an immediate armistice, and recommended negotiations to reestablish the Union "as it was." The theoretical clarity

51. "An Appeal to Christian and Patriotic Women upon Their Duties in Relation to the War," *Ladies' Repository* 22 (October 1862): 494. This is the mentality that prompted the enactment by federal and state governments of required loyalty oaths whose function was to "expose the covert traitors" and isolate them. Cf. Harold M. Hyman, *To Try Men's Souls: Loyalty Tests in American History*, pp. 139–98.

52. See Dunham, *Attitudes of the Northern Clergy Toward the South,* pp. 143–50. Also consult Sweet, *Methodist Episcopal Church and the Civil War,* pp. 47–62, and Vander Velde, *Presbyterian Churches and the Federal Union,* pp. 183–217.

of the issues was blurred by the nomination for president of General George B. McClellan, who immediately pledged in his acceptance letter to continue the struggle until the Union had been restored. With the typical genius of a political party to espouse opposites, the Democrats had given the nation a war candidate on a peace platform. Largely ignoring McClellan, the churches concentrated their fire on the Democratic program. Against the promise of a "delusive peace," the North Baptist Association of Massachusetts pledged itself to stand "like a flint" and vowed to "fight it out on this line to the end of the rebellion."[53] Virtually all churchmen who publicly expressed their preference agreed with the pastor who said of the would-be Democratic voter: "The man who casts his vote, in the election now pending, in favor of a peace not won by the conquests of our armies, does the rebel cause more service, if possible, than he would by joining the rebel army."[54] The *Christian Advocate and Journal* could declare without exaggeration once the ballots were tabulated: "There probably never was an election in all our history into which the religious element entered so largely, and nearly all on one side."[55]

The issue of the election, as the clergy saw it, was no less than the national destiny nobly won or meanly lost. The *Independent* likened the president to Joshua and the nation's situation to that of Israel engaged in subduing the Canaanites. "Joshua and his lieutenants are objects of intense abuse. What shall the people do? Shall they elect a chieftain who will make terms with the idolatrous Canaanites, whereby one-half of our territory, much of it already wrested from them, shall be restored to their control? Shall we give up Jericho, so miraculously given us of God; or Ai, for which we bloodily contended; or Bethhoren, down whose steps we pursued the flying chiefs?"[56] At the crossroads of its life, the chosen republic was required to affirm its election, to still the voice of the Canaanite in its midst, and to go forward in the divinely appointed struggle. Failure to "repudiate these traitors" within the

53. *Christian Watchman and Reflector,* October 6, 1864.

54. O. T. Lanphear, *Peace by Power,* "A Discourse Preached in the College Street Church, New Haven, Sabbath Evening, Oct. 9, 1864," p. 13.

55. *Christian Advocate and Journal,* November 17, 1864, p. 364.

56. *Independent,* October 27, 1864, p. 4.

holy nation would give victory to the South; and the effort to woo voters into the Lincoln column was, in the truest sense, an evangelistic labor "to recall every wandering, wavering soul from the error of ways that lead not to his death alone, but to that of his country and her principles."[57] In a sermon of thanksgiving for the capture of Atlanta, Gilbert Haven outlined the duty of the hour.

> The Church should unite as one man in this exigency. Prayers should go up daily for success in this election. Her salvation depends upon her faithfulness. She has had much to do with this revival of pure and undefiled religion. From the beginning her children have been found fighting for the cause of liberty and of man. She did more to develop the sentiment that was crowned in the elections of 1860 than all other influences combined. The great revival was a fitting and necessary prelude to that great election. Let her continue faithful and the work is done. Let her once more march to the ballot-box, an army of Christ, with the banners of the Cross, and deposit, as she can, a million of votes for her true representative, and she will give the last blow to the reeling fiend.[58]

This intense one-sided partisanship was eminently logical. An eschatological war required no less than an apocalyptic election in which the forces of good would "give the last blow to the reeling fiend."

Intolerance of those who cried for peace indicated a shift toward a harsher approach to the social order. It was one of the war's chief ironies that it stimulated an overwhelming outpouring of benevolence for the soldier and, to a lesser extent, the freedmen, even as it cut off the deeper roots of the humanitarian spirit. The clergyman eyed charity and compassion as suspicious virtues in need of restraint. They smacked too much of the effeminacy that had weakened the nation, and they pandered too easily to that bogus democracy in which the divine authority of government to command and to punish was lightly regarded. In his address at Dartmouth College in September 1861, the Reverend S. P. Leeds warned that antebellum peace had given America a "false philanthropy that has worked insidiously to sap our manhood." Armchair "pseudo-

57. *Christian Advocate and Journal*, October 27, 1864, p. 340.
58. Haven, *National Sermons*, pp. 481–82.

reformers" had wandered into fanciful utopian speculation that ill fitted them for action in the world. Their addled theories had softened the austerity of religion into vapid pronouncements about the fatherhood of God—"as if to be a father were only to be weak." This "unhealthy philanthropy" had spawned a sentimental pity for criminals, had seduced juries into laxity, and had persuaded executives to exert their pardoning power with unwarranted leniency. The war happily relegated these soft-headed people to the background "while men of deeds come to the front." The warrior in arms, the true man of action, was teaching tender souls that "speeches do not altogether rule the world." In his gory sacrifice, Americans perceived that truth would not triumph "except as baptized with blood."[59]

In an address before the American Tract Society, Dr. William Adams of Union Seminary pronounced a similar anathema on what he called "rosewater religion":

> Society has become enervated and demoralized by notions which have been put forth in the name of humanity. The community has become tolerant of crimes. Legislators, under a false notion of philanthropy, have taken action looking to the abolition of capital punishment, as if it were too cruel and vindictive for our modern civilization. . . . Instances have been numerous of notorious criminals arraigned for judicial trial, in whose behalf more sympathy has been expressed than for an outraged community. . . . No people have been more rapidly or thoroughly educating themselves for disintegration and anarchy, through an emasculated theology, degenerate notions concerning government—family government, civil government, Divine government—and law and justice, and authority, than we ourselves, in this long season of prosperity, and luxury, and enervation.

America could find its salvation only in rejection of this spurious humanitarianism that "has walked in silver slippers, [and] been attired in satin." Sentimental weakness had tended "to lure men to duty along a primrose path," and the present generation had discovered to its sorrow that the path was strewn with patriot bodies.[60]

59. Leeds, *Thy Kingdom Come*, p. 22.
60. *Christian Watchman and Reflector*, August 1, 1861.

In light of this iron-fisted philosophy, it is little wonder that the churches applauded the suspension of the writ of habeas corpus, the curtailment of disloyal newspapers, or the arrest of men like Vallandigham. All the "invidious sophism of independence," said J. B. Bittinger of Cleveland's Euclid Street Presbyterian Church, had to be eradicated. To those who protested that civil liberties were being abridged, Bittinger replied with a scoffing dismissal that the "so-called freedom of speech and press" was merely invoked as a mask for "foulness of vituperation" or "unblushing mendacity."[61] In a sermon to Brooklyn Methodists, the Reverend Cyrus D. Foss demonstrated an equal enthusiasm for the limitation of free expression. "We talk," he opined, "of the freedom of the press as something sacred. We have exalted it into a demi-god which is profanation to touch or to speak against. And what is it? It is but the freedom of fallible men, just like us, and some of them infamous men, to print their thoughts. Free speech and a free press are essential to the stability of republican institutions; but let neither insolently claim to be in such sense free as to be beyond any check. . . . The judicious exercise of unusual governmental powers of late cannot fail to exercise a salutary influence on all the interests of society. We shall be better governed hereafter."[62] These arguments provide an interesting rationale for the abridgment of liberty: if freedom were used as a cover for foul "vituperation" or misused by "fallible men," its contraction was vindicated. A people more in tune with their own constitutional heritage might have wondered whether freedom were truly free if it did not include the liberty to err.

If democratic rights were subject to restriction by the canons of virtue, the electoral process had to be scrutinized carefully. Protestants were convinced that peace at any price was the rallying cry of the dram shops and the slums of the large cities. From this dissolute element, it was believed, the bulk of McClellan's vote was drawn; and churchmen did not easily forget that this milieu, largely Catholic and immigrant, had provided the scene for the draft riots of July 1863. The coincidence of these disturbances with General Lee's invasion of Pennsylvania raised the possibility of a sinister cabal that

61. J. B. Bittinger, *A Sermon Preached before the Presbyterian Churches of Cleveland*, p. 11.
62. Foss, *Songs in the Night*, pp. 23–24.

had orchestrated the entire episode—invasion and riots—to destroy the Union. These were the thoughts troubling the editor of the *Christian Advocate and Journal* when he analyzed the returns from the presidential election. Though confident that the Lincoln victory heralded "the noon-day of life" for the United States, he read in the ballots a threat to the American way of life. That "our foreign born Romanist population" had cast their ballots for McClellan and had rioted indicated the presence of a "highly dangerous class" that had "very little sympathy with our free institutions." In his jubilation that the election had successfully concluded a significant "moral test of republican government," the editor proposed no specific solution, only a watchful eye on the disloyal class.[63]

Where this vigilance might lead, S. G. Arnold, a Washington lawyer, indicated at the close of the war. Writing in the *Methodist Quarterly Review,* he asserted that the war had taught Americans to surrender the "popular idea" that "all a people had to do to secure good government was to cast off monarchy and put on democracy." Arnold believed that Tocqueville's warnings about the dangerous potential of the tyranny of the majority had been amply verified by the massive corruption spewed forth from American cities during the war. These sad events recalled Americans to that first principle of Christian democracy—"reliance upon an enlightened, just, honorable, conscientious, virtuous, high-minded people." To the end that the state be founded on "integrity and virtue," these individuals should lose the vote—"deserters from the army, bounty-jumpers, smugglers, defrauders of the revenue, takers of bribes, duelists, gamblers, habitual drunkards, the sellers of spirituous liquors contrary to the statute, the keepers of disorderly houses, and many others." The editor of the *Review* approved the tenor of Arnold's recommendation but suggested in a footnote that a more thorough-going reform was needed.

> What aggravates the evil in our large cities, especially New York, is that an immense body of property holders occupy suburban residences and have no city vote. The men who own the city are thus disenfranchised in its government, while the real power is

63. *Christian Advocate and Journal,* November 24, 1864, p. 372. See also *Independent,* July 23, 1863, p. 4.

held by the Irish, the rumsellers, and the mob. A Popish vote well nigh controls our Protestant metropolis. Is it not time to so modify our municipal franchise at least as to secure the safety of property? Should not every owner of property in the city be a voter in the city at municipal elections? Nay, should not their number of votes be in some degree graduated to their taxation, whether of real or personal estate in the city? Something like this the restoration of order demands, and our security will require.[64]

In one sense, this article represented a single straw in the wind, and no serious effort was made to adjust suffrage to property. Still, that the proposal was made indicates how anxious Protestants were to create a disciplined and loyal citizenry who would not succumb again to the fractious ways of the antebellum era.

The happy failure of the churches to pursue this particular suggestion points to a larger noteworthy phenomenon whose results were not always so fortunate. For all their encomiums to authority and the corporate ideal, Protestants were often laggard, even inconsistent, in applying these ideas to specific issues of public policy. One might have expected that commitment to an organic view of society would provoke thoughtful criticism of the fundamental individualism of the American political economy. Specifically, this theory suggested that the federal government should undertake a major role in reforming the postwar South and in creating an institutional framework that would safeguard the freedmen. On the whole, Protestants never faced this problem squarely, if at all. Aside from traditional support of a high tariff and internal improvements in certain Republican (formerly Whig) circles, the basic laissez-faire structure of American economy and politics was reaffirmed. Thus the same Horace Bushnell who glorified the organic character of society also looked to the competition of the free market to eliminate slavery while George Prentiss would shortly be touting impartial suffrage as a panacea for the ills of Reconstruction.[65] Their example

64. S. G. Arnold, "The Suffrage Qualification," *Methodist Quarterly Review* 47 (October 1865): 582–93.

65. Bushnell, *Census and Slavery*, and George L. Prentiss, "The Political Crisis," *American Presbyterian and Theological Review*, n.s. 4 (October 1866): 645–46.

was typical of Northern Protestants who, in spite of their stress on order, continued to espouse policies that made them appear to be Adam Smith's unredeemed children. Beyond checking dissent and creating a more obedient patriotism, the clergy drew no implications from their authoritarian pronouncements.

Protestants, however, were oblivious to the anomaly; and perhaps we, too, should not be surprised at the mismatching of rhetoric and practice. Popular ideological commitments seldom hew to the canons of formal logic; and in R. H. Tawney's words, "Contradictions live in the heart of man in vigorous incompatibility."[66] In any event, war does not provide the ideal context for leisurely reflection. Faced with a massive rebellion, the churches seized, without full attention to the niceties of consistency, whatever intellectual weapons would shore up loyalty for the grim business at hand.

Moreover, there was a symmetry, though not perfect rationality, to the Protestant position. Long conditioned by individualistic modes of thought, churchmen spoke in these terms even when diagnosing the evils of individualism. They attributed the prior failure of the Union not to structural weakness but to the attitudes of citizens who harbored loose notions of democracy or who loved their country insufficiently. Accordingly the regeneration of the common life was to be won at the source of difficulty—in the hearts of the people. The underlying goal for America remained what it had been in the antebellum period: a society of free, disciplined people. But to that end, a new instrument had joined evangelical persuasion. Blood and iron were also channels of grace, and the war was functioning as the equivalent of a mass revival, making Americans fit for republican institutions. Thus when Protestants invoked corporate or authoritarian theories, they were not so much promising a structural reform as they were a transformation of consciousness, a heightened awareness of the "mystic chords of memory" that made Americans one folk.[67] By altering the spirit of society, the great struggle would permit a harmonious, unified culture to flourish under the form of individualistic democracy. It

66. Quoted in Page Smith, *A New Age Now Begins: A People's History of the American Revolution,* 1: 131.

67. The phrase is from Lincoln's first inaugural address; Basler, ed., *Abraham Lincoln,* p. 588.

was a shallow optimism that believed temporary austerity and a common foe would provide a lasting bond of cohesion; but fatuous hope is often born in war, especially in a conflict invested with eschatological symbolism. To a people who awaited millennial grandeur as the issue of their conflict, such expectations were neither unwarranted nor unrealistic.

Although the stress on authority and order was more ethos than program, it still had profound importance. It suggested a hard-nosed version of democracy in which dissent was suspect and the nation's revolutionary past slightly embarrassing. Obedient soldiering became virtually identical with patriotism, and conformity, not free expression, was the cardinal virtue. In the clergy's austere language lay a momentous confession: America had lost its Edenic innocence and had plunged into the dark vortex of history. To preserve its unique status among the nations, the new Israel had to become like them.

### AMERICA'S LOSS OF INNOCENCE

Northern clergy seldom entertained the thought that Union arms would fail, but they were unblinking in their acknowledgment that such a disaster would constitute a revocation of America's election. Henry A. Post said in the Presbyterian church in Warrenburgh, New York, on 16 September 1861: "We should sink to the level of the European nations: the hope of the world would turn from [into?] a nation too feeble, too inherently jealous, to preserve its high station as a democracy that ruled itself: the star of the western hemisphere would set amid lurid clouds, no more to rise." In view of this dreadful prospect, the American people had to renew their oath of fealty to God that he might "perform his covenant with his people."[68] Before a gathering at Amherst, President William A. Stearns pondered the frightening choice. "Are we," he asked, "to be broken down for our sins, and our free institutions become a hissing and a by-word over all the earth? Are we to be useful only as one more of those terrible examples which are set up along the track of history for the warning of mankind? Or is there yet a

68. Henry A. Post, *Sermon Preached in the Presbyterian Church, Warrenburgh*, p. 18.

great future before us, and is God leading us across the Red Sea of blood, that he may fit us, by suffering for prosperity?"[69] These sermons thundered at the new Israel the warning given to the old: the elect vessel commissioned to be a light among the nations must not become like them. An admission that America differed not from other nations would disclose the failure of its destiny. To be like the European countries was to sink the star of the Western Hemisphere. Either the United States was crossing its Red Sea—that is, America was the new Israel on the march—or it was no more than another piece of litter along history's way. No possibility of satisfying national existence, as simply one people among many, could be considered. If America were not different, it was nothing. In baptizing the Civil War with the bloody urgency of the Apocalypse, Protestants were fighting for more than the political integrity of the Union; the issue was no less than the survival of corporate identity and purpose.

A generation thoroughly drenched in biblical imagery should have better appreciated the irony of this particular Old Testament motif. Even as Israel vaunted its lofty distinction from the nations, it longed to become one of them, to acquire the political accoutrements that would make it a people in the sense that its neighbors were. "We will have a king over us," the Hebrew people said to Samuel at Ramah, "that we also may be like all the nations."[70] This bittersweet ambivalence toward other nations aptly represented the churches' attempts to define the American character and mission. With Samuel Harris, many Protestants gloried that their country was set apart from others by a lofty universal principle which alone "constitutes us a nation," and they rejoiced with Joel Bingham: "The dire spell of king craft was never woven over these wild, free, divine shores. No armies of insatiate conquerors ever thundered across these virgin plains. The oppressive maxims of old political systems, the prodigious inequalities of fortune which have divided the inhabitants of other continents into princes and beggars, the hoary prejudice of rank and caste—the long catalogue of govern-

69. William A. Stearns, *Necessities of the War and the Conditions of Success in It,* "A Sermon Preached in the Village Church before the College and United Congregations of the Town of Amherst, Mass.," p. 10.

70. I Samuel 8:19–20.

mental woes, these unsophisticated hills and valleys have never been called to learn."[71] Yet the vision of uniqueness was troubled by the apparent fragility of an American civilization that had come apart at the seams. America clearly needed to discover within its life a unifying power that would correspond to the symbols, memories, and constraints of European nations. "Our work as a Model Republic," said the Reverend Horace Hovey to departing volunteers in Coldwater, Michigan, "is but half done. We are yet to show the world that we have a cohesion and governmental power; that we are not a mere voluntary association for the promotion of temporary interests—not a mere debating society but that we are a veritable government, in which the majority rules through agencies established by law; and that armed rebellion can be punished here as well as in a monarchy."[72] To match the internal strength of other nations, America must endure the same yoke they had borne—the discipline of warfare. Protestants thus realized that their unique status no longer delivered them "from many of the vices and errors of European governments" and that America, like other countries, would not be permitted "to glide serenely on into the new order of society, which is imaged to us as the end of promise and prophecy."[73] By war's end, the same Joel Bingham who had exulted that armed cohorts had "never thundered across these virgin plains" was rejoicing that the usual weaponry of other states had done its work against the evils of American life. The weaknesses of the Union "have been ground to powder in the shock of battle, and trampled into the dust of the Southern plantations under the terrible marches of the national armies."[74] All the boasting about the North's armed might, the glorification of loyalty and military virtue, the suspicion of dissent and airy humanitarianism—these were the evidences that Protestants had accepted the need of an American counterpart to the integrative force of the traditions, armies, and centralized power

71. Bingham, *Hour of Patriotism,* pp. 16–17.
72. Horace Hovey, *Freedom's Banner,* "A Sermon Preached to the Coldwater Light Artillery and the Coldwater Zouave Cadets, April 28th, 1861," p. 7.
73. Goodrich, *Sermon on the Christian Necessity of War,* pp. 4–5.
74. Joel F. Bingham, *National Disappointment,* "A Discourse Occasioned by the Assassination of President Lincoln," p. 30.

that the European countries had employed to achieve viable nationalities. To preserve its special status as God's new Israel, the United States had to become like the nations.[75]

In particular, armed struggle was helping the national melting pot to fuse peoples of diverse origin into one American folk. Just as war had tempered the unity of other peoples, the current conflict enabled the United States to achieve greater internal uniformity. According to one Baptist, God purposed the "consolidation of the great national elements" and therefore had thrown a multiform populace "into one broad cauldron" that he might create an "amalgam of national character equal to the best of the European—the English."[76] Also using the British experience as counterpart, the Reverend William R. Williams expressed similar confidence in an address before the American Baptist Home Missionary Society in May 1862:

> We needed, as a nation, more of interpenetration—a more entire assimilation and unity. God has often used the terrible enginery of war apparently for this express end. The various races that are compounded into national unity on the British Isles were fused together by the conflicts and agonies of centuries, as the painter rubs together the colors on his palette; as the apothecary in the mortar bruises together his simples. . . . The furnace trials of the age are fusing and vitaefying [vivifying?] our homebred and our immigrant soldiers into a more solid and harmonious nationality. The men of the Rhine and of the Shannon are on the shores of the Potomac, and the Cumberland, and the Mississippi, learning that their common country is, as God's gift, to be defended by God's strength and in God's fear, and learning to appreciate, and emulate, and resemble each other.[77]

75. The ambivalence of American attitudes toward Europe are suggestively examined in Cushing Strout, *The American Image of the Old World*. The conception of American innocence in a corrupt world is discussed in R. W. B. Lewis, *The American Adam: Innocence, Tragedy and Tradition in the Nineteenth Century*. Also useful are Leo Marx, *The Machine in the Garden: Technology and the Pastoral Ideal in America*, and Henry Nash Smith, *Virgin Land: The American West as Symbol and Myth*.

76. *Christian Watchman and Reflector*, September 1, 1864.

77. Ibid., June 19, 1862.

It was probably no accident that England sprang to mind in this context, for most were certain that those of British descent would provide the basis for the "homogeneous character" of the United States.[78] Although other groups might contribute to or strengthen this synthesis, the "bold energetic Anglo-Saxon race predominating vastly over the rest" would happily set the tone of American life.[79]

The idea of a new national identity born out of old diversities was, of course, a perennial theme, one given classic formulation in Crève-coeur's evocation of "the American, this new man" or in Philip Schaff's vision of the United States as the "Phenix [sic] grave" of old nationalities. Similarly familiar was the belief that the English-speaking peoples possessed cultural superiority and should dominate the process of assimilation.[80] For Protestants in the 1860s, however, the forced heat of battle seemed to be the providentially new ingredient that would at last cause the melting pot to yield the desired product.

The United States was achieving an integrated nationality because its Edenic innocence had given way to a true American history—a common experience of suffering that created an organic bond among all citizens. In *An Oration Before the Alumni of Union College,* the Reverend D. H. Hamilton suggested in July 1861 that Americans reconsider the need for the shared memory of heroic exploits and glorious deeds. He recalled an occasion when a European taunted him with the assertion: "You [Americans] have no history." Hamilton had dismissed this comment with contempt and had informed his interlocutor: "It was to get rid of all the nightmare of the past, which you call history, that our Fathers fled to the wilderness beyond the Atlantic, that they might begin a new order of things untainted with the air of antiquity." Hamilton recounted the story

78. J. C. Lord, *On the Character and Influence of Washington,* "Delivered before the Union Continentals of Buffalo, on Sabbath, February 22nd, 1863," pp. 8–9.

79. West, *Establishment in National Righteousness,* pp. 5–11.

80. J. Hector St. John de Crèvecoeur, *Letters from an American Farmer and Sketches of Eighteenth Century America,* pp. 62–64, and Schaff, *America,* p. 51. An informative discussion of popular American attitudes toward various ethnic and national groups can be found in Ruth Miller Elson, *Guardians of Tradition: American Schoolbooks in the Nineteenth Century,* pp. 65–185.

to admit that he had erred, for the rebellion taught him that a nation without a past was a "naked orphan in the world." Such, he concluded, had been the status of the United States before Sumter. "We have heretofore had no history; only the incidents of our birth and childhood." Americans had wanted the active travail of a people struggling manfully to develop "the natural forces within them" and to master "the obstacles and emergencies" set before them. That common tradition could be attained only by austerity, unquestioning devotion, and even brutality. "We need," he said, "a little of that history which Sampson needed when he broke the cords of the deceitful Delilah, and carried off the gates of Gaza. We must make a little history like that which Bonaparte made when he ordered the 'whiff of grapeshot' fired INTO, and not over, the mobs of Paris." Only by replicating that "nightmare of the past" which the Europeans called history could America "redeem the present," "insure the future," and save themselves "from extinction."[81]

Samuel Harris suspected that the abstract nature of American nationality had left the country "void of all symbols that set forth its majesty and presence" and thus encouraged political fragmentation. Acquisition of a history—in D. H. Hamilton's sense of that word—would remedy this deficiency. American patriotism could hereafter be symbolized effectively by the war's battlefields and by an authentically American literature woven from the agonies of the 1860s. "In these events," predicted the Reverend Ray Palmer of Albany's First Congregational Church (New York), "history will find its themes; and poetry and eloquence their legends and examples; and fiction the inexhaustible materials which her imagination may combine." The ground upon which Americans trod would no longer be a neutral space—the empty wilderness or the virgin land—on which the drama of abstract ideals was played out; the ideals themselves would be soaked into the very earth by the blood there shed. Or as Palmer said: "Henceforth no soil beneath the wide arch of heaven will be more divinely suggestive than our own. Pilgrims from other lands will come to visit and survey *our* battle-

81. D. H. Hamilton, *An Oration Before the Alumni of Union College*, pp. 5–7.

fields, at Fort Donelson and Shiloh, Vicksburg, and Port Hudson, Murfreesboro, Antietam and Gettysburg, as we have gone to examine those of Thermopylae and Marathon, of Cannae and Pharsalia, of Bannockburn, Agincourt and Waterloo. So shall we take our place and influence among historic and classic lands."[82] Taking a place amid the historic and classic lands, America would, in short, become like the nations.

Horace Bushnell worked these various themes together in his address, "Our Obligations to the Dead," delivered to Yale alumni on 26 July 1865 when the guns had barely fallen silent. Bushnell argued that Americans before 1861 had possessed only disembodied ideas, a mass of arguments, insufficient to genuine nationality. Like unruly dogs, the states had been merely "kenneled under the Constitution" but did not participate in an authentic common life as one people. Americans forgot that ideas could be efficacious unto national unity only when translated into action, suffering, and death. "No argument transmutes a discord," Bushnell observed, "or composes a unity where there was none. The matter wanted here was blood, not logic." By the shared anguish of the war, ethereal concepts had turned into true nationhood. "These United States, having dissolved the intractable matter of so many infallible theories and bones of contention in the dreadful menstruum of their blood, are to settle into a fixed unity, and finally into a nearly homogeneous life." Furthermore, Bushnell accepted gladly the destruction of the jejeune optimism that America could remain "a Peace Society World" or untouched paradise. Baptism in the bloody rivers of history had produced the nationality of other peoples, and only this similar experience could vitalize America.

> If a gospel can be executed only in blood, if there is no power of salvation strong enough to carry the world's feeling which is not gained by dying for it, how shall a selfish race get far enough above itself, to be kindled by the story of its action in the dull routine of its common arts of peace? Doubtless it should be otherwise, even as goodness should be universal; but so it never has been, and upon the present footing of evil never

82. Ray Palmer, *The Opening Future: or the Results of the Present War*, "A Thanksgiving Discourse, November 26th, 1861," pp. 23–24.

can be. The great cause must be great as in the clashing of evil; and heroic inspiration, and the bleeding of heroic worth must be the zest of the story. Nations can sufficiently live only as they find how to energetically die. In this view, some of us have felt, for a long time the want of a more historic life, to make us a truly great people. This want is now supplied; for now, at last, we may be said to have gotten a history.[83]

As a result of this historic life, American nationality would gain fitting symbols embodying its essence and commanding the loyalty of citizens. Having acquired a sacral status, Civil War battlefields furnished "a gift for the ages to come." Thence future generations would journey to be "blest in remembrances of the dead" and to draw from the sanctified earth new dedication to the American enterprise. The stories of hallowed warriors fallen in battle—Reynolds, Kearny, Shaw, and many others—would inspire the nation to true dignity and heroic grandeur. Thus Bushnell foresaw the rise of a genuine American literature comparable to the flowering of letters inspired by the military achievements of the Elizabethan age or the literary awakening following the Napoleonic wars. In the arts the United States had "held the place of cliency," but this time was forever past. "Under that kind of pupilage we live no longer; we are thoroughly weaned from it, and become a people in no secondary right. Henceforth we are not going to write English but American." The nation's soil, its mountains, its sunsets—everything would offer a material representation of the American spirit, an incarnation of patriotism arousing "great sentiments, and mighty impulsions, and souls alive all through in fires of high devotion." Americans would become a race of bards discerning beneath the diaphanous veil of their geography a mystic harmony linking the physical landscape with the spiritual realities of the national experience.

As to poetry, our battle-fields are henceforth names poetic, and our very soil is touched with a mighty poetic life. In the rustle of our winds, what shall the waking soul of our poets think of, but of brave souls riding by? In our thunders they may hear the shocks of charges, and the red of the sunset shall take

83. Horace Bushnell, *Building Eras in Religion,* pp. 326, 327, 329, 332.

a tinge in their feeling from the summits where our heroes fell. A new sense comes upon every thing, and the higher soul of mind, quickened by new possibilities, finds inspirations where before it found only rocks, and ploughlands, and much timber for the saw. Are there no great singers to rise in this new time? Are there no unwonted fires to be kindled in imaginations fanned by these new glows of devotion? We seem, as it were in a day, to be set in loftier ranges of thought, by this huge flood-tide that has lifted our nationality, gifted with new sentiments and finer possibilities, commissioned to create, and write, and sing, and, in the sense of a more poetic feeling at least, to be all poets.[84]

Alan Trachtenberg has observed that the Civil War revoked America's "exemption from the travail of history," and the churches did not bemoan this abrogation.[85] They rejoiced that Americans had finally become a true *folk* rooted, according to the canons of romantic sensibility, in blood and place. What mere ideas could not perform, the spilling of blood had achieved. Americans would henceforth be a homogeneous people, strong, disciplined, obedient. Yet if the United States had become like the nations, it was also something more grand than an ordinary country defined by kinship or geography. The ideals that had now become incarnate in American soil and tradition were not merely the peculiar genius of one group; they were the principles of the Kingdom of God. The heights of Fredericksburg, Bloody Lane at Antietam, and the tangled thickets of the Wilderness were, to be sure, particularly American shrines; but they were also scenes of that larger campaign called Armageddon and thus had significance for all humanity. What had been done in those places, said Bushnell, carried the weight of universal importance, for the sacrifices offered there constituted "the grandest chapter" of world history.[86] In short, the United States had lost its exemption from the world's common lot for a unique reason: America had been immersed in the travail of history so that history might be, in Hegel's expressive word, *aufgehoben*—

84. Ibid., pp. 334, 335, 337–38.
85. Alan Trachtenberg, ed., *Democratic Vistas, 1860–1880,* p. 3.
86. Bushnell, *Building Eras in Religion,* p. 332.

that is, simultaneously annulled and fulfilled as the former things passed away and the new Jerusalem loomed on the horizon. Thus in the 1860s, Northern Protestants went forth glorying in military feats, powerful armies, and obedient citizens to inaugurate the reign of the Prince of Peace. It was not altogether a fortuitous combination of symbols.

# 5

## Search for the Jordan

As the last Southern strongholds fell to the Union army in the late winter and early spring of 1865, Northern churchmen gave thanks that the nation's tribulation was ending. The capture of Richmond at the beginning of April signaled the imminent collapse of the Confederacy and drew exultant words from the *Independent:*

> Who can ever forget the day? Pentecost fell upon Wall Street, till the bewildered inhabitants suddenly spake in unknown tongues—singing the doxology to the tune of "Old Hundred!" Shall we ever see again such a mad, happy delightful enthusiasm of a great nation, drunken with the wine of glad news. The city of Richmond. . . . Babylon the Great, Mother of Harlots and Abominations of the Earth . . . Rejoice over her, thou Heavens, and ye holy apostles and prophets: for God hath avenged you on her. And a mighty angel took up a great millstone, and cast it into the sea, saying, Thus with violence shall that great city be thrown down, and shall be found no more at all.[1]

Others applied apocalyptic imagery a month earlier to the capture of Charleston, South Carolina, where the first secession convention had met, but it was the same portent read amid the rubble of a different city: "Here and now is the vial poured forth on the seat of the beast."[2]

Years of sacrifice had apparently secured the national regeneration that fitted the Republic for its grand mission on the stage of world history. The Reverend Adoniram J. Gordon told the Jamaica Plain Baptist Church in Massachusetts that perfect freedom was about to

1. *Independent,* April 6, 1865, p. 4.
2. Haven, *National Sermons,* p. 521.

obliterate the "wilderness of servitude" and make American life "blossom as the rose."[3] In nearby Boston, the Reverend Edwin Webb preached the same day that God had rebuilt the United States into a holy temple whose perpetuity was guaranteed by the unflinching loyalty that the American people had learned in the war. Henceforth the national character would be marked by the "heroic spirit of the Spartan mothers" and the "endurance of the Roman soldiers."[4] Perfect liberty tempered by obedience unto law—these were the twin victories that confirmed America's election as the new Israel. Their achievement meant national salvation because they were the response of the entire populace to God's leading. "It was the people's war," said the *Ladies' Repository,* "they declared it, determined its principles and aims, paid for it, fought it, and triumphed." No president or political faction forced the issue upon them; they freely confirmed it as their own at the polls and in their effusion of blood and treasure. In this fact lay the "conclusive demonstration of the power and efficiency of republicanism." "The world looks on and learns," said the writer, "that the surest and safest foundation on which a government can rest is the intelligence and freedom of the people."[5] By its *Volkskrieg,* the Union had established its claim to be the central actor in the drama of redemption and had successfully mastered the chief crisis of its history.

Amid these ruminations, the Civil War received a final ritual enactment. The death of President Lincoln by an assassin's bullet

3. Adoniram J. Gordon, *The Chosen Fast,* "A Discourse Preached at a United Service Held at the Baptist Church, in Jamaica Plain, on the Occasion of the State Fast, Thursday, April 13th 1865," p. 17. A. J. Gordon was later to achieve prominence as an advocate of dispensationalism, an extreme variant of premillennial theory widely disseminated in conservative circles during the latter quarter of the nineteenth century. Since this movement was generally associated with theological reaction and usually took a dim view of modern culture, it is intriguing to hear Gordon's enthusiastic hopes for the Republic in 1865. According to his biographer, however, Gordon was not at this time a dispensationalist. Ernest B. Gordon, *Adoniram Judson Gordon* (New York: Fleming H. Revell, 1896), pp. 82–93. On dispensationalism, see the brief comments in the epilogue to this book as well as Kraus, *Dispensationalism in America,* and Sandeen, *The Roots of Fundamentalism.*

4. Edwin Webb, *Memorial Sermons,* p. 30.

5. "Editor's Study," *Ladies' Repository* 25 (August 1865): 511.

on Good Friday, 14 April 1865, was widely interpreted as the final
blood sacrifice by which the nation was purified and reborn to its
high mission. Subsequent hagiographic embellishments notwithstanding, Lincoln was peculiarly fitted for the role of martyred
president to which murder raised him. His wartime utterances had
given cogent expression to the common faith in America's world
mission, the transcendent worth of the Union, and the war as
crucial test for republicanism everywhere. If Lincoln frequently
enunciated these themes with less chauvinism and a greater sensitivity to the inscrutable nature of divine providence than did many
professional theologians, he was nevertheless voicing the same
democratic creed animating the religious community.[6] Thus in
death Lincoln quickly became the representative American who
incarnated the national genius in his own person and thereby re-
capitulated the suffering of every patriot. "As the philosopher learns
the plans of God from an unprejudiced study of Nature," observed
Edwin Webb, "so he learned the purposes of God from the instinct
of the people. . . . He did not mean to be ahead of the popular
feeling; for then there would be a reaction against his policy. He
did not mean to be much behind it; for then some other agent
might be sought, through which to give it expression; and so, regarding the voice of the loyal people, in this great crisis of the
Republic, as the voice of God, he kept his ear open and his eyes
attent, and marshalled his policy not quite abreast of the divinely
led masses."[7] To Joel Bingham, Lincoln was the "people's President,"
a latter-day Cincinnatus called from his plow to manage the affairs
of state in a spirit of republican simplicity learned from his humble
origins in the bosom of the electorate. It was therefore eminently
fitting, Bingham concluded, that this prototypical American, "after
having wrought out the painful salvation of the Republic, has been
offered, a bloody sacrifice, upon the altar of human freedom."[8]
Lincoln's death symbolized the expiation of the national sins, and
his blood—the token of every drop drawn by the sword during four

6. See William J. Wolf, *The Almost Chosen People.* This fine book is a
librarian's nightmare, for it has been subsequently reissued twice under different titles—*The Religion of Abraham Lincoln* and *Lincoln's Religion.*
7. Webb, *Memorial Sermons,* pp. 50–51.
8. Bingham, *National Disappointment,* pp. 35–36.

years of war—purchased a new and perfect nationality for the American people. As the Old School Presbytery of Nassau suggested: "He has been appointed to crown his career with martydom, to be laid as the costliest sacrifice of all upon the altar of the Republic, and to cement with his blood the free institutions of our land."[9]

As the spiritual center of the American experience, the life and death of Lincoln marked a victory analogous to the passion of Jesus, and clergy were not unmindful that the president had been shot on Good Friday. To Gilbert Haven, the parallel of Lincoln's final days to Holy Week was striking. As Jesus had made his triumphal entry into Jerusalem on the humble donkey, Lincoln entered Richmond in a similarly unostentatious manner ten days before his death. "Without music or banner, or military or civic pomp," the president had walked the streets of the Confederate capital virtually unattended, greeted by the "unshackled slaves" who danced "around him in an uncontrollable ecstasy of delight." Yet within the city unrepentant rebels, scowling "from their windows," nursed the animus that would reach out to kill him. When the appointed hour came, these miscreants poured their wrath upon him in the person of John Wilkes Booth, but their vengeance merely confirmed the magnitude of his achievement. "Without revenge, without malice, without hardness or bitterness of heart," the sixteenth president had met his death secure in the knoweldge that he had wrought the salvation of the Republic and that indeed his work was finished. Thereafter this great accomplishment should be memorialized on the day Christians celebrated the propitiation of sin for the entire human race. "The great day of the Church," explained Haven, "has become yet more solemn in the annals of America. Let not the 15th of April be considered the day of his death, but let Good Friday be its anniversary. . . . We should make it a movable fast and ever keep it beside the cross and grave of our blessed Lord, in whose service and for whose gospel he became a victim and a martyr."[10] Haven had pronounced an appropriate valedictory to the war fought simultaneously to save a nation and to inaugurate the millennium: religious and national concerns would be combined in one festival of thanksgiving for redemption.

9. *Presbyterian,* May 6, 1865, p. 4.
10. Haven, *National Sermons,* pp. 552, 575–80.

If Lincoln's death enacted the completion of national salvation, it also pointed to a work yet incomplete. By demonstrating that the spirit of rebellion still survived, the assassination warned Northerners that remaining vestiges of treason and slavery had to be purged from the land. Henry Boynton Smith wrote to his mother on 15 April: "It is an appalling disclosure of the depths of wickedness in the ardent advocates of the secession. I hope it will put a stop to that good natured sentimentality which was ready to receive back all these rebels and let them play over again their foul plots. Our only safety is in expelling the leaders or executing them."[11] A Methodist clergyman drew a similar lesson from the assassination. Until the "dastardly cowardice" of the rebellion had been made incarnate "in one infamous type whose name is BOOTH," many loyal persons had been prepared "to forget and forgive." Now Americans realized that one task yet remained—to extirpate the last broken pieces of the slavocracy, "root and branch, stem and flower, blossom and fruit."[12] Among many others, the Reverend Robert M. Hatfield believed that God intended to remove Lincoln because the president's generosity "unfitted him for this stern, harsh work" and that the Lord had replaced him with one whose austere character suited him for the task ahead. "It may be," said Hatfield, "that it was expedient that one man should die for the people, and that the whole nation perish not. God's interpositions on our behalf have been so marked and various during the last years that we cannot believe that he will now abandon us. While we mourn our Moses taken from us so strangely, we have confidence that the Joshua, raised up by Providence to take his place, will lead us safely into the promised land."[13] Andrew Johnson would prove a disappointing Joshua, but the symbolism was suggestive of the position that the nation was believed to occupy. Moses had brought the American Israel safely across the Red Sea and the wilderness. Final deliverance was at hand. One more effort, one more thrust of the hosts of God across the Jordan, would bring the elect people to their land of rest.

Clustered about the death of Lincoln was the ambivalent feeling that Protestants entertained as their fratricidal killing match came

11. Stearns, *Henry Boynton Smith*, p. 251.
12. "Editor's Repository," *Ladies' Repository* 25 (June 1865): 384.
13. *Independent,* May 4, 1865, p. 1.

to a close. The churches rejoiced that the conclusive victory had been won, "making this Immanuel's land," but the nagging feeling would not pass that something additional was required: one more mopping-up operation before the campaign could be declared officially ended.[14] In the remaining years of the decade, Protestants were to look for that one victory yet needed to crown their achievements; but the expectation of quick triumph was rewarded by protracted political conflict mocking these dreams. As the desired crossing of the national Jordan receded further into the future, the search for nostrums grew increasingly anxious and then subsided into fitful accommodation with a Reconstruction that defied prophecy.

### THE CHURCHES AND THE POLITICS OF RECONSTRUCTION

After the trauma of assassination had begun to fade, the churches turned their attention to the problem of determining what the nation should do with its victory. Three interrelated questions demanded answer. On what terms should the Southern states be brought back into the Union? What penalties should be imposed upon ex-Confederates? What policy should the federal government adopt toward the newly freed slaves? The ensuing national frustration was largely the result of the inability of these queries to yield the immediate solutions that Americans had learned to expect.[15]

A few believed that the best path to Reconstruction was a lenient policy of welcoming back the "erring sisters" with minimum penalties and virtually no federal regulation. Charles Hodge, who had an eye to the possible reunification of the Southern Presbyterian Church with the Northern Old School, called upon the nation to "be as magnanimous and generous in victory as we were brave and constant in conflict." Unduly harsh policies "exasperate instead of subduing; they exalt criminals into martyrs." He warned that the desired national reunification would be impeded by "the cry for

14. From a statement by the Presbytery of Carlisle (Old School) in the *Presbyterian*, May 6, 1865, p. 4.

15. My thinking on the subject of Reconstruction has been especially influenced by William R. Brock, *An American Crisis: Congress and Reconstruction;* John Hope Franklin, *Reconstruction: After the Civil War;* Eric L. McKittrick, *Andrew Johnson and Reconstruction;* and Kenneth M. Stampp, *The Era of Reconstruction, 1865–1877.*

blood" and that the South could become to the United States "what Ireland is to England": a permanently disaffected minority whose suppression would sap the resources and energies of the nation. Hodge wished a generous amnesty for all rebels and quick restoration to the Union of the former Confederate states once they ratified the Thirteenth Amendment.[16]

From the opposite end of the theological spectrum, Henry Ward Beecher echoed the call for generosity to the defeated foe. In the summer of 1866, when most Protestants had become convinced that the South needed careful regulation, he wrote to a convention of soldiers and sailors in Cleveland, Ohio, to urge speedy readmission of the seceded states and to deny the necessity of federal safeguards for freedmen. His rationale was instructive:

> We have entered a new era of liberty. The style of thought is freer and more noble. The young men of our times are regenerated. The great army has been a school, and hundreds of thousands of men have gone home to preach a truer and nobler view of human rights. All the industrial interests of society are moving with increasing wisdom toward intelligence and liberty. Everywhere, in churches, in literature, in natural science in physical industries, in social questions, as well as in politics, the nation feels that the winter is over and a new spring hangs in the horizon and works through all the elements. In this happily changed and advanced condition of things no party of the retrograde can maintain itself. Everything marches, and parties must march.[17]

After the Southern question had shown itself to be stubbornly complex, Northerners eventually retreated to Beecher-like affirmations of assured progress as a way of washing their hands of the dilemma; but in the year or two immediately following Appomattox relatively few were sufficiently weary to settle for such an easy solution.

Most Protestants believed that the rebellion merited punishment, and particularly in the several months following the murder of Lincoln, pulpits rang with demands for the execution of high Con-

16. [Charles Hodge,] "President Lincoln," *Biblical Repertory and Princeton Review* 37 (July 1865): 435–58.

17. Beecher, *Patriotic Addresses*, p. 739.

federate officials or for their banishment and the expropriation of their estates. The Reverend Henry Butler of the First Congregational Church in Keeseville, New York, suggested an appropriate Old Testament lesson for the hour: "America's spirit should be that of Samuel when he hewed the guilty Agag in pieces, sad, serious, determined, God-like." Such clerical utterances can be piled up ad nauseam, and Chester Dunham has already performed this task with chilling effect.[18] Although they accurately portray typical sermonic fare in the aftermath of the assassination, they provide, by themselves, a misleading barometer of the intent of Northern churchmen. Protestants wanted primarily a symbolic gesture vindicating the Union position—some judicial decision that stigmatized the South with a moral onus and summoned a concomitant repentance. The issue was whether legitimate authority, sustained at high cost, would continue to be honored. "During the last four years," said a clergyman in North Brookfield, Massachusetts, the day before Lincoln was shot, "God has been teaching the nation in an experience of blood, that there is truth in a blood theology. And the question is whether we have yet learned the lesson thoroughly. . . . Are we prepared as a nation to execute the law? Have we learned thoroughly the lesson of retributive justice which God has been teaching us? Shall our government, by letting these criminals go, lower the tone of moral sentiment which God has raised in the community by our experience of justice in his own wonder-working Providence?"[19] As the *Presbyterian* summed up the argument, easy forgiveness would "make the forms of criminal law a mockery."[20] Yet this satisfaction of justice need not be excessively bloody. Even in their most sanguinary mood Protestants wished the vast majority of Southerners excepted from punishment; and once the volatile passions aroused by Lincoln's death had cooled, few clergy called for the wholesale execution of the leadership. Leonard Bacon spoke for the matured sentiment of most Protestants when he said: "Manifestly, the government and the people are ready to deal liberally with their vanquished enemies. This is as it should be; the sweeping

18. Quoted in Dunham, *Attitude of the Northern Clergy Toward the South,* p. 186. See also pp. 183–91.

19. *Congregationalist,* May 5, 1865, p. 69.

20. *Presbyterian,* July 22, 1865, p. 2.

amnesty . . . [is] preparing the way, if I mistake not, for a complete reconciliation between the country and those who have been its enemies in arms, and for such a measure of mutual confidence between the North and the South as has never yet existed." Bacon inserted one crucial limitation to national generosity. The leadership, men "of intelligence and position," should not "be pardoned without being first convicted and sentenced; and some of these, when convicted, ought to be made examples of public justice."[21] It was significant that Bacon's proviso required only the formal act of sentencing and allowed that the penalties would be frequently commuted; only a few would actually "be made examples of public justice." Most Protestants were soon willing to settle for this type of justice—disfranchisement of prominent rebels and their disbarment from public office, at least until they had shown sorrow for their crimes. In comparison with exactions visited upon insurrectionists in similar circumstances elsewhere, these demands were astonishingly light.

The churches were also anxious that the South be reconstructed in such a manner that treason would not break forth anew or blacks be subjected again to the form, if not the name, of involuntary servitude. A Methodist from Cincinnati explained that possible trials of Confederates should not be evaluated as merely "a question of justice abstractly considered" but must be analyzed "in terms of what is best for the future of the country. If their execution will serve to teach the wickedness of treason and help to shield us from it in the future, execute them, and as many more as is necessary. If sparing their wretched lives will teach a better lesson of the strength and magnanimity of the Government, let them go."[22] After a trip to the South in the winter of 1865–66, Edward N. Kirk of Boston was similarly impressed that the national policy must aim beyond vindictiveness to the larger goal of securing the permanence of the triumphs won by force of arms.

> Reconstruction is the order of the day. But not to avenge our outraged country. . . . The reconstruction we want is, first that rebellion against the federal government shall be demonstrated

21. *Independent,* January 4, 1866, p. 1, February 1, 1866, p. 1.
22. "Editor's Study," *Ladies' Repository* 25 (August 1865): 510.

to be so costly, so despicable, so hopeless, that a thousand Cal-
houns, Macons, Ruffins, and Davises, can never again "fire the
Southern heart" to undertake it. Secondly, such a *quietus* put
upon the Hotspurs of the South, that in case of difficulty with
any foreign power, the mortified demagogues shall not be in
positions to avenge themselves by combining with those of the
foreign foe. Thirdly, a guarantee that the black man shall be a
citizen, fully and everywhere protected, as every white child is,
by the whole military power of the country, and in full possession of his rights of manhood. Fourthly, that that article shall
be put fully in force, by which the federal government is bound
to secure to each State a republican form of government.[23]

In short, Kirk and his fellow Protestants wanted guarantees that
slavery and disunion were forever quashed. To demand less would
be, as another clergyman put it, to lose the "valuable fruits of
these terrible four years of toil and blood and tears and household desolations."[24]

The failure of President Johnson and the South to meet these
"symbolic requirements," as Eric L. McKittrick aptly styles them,
produced a great uneasiness in the North.[25] There was no serious
opposition to the chief executive's generous amnesty to the rank
and file of the Southern people, but his pardons of leading planters
and ex-Confederates deeply troubled the North. Equally distressing
was the president's willingness to accept states back into the Union
on the sole condition that they void the secession ordinances and
ratify the Thirteenth Amendment. This forgiving policy did nothing
to preclude the return to power of the same men who had led their
constituents into armed rebellion, and it afforded no guarantee of
the rights of the newly freed slaves. Had Southerners conducted
themselves circumspectly, making some gesture of deference to
Northern sensitivity or had they demonstrated at least minimal
willingness to protect the civil rights of blacks, Johnsonian Reconstruction might have become palatable to the North. Instead the
conquered states pursued a course that inflamed the worst fears of

23. David O. Mears, *Life of Edward Norris Kirk, D.D.*, p. 315.
24. *Christian Advocate and Journal*, June 15, 1865, p. 188.
25. McKittrick, *Andrew Johnson and Reconstruction*, p. 21.

the president's critics. Electorates chose former Confederate officials for high office, and several legislatures enacted stringent codes relegating the Negro to a state of disfranchised peonage not unlike the slavery from which he had been ostensibly released. Northern Protestants were horrified at the easy return to power of "galvanized loyalists" whose recent Unionism was gilded thin over a traitorous past.[26] Nor could the churches accept with equanimity the signs of national failure to redeem the promise of full freedom to blacks. As the American Missionary Association declared through its official organ:

> The idea of emancipation which carries with it no protection of person and property, no advantage of the laws and institutions of the land—equal and impartial—is delusive and pernicious. In this age, and in this nation, there can be no meaning to liberty which leaves a man stripped of all civil rights, and free only as the beasts of the forest are free. Emancipation and liberty are but empty and mocking words if they do not convey the idea and rights of citizenship.[27]

These developments convinced the religious communities of the North that the South was beaten but unchanged; and to increase the agony, the nation had been given in Andrew Johnson "a doubtful sort of Moses, who seems to occupy himself more earnestly with striving to save the drowning host of Pharaoh than he does with leading Israel into the promised land."[28]

Reluctance to break openly with the administration delayed a violent clash between Johnson and his critics, but he made the breach inevitable by a series of provocative blunders. In February 1866 he vetoed first a bill continuing the Freedmen's Bureau and shortly thereafter a comprehensive civil-rights bill. These decisions telegraphed to the nation and to Congress Johnson's unwillingness to compromise—a point he underscored in coarse extemporaneous remarks denouncing his opponents as traitors. Then in May and July, first in Memphis and then in New Orleans, vicious anti-Negro

26. *Christian Advocate and Journal,* June 15, 1865, p. 188.
27. "Annual Meeting," *American Missionary,* 2d ser. 9 (December 1865): 268.
28. *Independent,* December 21, 1865, p. 1.

riots were greeted impassively by a president more inclined to fix blame upon the victims than the perpetrators. By the summer of 1866, the clear failure of Johnson's program induced Congress to enact its own policy. In addition to bills on the Freedmen's Bureau and civil rights, the House and Senate submitted to the states what would become the Fourteenth Amendment. This essentially moderate proposal granted citizenship to the freedmen, reduced congressional representation of states that denied the vote to former slaves, revoked officeholding privileges of those whose support of the rebellion had violated a previous oath to uphold the Constitution, and forbade the assumption of the Confederate war debt. As final acts of political indiscretion, the president urged Southern states to reject the proposed amendment, and he undertook a campaign tour—his famous "swing around the circle"—in which he horrified even his staunchest supporters by exchanging crude epithets with unfriendly crowds. In the November congressional elections, Johnson's estrangement from public opinion was sealed by the overwhelming landslide victory of his political enemies. The way was now open for the enactment in March 1867 of a program of Radical Reconstruction, invalidating existing governments in the South, placing the entire region under military rule, and forbidding readmission to the Union without state constitutions providing for impartial suffrage and disfranchisement of leading Confederates. The stage was also prepared for the eventual impeachment and acquittal by only one vote of President Johnson in 1868.

The events of 1866 crystallized opposition to Johnson among influential sectors of Protestant opinion. Although they had frequently been willing to mitigate his past behavior with patronizing references to his mistaken but "honest patriotism," they now covered him with opprobrium.[29] When Johnson vetoed the civil-rights bill, the *Congregationalist* demanded that the American people take up the gauntlet he had thrown at their feet. "Unless Congress shall at once make a stand upon the principles embodied in the Civil Rights Bill," warned the editor, "all that we have struggled for, in behalf of liberty during four years of war, will be put in jeopardy, if not fatally lost." Johnson's policy of "no further guaranty" was destroying the benefits of victory. "The real question at issue must

29. *Congregationalist,* July 14, 1865, p. 110.

be put squarely before the people. That question is not whether the seceded states are in the Union or out of it; nor whether suffrage is a necessary policy; nor whether the black man is the natural equal of the white; but whether those who sought to ruin the country shall be permitted to rule it? Southern politicians hope to win in Congress what the confederate generals lost on the field. Shall they have the opportunity?"[30] It was an ominous suggestion that black rights were subsidiary to the salvation of the nation from Southern Democrats; but for the moment the two concerns dovetailed perfectly, and Johnson was apparently sensitive to neither. The news of the riots was accepted as confirmation that the President had "fomented and sustained . . . wholesale murder" and that he should be classed among the "incompetent, obstinate, and violent rulers" with whom the Old Testament recorded another elect people to have been occasionally afflicted.[31] The *Independent* denounced the "mad career of Andrew Johnson," which culminated in the "St. Bartholomew in New Orleans," and Dr. George L. Prentiss of Union Seminary accused the nation's leader of acquiescence in "deeds of savage butchery . . . which finds [*sic*] not parallel this side of the Sepoy massacres in the dark places of Oriental heathendom." Prentiss concluded grimly that "sober minded, Christian citizens [are compelled] to turn deliberately to the Constitution and ponder, for the first time, the meaning of those 'other high crimes and misdemeanors' on impeachment for and conviction of which 'the President . . . shall be removed from office.'"[32] With studied understatement, the New York East Conference of the Methodist Episcopal Church summed up the emerging consensus: "We must now look to Congress and the people . . . [to assure] that the great moral results which philanthropists and far-seeing statesmen have ardently wished should follow the sanguinary contest, are not to be sacrificed to the animosities or ambitions of aspiring politicians."[33]

30. Ibid., March 30, 1866, p. 50.

31. *Christian Advocate and Journal,* August 30, 1866, p. 276.

32. *Independent,* August 9, 1866, p. 4; George L. Prentiss, "The Political Crisis," *American Presbyterian and Theological Review,* n.s. 4 (October 1866): 637. "St. Bartholomew in New Orleans" is an allusion to the massacre of French Protestants in Paris on St. Bartholomew's Day, 24 August 1572— an event to which Prentiss likened the anti-Negro riot in New Orleans.

33. Quoted in *Christian Advocate and Journal,* April 19, 1866, p. 124.

The national legislature apparently deserved the confidence reposed in it. The decision to disfranchise and disbar from office a
large portion of the Confederate leadership was greeted with relief.
The North was to be spared "the humiliating spectacle" of Confederate generals returning to the chambers of Congress.[34] These
"Canaanites" in the promised land would not be suffered, said the
Reverend John Gulliver of Chicago, "to lead our people into idolatry, to plot with foreign enemies, to conspire with domestic traitors,
to direct the knife of the assassin, and at last, perhaps, to overthrow
a government in which justice finds no sanctuary, and law no vindication."[35] Others were impressed that Congress had executed a
decree of justice sagely tempered with pragmatic flexibility. George
Prentiss was pleased with the section of the Fourteenth Amendment
that permitted revocation of the disqualifications by a two-thirds
vote of both houses because it put the Southern leaders on notice
that their return to American political life was possible only on
condition "that they see and acknowledge the error of their ways;
that they accept and intend to carry out in good faith the abolition
of slavery, the concession of all their rights to the freedmen, and the
repudiation of the debts contracted in the interest of the rebellion."[36] As George Ide viewed the matter, the proposal set in
motion "God's Method of Reconstruction" by keeping former
Confederates "in a state of abeyance and probation" until "they
are educated into harmony with the spirit of republican institutions
and the great ideas of humanity, civilization and progress."[37]

The second key feature of congressional Reconstruction was freedmen's suffrage. This goal was obliquely advanced in the Fourteenth
Amendment, which sought to induce the states to give the vote to
blacks by reducing proportionately the representation in the House
of states that denied the ballot to males over twenty-one years of
age on the basis of color. After the president's stunning rebuke at
the polls in the fall of 1866, this "shilly-shally bungling" approach,

34. From a resolution by the New Jersey Annual Conference of the Methodist Episcopal Church, quoted in ibid., April 4, 1866, p. 109.

35. *Independent,* April 5, 1866, p. 1.

36. George L. Prentiss, "The Political Situation," *American Presbyterian
and Theological Review,* n.s. 4 (April 1866): 310–12.

37. Ide, *Battle Echoes,* pp. 262–63.

as Congressman Thaddeus Stevens called it, was supplemented by more direct action.[38] The Reconstruction Acts of 1867 divided the South into five military districts whose commanders were authorized to register loyal voters, white and black, who would in turn elect representatives to a constitutional convention. As a prerequisite to securing readmission of their states, these conventions had to enact guarantees of impartial suffrage; and, finally, the new state constitutions were to be approved in popular referendum by a yet more carefully screened electorate. This final congressional program expressed the Northern confidence that these artificial bodies politic, purged of traitorous elements and committed by law to impartial suffrage, could effect a speedy restoration of the Union upon a durable and just basis. This approach was given constitutional recognition in the Fifteenth Amendment, which eliminated race or previous condition of servitude as a legal qualification for the ballot.

The churches heartily endorsed this aspect of congressional Reconstruction. They shared with nineteenth-century liberals everywhere an obsessive confidence in the power of the vote to work miraculous political regeneration. The New School Presbyterian Assembly declared in 1865: "Possessing these rights, they [the freedmen] will be in a position to be their own protectors. The enjoyment thereof will give them respectability, dignify their labors, elevate their desires, quicken their moral consciousness, and waken in their minds those hopes and high aspirations upon which the proper development of humanity so largely depends."[39] The editor of the *Christian Advocate* was certain that the statutory mandate of impartial suffrage was sufficient to ensure the rights of freed slaves, and he dismissed as groundless fears that they might be coerced into dependence upon the planter class:

> It is asserted that they will be conciliated by their former masters, and made politically subservient to them. We doubt not that such will be the policy of the masters themselves; we rejoice to believe it will be. What course would really be better for all

38. Stampp, *Era of Reconstruction,* p. 141.
39. *Minutes of the General Assembly of the Presbyterian Church in the United States of America, New School* (1865), 14: 43.

the ends of reconstruction? The chief interest of the country on the question has had reference to the enfranchisement and protection of the freedmen, now so large an element of the national population. If the whites of the South attempt to win their political interest, it must be by concessions to them by regarding their claims in the local governments. There could not be a better guarantee than such a Southern policy, to the aims of the North respecting the negro population. . . . That the negro votes can be generally or seriously abused by Southern politicians we do not fear. The freedmen know quite well the value of their new rights, and how they got them, and who gave them, and how to retain them. . . . We are willing to trust him to whatever influence the conciliatory policy of his former master can acquire over him; especially as not only Northern politicians, but Northern missionaries, will see to it that he shall understand well his own rights and interests.[40]

George Ide expressed the same confidence: "A race, acted on by the three mighty levers, Education, the Gospel, and the Ballot, must rise. No force of prejudice, no power of custom, no ban of exclusiveness can keep it down." Once these agencies were set in motion, as the Congress was doing, Ide was certain that the American political system would "tower up in MATCHLESS STRENGTH AND GRANDEUR, THE MARVEL OF THE AGES, AND THE HOPE OF THE WORLD."[41]

If the government fulfilled the promise of equal political rights for all and the churches performed the task of moral education, Protestants believed that their American Israel would cross its Jordan. George Prentiss, for example, called upon voters to repudiate the president's policies in the midterm elections of 1866, arguing that this action would open the way to impartial suffrage and, beyond that, the devoutly wished eschatological consummation of America's folk war:

> Let Christian patriotism and statesmanship do their part also, both at the ballot-box and in the council chamber; let political

40. *Christian Advocate and Journal,* April 4, 1867, p. 108.
41. Ide, *Battle Echoes,* pp. 279, 281.

and religious wisdom and zeal thus conspire together. . . . Then shall come to pass in this great Republic the prophetic words, written thousands of years ago among the hills of Palestine: In righteousness shalt thou be established; thou shalt be far from oppression; for thou shalt not fear; and from terror, for it shall not come near thee. . . . I will also make thine officers peace and thine exactors righteousness; violence shall no more be heard in thy land, wasting and destruction within thy borders; but thou shalt call thy walls Salvation, and thy gates Praise.[42]

Radical Reconstruction would thus bring the promised land in sight.

The failure of this dream must rank among the chief disappointments of American history, and the editor of the *Christian Advocate* inadvertently disclosed one reason that the passage of the Jordan was never made. He said of the laws Congress had passed: "The crisis of our country's last and greatest revolution is already past, and its results are crystallizing in the forms of institutions."[43] This belief was a terrible delusion, for nothing of the sort had happened. The government failed to create an institutional framework that might have made Reconstruction viable. Congress sought to carry out a revolution by statute alone, sustained for a few years by federal bayonets and the abortive efforts of the Freedmen's Bureau. Except for the short-lived bureau, the legislature created no new governmental organizations to supervise the rebuilding of the Union and attempted no fundamental realignment of the economic or social structure of the South. Reconstruction was undertaken almost entirely by fiat of law. "The right of citizens to vote," declared the Fifteenth Amendment, "shall not be denied or abridged on account of race, color, or previous conditions of servitude"—and there the matter rested without the institutional machinery that might have converted the dream into reality. When inveterate white racism and economic power were mobilized against the landless blacks and their few white allies, the Reconstruction governments, protected only by the shaky bulwarks of statute and a handful of federal troops, toppled one by one.[44]

42. Prentiss, "Political Crisis," pp. 645–46.
43. *Christian Advocate and Journal*, July 30, 1868, p. 244.
44. See Franklin, *Reconstruction*.

The weakness of the legal apparatus of Reconstruction is partly apparent in the fact that it decreed impartial, not universal, suffrage. Congress forbade the use of race or color as exclusionary tests and required that electoral qualifications be applied equally to black and white. The law did not, however, mandate the enfranchisement of blacks. In an article for the *American Presbyterian and Theological Review,* Doctor William Adams expressed the common view that this program represented the only equitable political adjustment. "We like," he said, "the expression *impartial* suffrage better than *universal* suffrage. Whatever qualifications may be thought proper for the high and solemn duties of a voter, let those qualifications be allowed to work, impartially, without regard to color. Those qualifications existing, let none be denied the right of voting, because of the complexion of the skin; and on the other hand we may well hesitate to confer that right on any because they are black, when wanting the qualifications which are expected of others."[45] According to the *Christian Watchman,* the proper rubric for Reconstruction was "impartial suffrage, no caste, no distinction of race or color in American politics."[46]

Deep prejudice existed among Protestants against indiscriminate extension of the ballot. That policy conceded too much to the kind of democracy that the war had made them distrust, and it flew in the face of the fundamental dictum that republican institutions could be safely entrusted only to people of intelligence and probity. If the war had vindicated the American proposition "that freedom alone secures to man the circumstances necessary for the highest development of his nature," the conflict also proved according to Methodist I. W. Wiley that "it is Christianity alone which can fit a people for the institutions of freedom."[47] Impartial suffrage was the "true doctrine," in Samuel Spear's words, precisely because it met both conditions of this basic axiom.[48] It granted the ballot on

45. William Adams, "The War for Independence and the War for Secession," *American Presbyterian and Theological Review,* n.s. 4 (January 1866): 91.
46. *Christian Watchman and Reflector,* January 3, 1867.
47. I. W. Wiley, "Thoughts for the National Birthday," *Ladies' Repository* 25 (July 1865): 394.
48. Samuel T. Spear, "The President and Congress," *American Presbyterian and Theological Review,* n.s. 5 (January 1867): 48.

terms equal to all but also permitted the exclusion of the ignorant, the vicious, or the base. The *Congregationalist* expressed a common fear that universal enfranchisement, even for the worthy cause of giving the vote to blacks, would begin a process destructive of American liberty:

> We do not quite fancy the phrase "Negro Suffrage" as the watchword of a party. If it means that the privilege of suffrage is to be conferred upon all black men, then the logical inference is that suffrage should be universal; for surely no white man nor red man, should be excluded from a political privilege to which all black men are admitted. A discrimination in favor of black as a color is as false in principle as discrimination against it. But what sober minded person is in favor of removing all restrictions from the elective franchise, and making suffrage absolutely universal, without regard to nativity, to intelligence, or to moral qualifications? Who will claim that every white man in the slums of northern cities, and every negro in the cabins of southern plantations, ought to vote, or could be allowed to vote with safety to the commonwealth?[49]

Impartial suffrage appeared to be the only method of achieving equality without destroying the political integrity of Christian America.

Protestants wished to secure republican government as they understood it, but they had unwittingly placed a huge stumbling block in the path of political equality for Afro-Americans. The theory of impartial suffrage denied that the vote was an essential civil right and made it a "prerogative conferred by society in its own interest."[50] This policy commended itself as a safer, more cautious approach to stable democracy, but it wanted the unambiguous clarity of the position that made the vote the just claim of every American. Once it was admitted that the ballot could be separated from the inalienable rights of citizenship, the idea of political equality was thrown into a morass of legal difficulties; and the entire argument was already set on premises congenial to those who wished to keep blacks

49. *Congregationalist,* September 1, 1865, p. 138.
50. Ibid.

off the voting lists. In particular, the principle was riddled with possible loopholes that might be skillfully exploited once the former Southern leadership class returned to power. Since each state could determine its own criteria of impartiality, the way was clear for the poll tax, the so-called grandfather clauses, literacy tests, and other ingenious subterfuges by which the freedmen were systematically stripped of the franchise after 1865. A constitutional amendment guaranteeing the vote to all native-born Americans—or, more realistically in the context of the nineteenth century, to all males—over twenty-one years of age would have been no panacea for national ills, but it could not have been so easily evaded as the more amorphous language of the Fifteenth Amendment.[51] This step, however, neither the Congress nor the churches were prepared to take.

Whether suffrage were universal or impartial, the ballot represented an inadequate guarantee of a reconstructed South in which blacks could be equal participants. The Freedmen's Bureau, created by Congress in March 1865, was the nation's one attempt to move beyond reform by statute. Headed by Major General Oliver O. Howard, the bureau was given "control of all subjects" relating to the former slaves. Potentially the agency could have facilitated land reform, education, and the protection of civil rights; it might also have served as an ombudsman, bringing before the nation the needs and grievances of Afro-Americans. Except for its educational assistance, however, the bureau fulfilled none of these roles. Howard made a halfhearted attempt to grant homesteads from lands seized during the war. But when the president opposed him, the general retreated, dispossessing those already occupying confiscated estates. Instead of the expected "forty acres and a mule," Southern Negroes received government pressure to work as contract laborers for their former masters. When a commissioner championed the black cause too earnestly, he found himself relocated or fired. The agency that might have been a powerful lobby on behalf of the freedmen was used to reconcile them to the fact that no fundamental reform of Southern society would be undertaken except for the legal end of slavery and the enactment of impartial suffrage. The superior ability and moral integrity of Howard casts a poignant aura about this

51. This point is cogently argued by Brock, *An American Crisis,* esp. pp. 296–97.

national failure. The dreams were lost not by men of ill will but by the well-meaning naivete of "the best and the brightest" that America had to offer.[52] Protestants did not analyze the bureau too carefully. They condemned Johnson's veto of the bill extending its life and made note of its necessity—especially when news of race riots or the appalling destitution of blacks reached their ears—but their endorsements were often given with the laconic brevity of the New School Presbyterian Assembly of 1866: "We rejoice that the active functions of the Freedmen's Bureau are continued."[53] These cursory but warm notices were born of the confidence that the agency was in the care of the ideal "Christian soldier . . . one of the best in our army."[54] With such a trusted evangelical Christian as Oliver O. Howard at the helm, the churches need not trouble themselves unduly about the bureau's work. In fact the universal esteem in which he was held tended to create, as the *Independent* observed in an insightful moment, the false assurance "that the affairs of the freedman are better than the facts justify."[55] Beneath the general chorus of approval, however, there was an uneasy fear that the government could not, in a free society based upon laissez-faire principles, maintain indefinitely a program designed to benefit a particular group of citizens. When President Johnson vetoed the bill extending the life of the bureau, the *Congregationalist* opposed his action but granted that he had raised valid concerns:

> To this policy there are objections upon financial and moral grounds, which the President has set forth in his veto message with a good deal of plausibility. It must be admitted that to keep a large class of the community under the special tutelage of the government, is foreign to the genius of our democratic society; that the government should not be made an eleemosy-

52. See William S. McFeely, *Yankee Stepfather: General O. O. Howard and the Freedmen.*

53. *Minutes of the General Assembly of the Presbyterian Church in the United States of America, New School* (1866), 14: 263. For the effect of the riots as a goad to sentiment for keeping the bureau functional, see *Christian Advocate and Journal,* July 12, 1866, p. 220.

54. *Presbyterian,* August 26, 1864, p. 2.

55. *Independent,* June 14, 1866, p. 4.

nary institution, nor the blacks be encouraged in the habit of looking to the government for the supply of their wants. It is far better for the blacks themselves, and for the community in which they live, that they should be taught self-reliance, and left to work out their own future, *provided* they can be made secure in the enjoyment of their freedom, and their rights as men. This security can be assured by giving them the right of suffrage, upon the basis of intelligence. In place of protection from the general government, let them have the power of protecting themselves through the ballot-box. This simple guaranty will work the solution of all the difficulties of their position. Those who are dependent in any degree upon their votes, will be slow to injure or oppress them. And we greatly prefer this method of caring for the negro to that of governmental protection.[56]

Unfortunately President Johnson was "as much opposed to granting suffrage to the negro, as he is to giving him the special protection of the government."[57] Therefore, the paper reluctantly concluded that the bureau should remain a tool of national policy. This line of argument implied, however, that the agency was only a stop gap to be discarded once the Union had been restored on the basis of impartial suffrage. Congress, in fact, pursued such a policy. After the Reconstruction Acts of 1867, the bureau was gradually absorbed by the military forces occupying the South, and many of its functions were entirely discontinued.

In spite of their frequent praise of a corporate ideal, the denominations' political vision was still restricted by laissez-faire principles, and that limitation was strikingly confirmed by their failure to demand that the bureau be an instrument of significant land reform. Protestants, of course, wished blacks to have their own homesteads, and there was some alarm when it became clear that Johnson's generous pardons had in effect restored "the abandoned or confiscated" properties to their former owners and had thus paralyzed "the power of the Bureau by taking out of its possession nearly all the lands."[58] Nevertheless, clergy seldom more than mentioned this failure as they hastened to stress some other, presumably more

56. *Congregationalist,* March 2, 1866, p. 34.
57. Ibid.
58. "Condition of the Freedmen," *American Missionary,* 2d ser. 9 (November 1865): 241.

essential, aspect of the agency's work—such as educational assistance or protection of political rights. It was a rare minister who affirmed without qualification: "A hold upon the soil is worth far more to the negro than a hold upon the ballot box. Give him the latter, if you can; but do not fail to give him the former."[59] In stating the issue so bluntly, the Reverend John Gulliver underscored the reason so few of his colleagues advanced to his position. His rationale diverged from the received opinion that economic and social progress would automatically follow the granting of political rights and moral instruction. George Ide had said of the ballot and Christian education: "Capital and labor will soon adjust themselves to the new order of things. All friction and disturbance will cease."[60] To bestow confiscated land indiscriminately, as Gulliver advocated, was to reverse this fundamental axiom; it made economic status the cause rather than the effect of moral industry and political freedom. Understandably then, the vast majority of Protestant spokesmen had nothing to say about land reform.

The American Missionary Association provides a representative example of the extent to which Protestant interest in homesteads for blacks was restricted by the belief that economic issues were ancillary to questions of political freedom and individual character. The most consistently pro-Negro ecclesiastical organization, the AMA did encourage several private ventures to purchase land for freedmen; but in September 1868, after the issue had been discussed in the pages of the official journal, the editor declared:

> We cannot emphasize too strongly the remark that a mere patch of land is not all that the colored man needs. Gerrit Smith tried that long ago, with some of the free negroes in the State of New York. Indeed, if we remember aright, he added a gratuity of $50, with each piece of land, and yet the experiment, as a whole was not successful. . . . In short, should not the purchase of lands for the Freedmen by Northern benevolence be confined mainly to aiding the enterprising few who have a little capital and a good deal of energy—such as our teachers, and others, could readily select in the different localities—and should not the main efforts of the North be given to the educational and religious elevation

59. *Independent,* April 12, 1866, p. 1.
60. Ide, *Battle Echoes,* p. 245.

of the "unfortunate masses," that, mind and heart being developed, they might win their way to lands and houses, as well as to other and better things?[61]

Protestants believed of economics: seek ye first the kingdom of individual morality and political freedom, and all these things will be added unto you. Thus, private, selective benevolence, carefully geared to avoid stifling initiative or disturbing the equilibrium of God's ideal social order, marked the outer limits by which agrarian reform was bounded.

The Protestant community did not have the ideological resources to envision a program more extensive than the one already passed. The enactment of Reconstruction Acts of 1867 prompted an expansive interpretation by the editor of the *American Missionary*. "The final act of the great drama" of redemption, he observed, "seems to draw toward its termination." Now that "the fullest individual freedom" had been won on the battlefield and in the legislative hall, the remainder of the struggle would require other weapons. "The civil and military struggles having achieved their ends, the crowning effort is to be made in the spiritual [realm]."[62] Ostensibly an affirmation of hope, this confidence was really an admission that prevailing religious thought possessed no intellectual capital to support further political or social reform. The churches were saying that the Congress, in decreeing impartial suffrage and the equal protection of the laws, had done all that government could accomplish. The day of legislation had passed, and the suasion of the Gospel was the only weapon remaining to counter unresolved problems.

### MISSIONARY CAMPAIGN IN DIXIE

After Appomattox, the leaders of the churches were eager to broaden their missionary onslaught into the South. "Now is the time

61. "Lands for the Freedmen," *American Missionary*, 2d ser. 12 (September 1868): 207. For further information on the AMA's efforts to secure land for a select group of freedmen, see Richard B. Drake, "The American Missionary Association and the Southern Negro, 1861–1888" (Ph.D. diss., Emory University, 1957), pp. 115–19. For an account of similar private ventures among other nonecclesiastical agencies, consult McPherson, *Struggle for Equality*, pp. 412–16.

62. "Let Us Make Man," *American Missionary*, 2d ser. 11 (August 1867): 179.

for this great, loving, self-denying effort," said the AMA. "Everything has been unsettled by the war. The elements of society are now soft and plastic, ready to be molded and stamped."[63] Even the conservative *Presbyterian* was caught up in the fervor of the hour: "The greatest missionary field on the globe lies now beyond the Potomac, and we hope our Church will have the wisdom to occupy it, and redeem the millions of its impoverished and sorrowing inhabitants for Christ."[64] When the American Home Missionary Society surveyed the area, it saw a fertile Canaan ripe for the taking: "The Army, the President, and the Congress have marched in solemn procession before the ark around this Jericho." By a blow on the ram's horn, they had brought down the political structure of the Confederacy and had left "the old religious institutions in large portions of the South . . . virtually dissolved."[65] The Northern churches needed only to go in and possess the land.

This campaign to evangelize the South—and beyond it, the world— was greatly inspired by nationalistic motives. According to the Reverend Samuel Wolcott of Cleveland, Ohio, the American Home Missionary Society was "the synonym of patriotic love. . . . It lives for our country—for her safety, for her honor, for her advancement in knowledge and power and virtue, for her highest elevation, for her perfected development in whatever is lovely and of good report." The "sublime ideal" of the society, he concluded, was to awake in America those "invincible forces" that would truly make the Republic "the hope and goal of humanity."[66] As Wolcott's "sublime ideal" implied, the Christianization of the South merged into the larger task of evangelizing the entire world. In fact, the distinction between domestic and foreign missions became almost meaningless in the atmosphere of fervent zeal with which the postwar Gospel crusade was begun. Without guile Protestants believed that the Civil War had raised the United States to such commanding preeminence that the perfected spirituality of the nation would

63. "Appeal for $750,000," *American Missionary*, 2d ser. 9 (October 1865): 227.
64. *Presbyterian*, April 29, 1865, p. 2.
65. "An Appeal for Ministers," *Home Missionary* 38 (August 1865): 88.
66. Samuel Wolcott, "The Renovating Forces in the Republic," *Home Missionary* 39 (August 1866): 86.

roll like an irresistible tide across the globe. The Reverend Edmund
K. Alden of Boston explained:

> It is no vain boasting; it is simply the plain sober fact that the
> forward thought of the world in civilization, in government, in
> liberty, in education and in religion is on this continent. Pre-
> viously existing as a pleasant dream in the minds of the people,
> it became a settled eternal verity through the teachings of our
> recent national conflict. . . . We have reached the time when
> patriotism and philanthropy are one; when Home Missions
> and Foreign Missions are identical; when what we do for Amer-
> ica, we do for the world.

In the purification of America lay the salvation of the world—an
ironic doctrine capable of almost literal reading, for according to
Alden the United States was soon to absorb politically rather large
chunks of the rest of the earth. The purchase of Alaska convinced
him that Canada, Mexico, and perhaps other nations would be
annexed to the great Republic.[67] It was not an uncommon dream.
When he spoke before a Cincinnati audience to state the signs of
encouragement in missionary labor, Bishop Matthew Simpson
predicted that the American flag would fly eventually "over the
whole Western hemisphere." The circle of power might stretch still
farther, he tantalized: "We must take the world in our arms, and
convert all other nations to our true form of government. . . . The
day is coming when the matrons of liberty shall hide this flag, as
the loyal mothers of the South hid it; and the mothers of Europe
will teach their boys the name of Washington, and learn [sic]
them to love our flag, till it shall be respected and honored to
earth's remotest bounds."[68]

With the current of world history bearing them ineluctably forward, Protestants were confident that they possessed the ability
to perform almost any task given to them. The American Baptist
Missionary Union believed that the war had "disclosed our missionary resources, both as respects means and laborers; enlarged our
conceptions of the nature of our Christly work; quickened our

67. Edmund K. Alden, "The Indefinite Grandeur of the Home Missionary
Work," *Home Missionary* 40 (September 1867): 109–16.
68. *Christian Advocate and Journal,* December 20, 1866, p. 401.

Christian sympathies, and trained our people to those larger enterprises beyond their own local wants."[69] Writing for the *American
Presbyterian and Theological Review,* the Reverend Robert R.
Booth compared the evangelization of the world to Sherman's
march to the sea. A comparable outlay in money and men would
unquestionably bring the Gospel to every human being within
twenty years and "bring the latter day of glory down upon the
earth."[70] This global optimism encouraged the belief that the
mission to the South would be a short operation preparatory to
greater things. An anonymous Methodist epitomized the prevailing
mood: "As the Northern people at the call of divine Providence
and President Lincoln have given men and money till the rebellion
is ended; so will our people at the call of divine Providence and of
our Bishops give men and money until the South is saved from her
political and moral heresies and sins, and made the dwelling place
of peace, liberty, and righteousness."[71]

Accordingly the denominations adopted a harsh, frequently contemptuous attitude toward the Southern religious bodies. The New
England Methodists suggested that "even a seeming recognition"
of the legitimacy of the Methodist Episcopal Church South was
"contrary to every act of justice and piety" because that communion was "born of slavery, organized and officered as a pro-
slavery church."[72] J. S. Backus, a leading figure in the Baptist Home
Missionary Society, averred that a willingness to accept the perpetu-
ation of the Southern convention was identical to the spirit that
would "reproduce and sustain the Southern Confederacy."[73] The
Old School Presbyterian Assembly ruled that any Southerners
seeking affiliation with the Northern church must repent of their
political sins, and it prescribed stringent penalties for any of its

69. "Fifty-first Annual Report," *Missionary Magazine* 45 (July 1865):
193.

70. Robert Russell Booth, "The Relation of the Work of Missions to Christianity," *American Presbyterian and Theological Review,* n.s. 5 (July 1867):
456–57.

71. *Christian Advocate and Journal,* September 14, 1865, p. 290.

72. Quoted in ibid., May 10, 1866, p. 145. On similar Methodist attitudes,
see Morrow, *Northern Methodism and Reconstruction,* passim.

73. Quoted in Robert A. Baker, *Relations Between Northern and Southern
Baptists,* p. 103; see also pp. 99–121.

judicatories disregarding the order.[74] The *Independent* spoke for most Protestants when it urged that Dixie be treated ecclesiastically as "territory occupied by the Church of Rome or the followers of Mohammed."[75] Under this contumely, the apostate Southern churches were expected to wither into insignificance. A writer for the *Ladies' Repository* predicted that the Northern denominations had merely "to watch this process of disintegration, [and to] gather up the fragments of the crumbling Church."[76]

Nor was the successful evangelization and education of the freedmen in question. Years of romanticizing the Negro as a naturally religious, simple creature induced the expectation of an exceptional spirituality—"a deep personal experience, and a complete reliance on the guidance and the efficient power of the Holy Spirit."[77] Furthermore, the supposed childlike character of blacks seemed destined to make them eagerly imitative disciples of their Yankee benefactors. Churchmen were impressed by the confirmation of initial missionary reports, such as this from a worker in Missouri: "They are deeply anxious to learn, and willing to practice, the truth. They are the nearest like clay in the hands of the potter of any people I ever saw."[78] Although these caricatures fed white paternalism and obscured the cohumanity of the Afro-American, they fulfilled the prime purpose for which they were invoked— to increase the self-confidence of the churches in their righteous mission and inevitable victory. Who could doubt that a people whose "docility and . . . religious sensibility are the admiration of all" would speedily succumb to the missionary's benevolent teaching?[79]

74. *Minutes of the General Assembly of the Presbyterian Church in the United States of America, Old School* (1865), 17: 562–64. For similar action by the New School, consult its *Minutes* (1865), 14: 21. The subject is treated at some length in Vander Velde, *Presbyterian Churches and the Federal Union,* pp. 183–279.

75. *Independent,* September 14, 1865, p. 4.

76. "Editor's Respository," *Ladies' Repository* 25 (November 1865): 704.

77. Letter from the Reverend William T. Gilbert to *Christian Advocate and Journal,* August 3, 1865, p. 241.

78. L. Newcomb, "Missouri," *Home Missionary* 39 (May 1866): 12.

79. *Minutes of the General Assembly of the Presbyterian Church in the United States of America, New School* (1866), 14: 314.

The denominations of the Southern whites would fall apart or be converted to the truth, and blacks would be evangelized into miniature versions of their stepparents from the North. Meanwhile, American Protestantism would extend its spiritual influence to the ends of the earth. For a brief time after the killing stopped, the churches were drunk with heady visions.

### FRUSTRATION AND RETRENCHMENT

The dual program of Radical Reconstruction and missionary labor in the South lends itself to easy criticism in the retrospect of a century; but in fairness much must be said to its credit. The three constitutional amendments adopted between 1865 and 1870 may have offered an inadequate solution to the American dilemma, but it is doubtful that they could have been ratified at any other time in U.S. history. In spite of defects, they provided the legal staging area for subsequent attacks against racial discrimination. The crusade to educate and evangelize the South, particularly the freedmen, spawned numerous schools without which the obstacles to Afro-Americans might have been even greater. The names of these institutions—Fisk, Atlanta University, Morehouse, Hampton, and Biddle, to name only a few—call an honor roll bearing witness to the self-sacrifice of Northern philanthropists and the still more heroic effort of blacks to combat the forces that perpetuated their bondage. Yet when the best has been said, it is still not enough to avoid the conclusion that the prescription for Reconstruction fell sadly short of the requisite measure of equity. In a classic analysis of postwar federal policy, Albion Tourgée, one of the self-described Northern "fools" who had believed a golden age was aborning in Dixie, laid bare the ultimate cause of failure to achieve Lincoln's dream of a more perfect Union:

> After having forced a proud people to yield what they had for more than two centuries considered a right,—the right to hold the African race in bondage,—they proceeded to outrage a feeling as deep and fervent as the zeal of Islam or the exclusiveness of Hindoo caste, by giving to the ignorant, unskilled, and dependent race—a race who could not have lived a week without the support or charity of the dominant one—equality of political right! Not content with this, they went farther, and, by erecting

the rebellious territory into self-regulating and sovereign States, they abandoned these parties like cocks in a pit, to fight out the question of predominance without the possibility of national interference. They said to the colored man, in the language of one of the pseudo-philosophers of that day, "Root, hog, or die!" It was cheap patriotism, cheap philanthropy, cheap success![80]

The gallons of printer's ink that have been spilled in criticism or defense of Reconstruction policy cannot evade the harsh truth that lies behind Tourgée's assessment. However, well intentioned national policy might have been, its tragic corollary was the triumph of *Herrenvolk* democracy. For that failure, the churches must accept their share of blame.

The tokens of failure began appearing early and with such persistence that the clergy were forced to try to make sense of events that did not follow the expected scenario. The actions of congressional Reconstruction were to have forestalled further difficulty. The *Christian Advocate* had predicted that the ratification of the Fourteenth Amendment "will . . . settle in a satisfactory form all the great issues before the country," and the *Congregationalist* believed several months later that the 1867 legislation had virtually raised the freedman from "a boot black and menial" to the "chair of state."[81] "What then," the editor of the *Congregationalist* had exulted, "shall hinder the party of progress from taking immediate control of the South, and working out there the glorious results which it has accomplished in the free North?"[82] Continued Southern resistance to federal laws dismayed these naive hopes, and by the end of summer 1867 the *Advocate* had exchanged its optimism for gloom. Observing that the South yet strove to crush the blacks and the few white Unionists, the paper noted sadly: "Slavery appeared enormous enough to the civilized world before the war, but we are only now learning how profoundly and fatally its barbarous power

80. Albion Tourgée, *A Fool's Errand*, p. 126. The "pseudo-philosopher" was Horace Greeley, the influential editor of the *New York Tribune* and an unsuccessful candidate for the presidency in 1872.

81. *Christian Advocate and Journal,* December 6, 1866, p. 388; *Congregationalist,* April 19, 1867, p. 62.

82. *Congregationalist,* April 26, 1867, p. 66.

could strike through the hearts and heads of a people."[83] Even the *Presbyterian* broke its self-imposed silence on political issues to declare: "Our triumph was premature . . . and now a new class of dangers has assailed us. The spirit of rebellion, although checked was not subdued, and taking advantage of the conflicts which have taken place in our government itself, is perhaps as intense as ever." Americans must pray, said the weekly, for "a second interposition" of divine grace like that manifested during the war in order to save the nation.[84] The Jordan had not yet been crossed; and that expatriated New Englander, Truman M. Post, wrote from his vantage point in St. Louis: "By God's outstretched arm they [the American people] have been delivered, have been led triumphant through the sanguinary gulf of revolution, and for the hour have taken up the exult of Miriam. But still they are in the wilderness, sore bested it may be with hunger and weariness, and the land of promise is afar."[85]

Nor were the reports of evangelistic work among the Southern whites cheering. From Missouri a laborer of the American Home Missionary Society wrote: "What can a minister hope for, in such a field, but a discouragingly slow process of reconstruction? How can a man build with confidence and hope on quicksand?"[86] A Northern clergyman in Virginia had little more cheering than these words to offer: "The people are ignorant, superstitious and prejudiced. I trust that I am doing some good among them, though the fruit of my labors may not immediately appear."[87] The catalog of lamentations grew in volume with the years, and a report to the 1868 Methodist General Conference on work among the Southern masses, though trying to put a good face upon the supposedly "astonishing results" achieved, was forced to admit:

> The passions and sectionalisms born of the war survived it. The Churches in the South which committed themselves to the twin wrongs—slavery and rebellion—came back to reassert

83. *Christian Advocate and Journal,* September 19, 1867, p. 300.
84. *Presbyterian,* August 31, 1867, p. 2.
85. Truman A. Post, *Truman Marcellus Post, D.D.,* p. 335.
86. O. A. Thomas, "Missouri," *Home Missionary* 39 (June 1866): 39.
87. W. H. Maverick, "Virginia," *Home Missionary* 41 (February 1869): 245.

themselves; to repeat their mischievous dogmas; to rebuild on the old foundations, and, it is to be feared, with similar, untempered mortar, the shattered fabrics of their several ecclesiastical systems; to resist, with every possible appliance—and theirs are neither few nor small—and, also, to the bitter end, the introduction and establishment of our system upon that soil. Nor are their appliances by any means few or impotent. It deserves to be known that some of our preachers and teachers in the South have been driven from their work, and others have been brutally murdered, while peacefully pursuing their chosen labor among the people of their care. Prejudice and sectional proscription are formidable weapons in the hands of men rendered earnest and desperate by defeat and disaster.[88]

These dolorous reports confessed what statistics demonstrated clearly: except for scattered pockets of Unionists and aside from the larger cities where Northern émigrés constituted the bulk of their congregations, the Yankee denominations were almost universally shunned by the white people of the South.[89]

This hostility fell with special force upon the despised "nigger teachers" and thus severely handicapped their work among the freedmen.[90] Many Southern churchmen wished some form of educational or religious ministry to the Afro-American, but they wanted control of any programs for this end. The Yankee teachers and preachers were dismissed as interlopers come to wreck further the social harmony of the South and to fill the former slave's head with disruptive notions of equality.[91] In 1867 the Committee on Freedmen of the Old School General Assembly gave testimony to the corrosive effect of this continued opposition to its work: "The

88. *Journal of the General Conference of the Methodist Episcopal Church, Held in Chicago, Ill., 1868*, p. 563.

89. See Morrow, *Northern Methodism and Reconstruction*, pp. 96–124, 234–50.

90. From a report by Bishop Matthew Simpson on the Mississippi Annual Conference of the Methodist Episcopal Church in *Christian Advocate and Journal*, January 28, 1869, p. 25.

91. For examples of the Southern attitude, consult Baker, *Relations between Northern and Southern Baptists*, pp. 122–33, 166–83, and Ernest Trice Thompson, *Presbyterians in the South*, 3: 308–31.

complete social ostracism of any minister who enters the field, if he does his duty, is hard to bear. To be despised by a wicked world, through grace, leads the servant of Jesus to be strong; but to be disgraced in the eyes of those who profess to follow the common Lord, saps the strength and wounds the soul." The effect upon the laborers was predictable: "Some have gone without counting the cost, and been soon discouraged." The report pinpointed another stumbling block—the inadequate support given by the Northern churches to those struggling against discouraging odds. "To preach the gospel in Africa," the committee noted with a touch of irony, "makes a hero in the Church, and gives one a place in the prayers of all Christian households, but to preach the same gospel to the benighted Africans in our own land, secures neither honor nor sympathy from the large body of Christian people." The fact that fewer than one-quarter of the Old School churches had contributed financially to the work of the committee in the closing fiscal year underscored the validity of this complaint.[92] Finances remained a constant source of embarrassment to all church-related organizations working on behalf of blacks, especially once the assistance from the Freedmen's Bureau began dwindling and after the secular American Freedmen's Union Commission disbanded in 1869. Special bequests smoothed the gaps from time to time, but the story of these various benevolent societies is a record of meager salaries, ceaseless pleas for more money, budgets barely met, and eventual retrenchment.[93]

Missionary toil also gave lie to any hope that the freedmen would soon absorb the culture of their Yankee teachers, and the supposedly untutored natural piety of blacks began to appear to be crude paganism. After attending a worship service among the freedmen, a teacher employed by the AMA in Louisville, Kentucky, voiced her misgivings: "The idea seemed to be inherent with them, that the duty of Christians consists primarily in boisterous prayers and weird singing and shouting . . . rather than in pure and upright living."[94]

92. *Minutes of the General Assembly of the Presbyterian Church in the United States of America, Old School* (1867), 18: 443.

93. See, for example, Beard, *Crusade of Brotherhood,* p. 251, and Morrow, *Northern Methodism and Reconstruction,* pp. 164–65.

94. "From Miss S. G. Stanley," *American Missionary,* 2d ser. 10 (September 1866): 200.

The charge was lodged more bluntly by the Committee on Freedmen of the Old School Assembly. "The rags of their heathenism are neither worn out nor thrown away. . . . Superstition permeates their whole society, and manifests itself as an atmosphere about the world of piety they inhabit. Visions, revelations, and rhapsodies sweep through their confused ideas of worship, until their religion becomes an inebriation."[95] Northern churchmen were furthermore appalled by what they perceived to be the freedman's degraded home life. One teacher submitted a grim portrait intended to describe the typical black family:

> The father, mother, three children and dog occupy the one room of the cabin. Both parents smoke; both boys run loose in the street with the pigs. . . . The small room is crowded with broken furniture, cast off finery, crockery, and indispensables. Neither parent can read. A few well-thumbed readers are all the literature the house contains. No paper comes, to quicken their ideas. Life is a round of menial duties for the mother, and of hard work for the father. Ambition seems dormant, and progress is out of the question.[96]

The hard conditions of postbellum life in the South attest to the likely accuracy of this description and probably its frequent recurrence. Unfortunately the minister or educator usually read the marks of physical deprivation as a want of virtue to be remedied by re-creating the Afro-Americans in his own image, and the editor of the *American Missionary* prefaced this story with the opinion: the freedmen "must be made as nearly as may be like Northern teachers and Northern thinkers. Habits of neatness, system, thrift, are invaluable."[97] Missionary experience had disclosed the internal logic long present in popular stereotypes of the Negro. The innocent child of nature converts with relative ease into the semibarbarian of the wild.

As concern with the moral condition of Southern blacks grew

95. *Minutes of the General Assembly of the Presbyterian Church in the United States of America, Old School* (1867), 18: 447.

96. "Home Influence Among the Freedmen," *American Missionary,* 2d ser. 11 (March 1867): 59.

97. Ibid.

more acute, the campaign to educate and evangelize them was defended more frequently on the grounds that they presented a serious potential threat to the Republic. The same report to the Old School Presbyterian Church that cast aspersions upon the freedmen's religion warned that they were promising candidates for subversion by that archenemy of democracy, Roman Catholicism. "We are fully persuaded," the report ended somberly, "that there has seldom been found a people who, as a mass, are more fully prepared to embrace and enjoy the mysteries and promises of the Man of Sin."[98] These words were written in the wake of the Second Plenary Council of the American Catholic hierarchy in Baltimore in 1866 where the bishops had endorsed the principle of a mission to freedmen.[99] Although the plan remained more pronouncement than fact, other Protestants took up the fear of the Presbyterians and invoked the specter of a massive Jesuitical onslaught that might win blacks to Rome.[100] Behind these fears lay the more general anxiety enunciated by a Baptist clergyman: "We must educate and Christianize this ignorant mass of voters, or see the nation, sooner or later, go down before them and others like them."[101] Those who had been the objects of the churches' compassion were being transformed into a troublesome presence.

In a passing notice in 1867, the Home Missions Committee of the New School Presbyterian Church issued a brief statement that shed much light on ecclesiastical failure in Dixie. "The work at the South," observed the report, "has been more encouraging among the freedmen, where they have been able to send their [own] missionaries, than among the whites. But the colored missionaries are very few, and the prejudice against all Northern men, among all the whites at the South, both loyal and rebel, is such as to hinder the usefulness and comfort of missionaries sent from the North."[102]

98. *Minutes of the General Assembly of the Presbyterian Church in the United States of America, Old School* (1867), 18: 448.

99. John Tracy Ellis, *American Catholicism*, pp. 99–100.

100. "The Necessity of Great Enlargement in the Work Among Freedmen," *American Missionary*, 2d ser. 11 (February 1867): 34–35.

101. *Christian Watchman and Reflector*, March 3, 1870.

102. *Minutes of the General Assembly of the Presbyterian Church in the United States of America, New School* (1867), 14: 555.

The unyielding hostility of whites and the inability of the Northerners to relate with maximum effectiveness to the freedmen were
the interlocking facets of a dilemma fatal to the hopes of the evangelical enterprise. A year earlier in a typical burst of optimism,
Henry Ward Beecher had promised: "There is a divine Christ power
which allays hatred, disarms prejudice, and can work the conversion
of the poorest and lowest in the South as well as in the North."
This trust in a "regenerative power that will spring into activity as
soon as it is touched" was being sorely tried, if not refuted.[103]

By 1868 evidence clearly demonstrated that the missionary campaign in the South was faltering and that congressional Reconstruction had met serious obstacles. These events produced anxieties
easily personified in the person of the seventeenth president. This
"piece of rottenness under the nose of God," as the aging Charles
Finney called Andrew Johnson, became the symbol of the frustra-
tions experienced by the nation.[104] The president was the false
Joshua upon whose shoulders had fallen the responsibility of leading
the American Israel to its promised land, and he had proven recreant
to his trust. "Andrew Johnson could have taken this nation with
him," said one Protestant, "over the ruins of a prostrate rebellion
to the land of milk and honey—with all rights assured to all men,
while no incentive existed for a war of races, where one people
would not feel that its destiny was for evermore to dig amid tears
and sorrow, to eat the bread of humiliation, to see children come
to them without opportunity or hope of education and improvement. All of this Andrew Johnson might have done."[105] Although
the president's political errors were legion and perhaps constituted
an impeachable offense if the constitutional definition of it is construed broadly, it was scarcely fair or realistic to place the onus of
failure entirely upon him. The inadequacies of congressional policy
assured an unsatisfactory Reconstruction in any case; but the
president's gross insensitivity to public opinion made him the
logical scapegoat on which to pour out accumulated rage. Accordingly, when impeachment came, numerous church bodies and
ecclesiastical newspapers urged the removal of this great criminal

103. "Speech of Rev. Henry Ward Beecher," *American Missionary* 2d
ser. 10 (June 1866): 131.
104. Quoted in *Independent*, January 21, 1869, p. 4.
105. Ibid., April 12, 1866, p. 4.

whose "habitual falseness to his high trust" had nearly ruined the country.[106] At the quadrennial Methodist General Conference meeting in May 1868, as Johnson's trial reached its climax, one delegate urged that the Senate rebuke the chief executive's "tyrannical usurpation," and the conference set aside an hour of prayer that the upper chamber might perform its duty; no one needed to specify what that duty was.[107]

Among its clerical supporters at least, the impeachment movement was driven on by the hope that at last a quick remedy for the ills of Reconstruction had been found. "Congress," said the *Christian Advocate* in September 1867, "has but to proceed in the way clearly marked out to it, and all will go forward safely and surely to the end."[108] The *Independent* expressed its optimism more forcefully: "Under the presidency of Mr. Wade [the presiding officer of the Senate who would accede to the presidency in the event of Johnson's ouster], the Union is to be quickly restored. The Southern States, which Andrew Johnson has so long kept out will come back with music and banner. One after the other, in rapid and joyful succession, they will take their old places. But these new states will not be like their old selves. They are henceforth regenerated creatures."[109] Such pronouncements give a clue to a question that has vexed historians: why was Johnson impeached? The chief executive had been thoroughly repudiated by the electorate; Congress had already enacted its own program and hobbled his power to interfere by restrictive legislation; less than a year remained until the next election; and General Ulysses S. Grant was widely touted as the putative successor to the discredited Johnson. "With more than a two-thirds majority against him in both Houses," Samuel Spear observed before the impeachment fever, "Congress can better afford to let the President live out his Constitutional days; and then he will die without any excitement, trouble, or expense to the people."[110] In the spring of 1868, that argument

106. *Congregationalist,* May 14, 1868, p. 156.
107. *Journal of the General Conference of the Methodist Episcopal Church, Held in Chicago, Ill., 1868,* pp. 152–53.
108. *Christian Advocate and Journal,* September 19, 1867, p. 300.
109. *Independent,* May 14, 1868, p. 4.
110. Spear, "The President and Congress," *American Presbyterian and Theological Review,* n.s. 5 (January 1867): 44.

should have seemed equally compelling, but impeachment answered to another logic. Americans, encouraged by their churches, were searching for a decisive action that would forever resolve the ambiguities of Reconstruction and permit the nation to achieve its rightful destiny. In pursuing policies directly opposed to strong majority sentiment, Andrew Johnson made himself the appropriate victim whose sacrifice would hopefully assure that swift and final victory.

The failure to remove Johnson did not lead to mournful hand wringing, however. Most papers and ecclesiastical bodies chose to ignore his narrow acquittal. Their attention was already focused elsewhere. As the Senate trial closed, the Republican national convention was assembling to nominate Grant for the presidency. Protestants left off the pillory of the false Joshua to rejoice that the true had at last come forward to receive the mantle of the fallen Moses. To secure this happy end, the bloody shirt was waved with a vengeance. Democrats were denounced as the "Pro-Slavery Rum party" which true Christians must avoid, and the election was depicted as a continuation of the struggle to suppress the rebellion: "It remains to be seen whether a nation that has poured out its blood and treasure like water to defeat them in the field will surrender to them, and their allies, who had not the courage to fight with them, at the polls."[111]

When the election produced the expected Grant victory, the clergy rejoiced that the end was at least near. According to the *Christian Advocate,* Grant's election meant an early adjustment of remaining difficulties. Now that Republican success sealed as "a fixed fact" black suffrage, the Ku Klux Klan would no longer maraud the Southern countryside. Now the nation could go forth to cultivate that "spirit of kindness and good-will" in which would be submerged "the bitterness of partisan strife."[112] The *Congregationalist* saw in the returns the promise of a "reign of order." "The loyal Southerner, white or black, may sit hereafter under his own vine and fig-tree, none daring to molest or make him afraid. Slavery being dead which before rendered security impossible, and the

111. *Independent,* February 20, 1868, p. 4; *Congregationalist,* July 16, 1868, p. 228.
112. *Christian Advocate and Journal,* November 12, 1868, p. 364.

malignant spirit which animates the 'lost cause' having now received a deadly wound, the blessed day seems close at hand when constitutional liberty and personal freedom are to be enjoyed throughout the whole land, by all the people."[113] For Gilbert Haven, the triumph of the Republican candidate prompted a reexamination of "America's Past and Future." Assessing Grant's career from his military successes to his recent victory at the polls, the Methodist clergyman read in it the portents of America's destiny assured:

> He has kept intact our vast boundaries, and insured their vaster expansion. He has changed the contempt of all nations into respect and implanted a dread of our prowess and our ideas that is a sure precursor of a fast-hastening change in all their states conformable to our triumphant principles. He has insured the essential extension of America over the world. Already the United States of Europe are openly advocated in congresses from all her people, and that more distant and dubious title, the United States of Asia, looms up mistily on the far horizon. Even the United States of Africa will be born in due time into the family of republics; while the United States of America shall encompass the whole continent in her oceanic lines. Thus from the victory over the rebellion will arise a fraternity of nations, few in number, divided by no alienation of language, government, or faith; ultimately to become one with each other, with Christ, with God.[114]

These were high accolades for the cigar-smoking soldier and, like so many other Protestant dreams, were inflated beyond the possibility of realization.

The eagerness with which the Grant victory was greeted betrayed a weariness of the flesh and a wish to be done with strife. The Republican candidate had artfully exploited the psychological exhaustion of the electorate, promising that his administration would end agitation by allowing the existing laws to work unhindered. The promise of tranquility appealed to the churches, and there was an almost audible sigh as the *American Missionary*

113. *Congregationalist*, November 12, 1868, p. 364.
114. Haven, *National Sermons*, pp. 614–15.

concluded from the preliminary returns that Grant had been elected. All the friends of freedom

> will rejoice, with us, in the result of the October elections, giving assurance as they do, that we shall have peace, and a cessation of that brutal warfare in the South, that has been waged against all loyal men, especially those of color; and that thus will be removed, the only real barrier that has stood in the way of . . . our religious and educational work there. Give us peace and quiet, and we confidently believe, that ministers and teachers, schools and churches, will do more for the satisfactory reconstruction of the South, than any system of legislation that can be devised. . . .[115]

The *Christian Advocate* sketched the same goal several months earlier: "With General Grant we longingly desire peace. And because we desire it we are tenacious of the conditions essential to peace. Among these at this moment must be included and made prominent the letting alone, to work out its completed course, the Congressional scheme of Reconstruction."[116]

This was an essentially conservative position, assuming that institutional reform was complete and would, if left untouched, work out successfully the remaining problems. In spite of evidence that the Reconstruction program was bankrupt, the churches continued to believe that a man of integrity would make the policy viable. The idea was comforting. With Johnson gone and the hero of the war come to power, everyone could rest. Comments about Reconstruction politics waned rapidly in the aftermath of the Grant victory; and by 1869 the familiar themes were only occasionally trotted out in the religious press. The result was perhaps inevitable. As Truman Post had written in 1866: "It is a sad truth that men, for the most part, are not heroes or martyrs. From the extraordinary tension requisite to act the part of such, they must in time relax from sheer exhaustion."[117] One can fight only a limited number of "final" battles before the collective psyche is drained.

The churches' weariness with sectional strife can also be traced

115. "Cheering," *American Missionary,* 2d ser. 12 (November 1868): 250–51.
116. *Christian Advocate and Journal,* August 6, 1868, p. 252.
117. Post, *Truman Marcellus Post,* p. 333.

in a greater willingness to seek accommodation with the Southern Protestantism previously denounced as a spiritual Babylon. The American Baptist Home Missionary Society sent to the Southern Convention in 1867 a committee offering amity and fellowship; two years later the former proposed that the two bodies devise a system for the joint commissioning of laborers within the bounds of the defeated Confederacy.[118] In 1869 the Methodist bishops dispatched a delegation of their number, including the flag-waving Matthew Simpson, to present an olive branch to the General Conference South. George R. Crooks commented of the event: "The extinction of slavery has removed the permanent cause of antagonism; and the power of attraction which comes of unity in doctrine, discipline, and usage begins to be felt. . . . They [the bishops] wisely propose an oblivion of the past, and recognize the fact that we are living in a new time and under altered conditions."[119] The Old School Presbyterians quietly retreated from their 1865–66 declaration that Southerners could not be received into communion without a profession of loyalty to the federal government and a confession of sin. In 1868 the Assembly acknowledged the legitimacy of its southern counterpart. And two years later, after the merger of the Old and New Schools, the reunited church sent to the Southern branch a committee bearing the message that no rule or pronouncement of previous assemblies would have any authority unless it was approved by both schools.[120] In effect, this was a face-saving method of nullifying wartime strictures offensive to the South. Such gestures were received with decided coolness—and often abuse—by those to whom they were directed, and rancorous exchanges across the Mason-Dixon line continued for years. It was not until 1876 that the two branches of Methodism reached formal mutual recognition; Northern Presbyterians did not achieve fraternal relations with their brethren in Dixie until 1883; and it was 1894 before the Southern Baptist Convention and the American Baptist Home Missionary Society reached a settlement of differences.[121]

118. Baker, *Relations between Northern and Southern Baptists*, p. 104.
119. Letter to *Independent*, June 3, 1869, p. 1.
120. *Presbyterian Reunion: A Memorial Volume*, pp. 447–48.
121. Morrow, *Northern Methodism and Reconstruction*, pp. 87–88; Thompson, *Presbyterians in the South*, 2: 223–64; and Baker, *Relations between Northern and Southern Baptists*, p. 193.

Still these early peace feelers from the North indicate a profound shift in sentiment. Protestants no longer spoke confidently of disintegrating or absorbing apostate Southern churches. It was the hour for making truces, not launching armies of conquest.

The American Home Missionary Society admitted more candidly than any other organization that it had overextended its Southern commitment. "At the close of the war of the rebellion," confessed the society in December 1867, "it was supposed that the peculiar obstacles to the work of Home Missionary effort at the South were removed. . . . Accordingly, the Executive Committee promptly undertook this new task. . . . But the fires of the rebellion, which had only been smothered, continued to burn, and subsequent political events fanned their embers to a fiercer flame. The tide of emigration to the South was arrested and turned back. All evangelical effort, under the auspices of Northern men and institutions, was paralyzed." Therefore the society decided that it was "inexpedient, at present, to make large outlays in that quarter."[122] The proposal to cut its losses in the Southern field represented a sharp change from that heady optimism two years earlier when the society had announced that the region was a defenseless Jericho, easy prey to the Northern hosts.

Protestants were also less inclined to attack white supremacy and racial segregation in the South. In November 1869 the *Christian Watchman* urged Northern Baptists to seek the advice and approval of their coreligionists below the Mason-Dixon line in determining the proper methods of aiding blacks. "Our theory for a long time," said the editor, "has been that the freedmen have at the South many of their best friends, men whom Northern philanthropists would do wisely to consult with respect to the best modes of giving to the emancipated the civil rights and the kind and degree of culture which will subserve their true interests."[123] By 1872 the American Baptist Home Missionary Society unashamedly courted Southern support by declaring that "not a doctrine or sentiment is intended to be taught [in the freedmen's schools] to which any Baptists could consistently object." The message was apparently

122. "The Southern Field," *Home Missionary* 40 (December 1867): 196.
123. *Christian Watchman and Reflector,* November 25, 1869.

credible to those to whom it was addressed, for some of the state associations in the South endorsed the work.[124] After 1868 the American Missionary Association subtlely, probably unconsciously, began changing its rhetoric from an aggressive to a defensive posture. The freedmen, said one editorial in the *American Missionary,* "need the moral and religious stamina that will lift them above seductions; and nerve them to endure suffering. These missionaries and teachers are their leaders, cheering them in dark hours, holding before them the hope of an education, and strengthening them with divine truth."[125] This was the description of a crusade become a holding action, of an effort to maintain enclaves of patient endurance in the midst of a hostile environment. By cultivating the religion of the catacombs, the association had chosen perhaps the only path open to it but had also tacitly admitted that the oppressive social system of the South was not to be attacked head on. The way was paved for the organization's total sellout to the forces of reaction in the mid-1870s. When General Samuel C. Armstrong was elevated to the chief position of leadership in 1876, the association proclaimed publicly that the task of educating and evangelizing blacks should be devolved upon the whites of the south.[126]

The changes in policy increasingly placed the stigma of his oppression upon the Afro-American himself. If he demonstrated his worthiness, he would eventually achieve his just share of society's benefits. Bishop Davis W. Clark, chairman of the Methodist Freedmen's Aid Society, warned in December 1867 that the laws of the universe decreed that the Negro should "have no power to preserve his freedom" unless he were industrious, intelligent, and moral.[127] The following winter a Northern clergyman after traveling among the freedmen wrote: "If the colored people of the South are doomed to an inferior position, by their ignorance or their vices; they and their votes will be controlled by the more cultivated and competent whites; and no plans of reconstruction, no legislation at Washington,

124. Baker, *Relations between Northern and Southern Baptists,* p. 124.
125. "The Southern Situation," *American Missionary,* 2d ser. 12 (September 1868): 203.
126. See Richard B. Drake, "Freedmen's Aid Societies and Sectional Compromise," *Journal of Southern History* 29 (May 1963): 175–86.
127. *Christian Advocate and Journal,* January 2, 1868, p. 2.

can permanently prevent this. In the long run, capacity is sure to secure position and power."[128] With remarkable brevity, Edward Kirk capsulized the point of the argument: "Once . . . [the slave] was worth as much as a horse, and consequently somebody took care of him. Now nobody takes care of him. The negro—the improvident negro in America must sink."[129] The former slaves were hemmed in by the ineluctable logic of the argument: because the improvident sink and the industrious rise, blacks at the bottom of the economic ladder must be improvident.

The transformation of attitudes toward the black and white communities of the South was far from complete. The bloody shirt would be waved at least quadrennially at the presidential canvass until the 1890s.[130] Still by 1869, significant changes were in the wind. Peace feelers had gone out to former enemies; and Afro-Americans, erstwhile claimants to justice, were becoming an annoying problem to be gotten rid of by the shortest route possible. The fundamental difficulty was that Protestants were tired. They had fought the most costly war in national history, had exhausted their schemes of Reconstruction, and now craved nothing more than a season of ease in Zion. The churches, however, had given too many of their sons to the cannon's maw to allow that the precious dream was only an illusion. Even as they accommodated themselves to a reality less than the total victory for which they had struggled, the clergy continued to assert wistfully that the land of promise must surely be close at hand. In April 1868 the Reverend Daniel Curry wrote:

128. *Independent,* March 18, 1869, p. 1.
129. "Anniversary at Boston," *American Missionary,* 2d ser. 11 (July 1867): 146.
130. The Republican party vacillated between overtures to the South and denunciations of its treatment of blacks. This uncertain posture reflected the party's tenuous position in national politics and the concomitant necessity of trying to build, either among whites or blacks of the old Confederacy, a viable Southern base. Once the political realignment of the 1890s gave Republicans an electoral majority exclusive of Dixie, the bloody shirt was permanently retired. See Stanley P. Hirshon, *Farewell to the Bloody Shirt: Northern Republicans and the Southern Negro, 1877–1893.*

We are not blind to the disorders and distractions that prevail in the "unreconstructed" states, and we are not surprised at them nor discouraged by them. But though passions seem for the time to bear rule, and partisanship to triumph over both patriotism and private interest, we still have hope. Passions are but for a season; reason and self-interest are perpetual, and must prevail at length. . . . Our Joshua [Grant] still lives, and through him, we trust, our God will soon give rest to his people.[131]

These lines bear poignant testimony to a hope in which too much was invested to let it die. The passage of the Jordan simply *had* to be made; but even the most optimistic realized that river was more elusive than imagined, and the American Israel wanted to rest, not march.

131. Daniel Curry, "The Africo-American," *Methodist Quarterly Review* 50 (April 1868): 252.

# 6

## "Wanted—A Moral Purpose"

Near the close of a professional life that had spanned the years between the antislavery agitations of the 1830s and the election of Ulysses S. Grant, the Reverend Albert Barnes delivered a final interpretation of the previous four decades. A fledgling nation whose "experiment of self-government had not been fully tried" had been transformed by the war into a transcontinental colossus whose strength "has been put to the utmost test" and emerged victorious. These years had welded together "one great united people, destined in all human probability to accomplish more for the good of man than all the nations of antiquity have done, or than is to be accomplished by any existing people on the globe." Americans on the threshold of maturity could gladly begin their productive years with great hope. "Never in the history of the world," said Barnes, "did young men enter upon their career with so much to cheer them, to animate them, to inspire them with hope, to call forth their highest powers for the promotion of the great objects which enter into the civilization, the progress, and the happiness of man." Similar claims to be the undisputed redeemer nation rolled on in a sea of self-congratulatory chauvinism.[1]

This joyous tide could not drown entirely suspicions that all was not well in Zion. Doubts about the efficacy of Reconstruction fit into a larger picture of half-suppressed questions. Between hymns to the vindicated elect nation were ominous notices that the folk loyalty purchased by blood was being dissipated amid corruption, materialism, unmeltable ethnic groups, disruption of familial ties, and the menace of Roman Catholicism. Yet the reality of danger never dulled the rhetoric of triumph. In fact, the presence of new enemies—and the resurgence of old ones—heightened self-ascriptions

1. Albert Barnes, *Life at Threescore and Ten,* pp. 106, 109–10, 136.

of greatness, perhaps because Protestants could not accept the shattering truth that their Civil War had not been a redemptive *Volkskrieg* sealing the American destiny. Owen Chadwick's remark about the spiritual crisis of Victorian England is equally appropriate to the condition of American churches in the postwar era: "Within this earnestness was the haste of beleaguered men. Though Christians felt assured of their safety, they could hear wolves prowling in the undergrowth and built their protective hedges a little higher."[2] Thus the 1860s ended with continued affirmations of an imminent millennial destiny for the great Republic–a confidence, however, papered defensively thin over alarming questions.

NEW PROBLEMS AND OLD

Except for occasional blasts against the Roman Catholic Church as the protector of foreign-born draft rioters, Protestants had largely ignored their former adversary during the war. Richmond, not Rome, had become the seat of the beast. Once hostilities were closed, the advent of 1866–the year long designated by certain prophetic speculators as the time of the consummation–drew the churches' attention back to their old enemy. These prognostications acquired new significance at the outbreak that year of another Italian war, furthering the political unity of the peninsula. "It is certainly an interesting circumstance," noted the *Congregationalist,* "that the year which has stood out so prominently in the computations of so many writers, during the last two hundred years, should be marked by the opening of a great war in Europe–a war in which the Papacy is obviously threatened, and its temporal sovereignty doomed apparently to a speedy extinction."[3] The "great war" proved a short imbroglio in which Venetia was wrested from Austria, but this outcome left the papal states the only territory yet to be annexed by the Italian government. Furthermore, Prussia inflicted another defeat upon Catholic Austria at Sadowa in July and thus ensured that the process of German unification would be controlled by a Protestant state. Surveying these events, a Methodist clergyman asserted in January 1867 that the previous year had indeed been a

2. Owen Chadwick, *The Victorian Church,* 1: 527.
3. *Congregationalist,* July 20, 1866, p. 114.

time of prophetic fulfillment. The world marched "toward enlightenment, freedom, and evangelization."[4] Surely the death knell was sounding for the man of sin.

To the detriment of predetermined interpretations of the Apocalypse, 1866 was also the year of the Second Plenary Council in Baltimore, which served notice that Catholicism was not a dying faith. Toward the close of the decade, the hierarchy in several areas also renewed the earlier efforts of Archbishop Hughes to break the de facto Protestant monopoly of secondary education. In New York State, the Catholic Church lobbied for aid to parochial shools—a clear intimation, thundered one Baptist, of Romanism's intention to manipulate "party demagogues" to secure the demolition of the common school system.[5] Catholic pressure in Cincinnati persuaded the board of education to eliminate daily readings from the Protestant version of the Bible. Writing of this celebrated case that would multiply litigation well into the 1870s, the *Christian Advocate* denounced the coalition of "Roman Catholics and infidels" whose ultimate goal in the extrusion of the Scriptures from the classroom was "the entire destruction of the school system, and the division of the public money among sectarian institutions." The Cincinnati decision augured a total calamity and forced the editor to question whether the recent baptism of blood had genuinely purified the nation. "The war, or the rapid development of wealth," he lamented, "has desperately weakened the tone and power of conscience and created an unwholesome atmosphere."[6]

The churches had endured the final crisis only to discover that another danger lay beyond. The nation "has successfully passed one fearful period of peril," observed the Reverend S. D. Hillman of Dickinson College, "and lo, another threatens." He foresaw in the coming ten years a powerful influx of Catholics and pagans from "the old centers of exodus in Europe . . . far outstripping the proportionate numbers they have sent before."[7] This incoming tide appeared to be a plot contrived by the Curia to save Catholicism

4. *Christian Advocate and Journal,* January 3, 1867, p. 4.
5. *Christian Watchman and Reflector,* July 1, 1869.
6. *Christian Advocate and Journal,* November 18, 1869, p. 364.
7. S. D. Hillman, "The United States and Methodism," *Methodist Quarterly Review* 49 (January 1867): 48–49.

from its impending doom. The *American Missionary* believed that the pope, if successful in his campaign to convert North America, would shortly take up residence in the United States and warned somberly: "He has no idea of carrying the key of St. Peter without at the same time carrying the sword. . . . With a majority of voters here, why should not the head of the church become the head of the nation, and wield a power to make her enemies tremble?"[8] From the apparent decline of Catholicism abroad and alarming evidence of its aggressive success at home, the corresponding secretary of the American and Foreign Christian Union deduced the same sinister designs:

> Yet their only hope in all the earth is these United States, and they will contest the ground with the energy of desperation. And though they must ultimately fail, and Babylon must fall, yet unless the Protestant pulpit and press awake, and do more to arouse the nation to our danger, to confront Romanism in all its designs, and to warn Protestants and others of its purposes and encroachments, we shall awake one of these years to find Papists in all the high places of the nation, with the control of cities and states, our Sabbaths abolished, our educational system in ruins, Romanism established and sustained by law, (as it already is partially in several places,) our religious freedom gone, and all to be recovered only as they have been regained elsewhere, through revolution and bloodshed. And the American people cannot awake one day too soon if by timely and well-directed efforts they would avert such a calamity. Resistance now, or a religious war within twenty years, is the alternative before us.[9]

These terrors were scarcely allayed when rumormongers in the summer of 1868 bruited the story that the Catholic Church had authorized the American bishops to raise a hundred thousand volunteers to be sent to Rome in service of the pope. To many Protestants, it was plain "that we are attacked by a large well-disciplined army.

8. "Rome in the Field," *American Missionary*, 2d ser. 12 (January 1868): 15.
9. H. Mattison, "Romanism in the United States," *Methodist Quarterly Review* 50 (October 1868): 531–32.

They are fighting hard to conquer us, and to secure the government of our land. It is our duty to meet them, and to contest every inch of their progress."[10]

The threat from Europe was augmented by another peril: Chinese laborers were coming to California in great numbers. Although the churches usually decried the mistreatment of these immigrants— some were prepared to grant them early citizenship—there lay behind the appeals to place among them more home missions a fear that yet another enemy had arrived.[11] In a sermon delivered before the Old South Church of Boston, the Reverend J. M. Manning predicted a titanic conflict between Eastern and Western cultures. Advances in transportation and communication placed the United States and China in a contiguous position from which "the battle we join with them will be inevitable and incessant." Manning believed that the struggle would be a "hand to hand encounter" in which fixed lines dissolved—Americans in China, Chinese in America. From this transoceanic struggle "the decision must come, whether Christ or Confucius, Buddhism or Christianity, shall be supreme over both nations." At minimum, the churches should erect a missionary quarantine line to prevent the further infiltration of heathenism eastward from California, "or all our goodly heritage will be overflowed, and the question with us will be, not how we may convert China but how we may prevent China from converting us!"[12] Fear of this magnitude was relatively infrequent, but these occasional oracles indicated the presence in embryo of a "yellow-peril" mentality and provided still another disturbing token that the war

10. *Presbyterian*, May 16, 1868, p. 4, June 27, 1868, p. 4.

11. For a strong endorsement of citizenship for Chinese-Americans, see the letter of G. S. Abbot to the *Christian Watchman and Reflector*, October 14, 1869. See also "The Chinese in America," *American Missionary*, 2d ser. 13 (November 1869): 250–51, and *Independent*, July 29, 1869, p. 4. On American attitudes toward the Chinese, see Stuart Creighton Miller, *The Unwelcome Immigrant: The American Image of the Chinese, 1785–1882.* Miller argues that the Chinese Exclusion Act of 1882 was not merely the result of lobbying by California interests but was the outcome of long-developing, unfavorable stereotypes of the Chinese.

12. J. M. Manning, "Present Aspect of Christian Missions," *Home Missionary* 40 (April 1868): 277–82.

had not moved the Republic into the broad, sunlit uplands of the
millennium.

These strangers in the land called into question the melting pot's
ability to do its work and made some wonder if the war had truly
succeeded in welding the nation's diverse populace into one people.
Although most continued to believe that the American environment
"dissolves and dispels" the danger of immigration, a number of
worried voices suggested otherwise.[13] Agitation for immigration
restriction was rare, but fear of the foreigner and his supposed vices
was common. The words of Presbyterian S. M. Campbell of Roches-
ter, New York, indicate the prefigurements of a nativist spirit even
though the pastor proclaimed his adherence to an open-door policy:

> This is a Christian Republic, our Christianity being of the Protes-
> tant type. People who are not Christians, and people called
> Christians, but who are not Protestants, dwell among us; but
> they did not build this house. We have never shut our doors
> against them, but if they come, they must take up with such
> accommodations as we have. . . . If any one, coming among us,
> finds that this arrangement is uncomfortable, perhaps he will do
> well to try some other country. The world is wide; there is
> more land to be possessed; let him go and make a beginning
> for himself as our fathers did for us; for, as for this land, we have
> taken possession of it in the name of the Lord Jesus Christ; and,
> if he will give us grace to do it, we mean to hold it for him till
> he come.[14]

The Reverend Edward P. Goodwin of Columbus, Ohio, attacked
dangerous notions "about making the American the real cosmo-
politan, by putting into him the blood of every nation." Allowing
that the theory was beguiling, Goodwin asked the question troubling

13. *Christian Advocate and Journal,* February 18, 1869, p. 52.
14. S. M. Campbell, "Christianity and Civil Liberty," *American and Presbyterian Theological Review,* n.s. 5 (July 1867): 390–91. Such sentiments as
these had contributed to a wave of nativist agitation before the Civil War
(Billington, *The Protestant Crusade*) and would play a role in a renewed outburst of the phenomenon toward the end of the century. See John Higham,
*Strangers in the Land: Patterns of American Nativism, 1860-1925.*

the religious community: as long as the foreign born maintained their special vices, particularly Roman Catholicism, "How much will they undergo assimilation?" The answer was "patent on the face of it": "They can no more become genuine republicans than the night can become the day."[15] One suspects, however, that the real offense of the newcomers was not their antirepublicanism or their sins but their refusal to surrender their ethnic cohesiveness. In April 1869 the *Congregationalist* suggested that the greatest threat to the nation was the continued sense of distinct peoplehood among the immigrants. "Only by fusing all foreign elements into our common nationality," said the paper, "and making our entire population in spirit and intent Americans, shall we preserve our unity and concord as a nation." No one deserved the right to citizenship who "proposes to cast a German vote, or an Irish vote, or a French vote, or to combine with others in a party to represent and perpetuate his foreign nationality in our politics."[16] The one folk supposedly fused by the war—"the men of the Rhine and of the Shannon . . . [together] on the shores of the Potomac"—was still merely an ideal, and one apparently sinking under the weight of reality.[17]

Perhaps more unsettling were indications that the elect people had enemies within as well as without. The war was hardly ended before Protestants began wondering if their fellow citizens had indeed learned the expected self-discipline, republican simplicity, and higher morality. The experience of the camp had taught heroic self-sacrifice, but it had also heightened secular preoccupations potentially subversive of spiritual values. "The political troubles through which we have passed, and are still passing," said the *Presbyterian,* "have greatly distracted the thought of the community from the great and principle concern . . . as in a great measure to produce forgetfulness of Christ's Kingdom. The injurious effects of this have been obvious. Things seen and temporal have gained ascendency over things unseen and eternal."[18] Similarly national affluence, poured out recently for

15. Edward P. Goodwin, "Home Missions for the Sake of the World," *Home Missionary* 40 (August 1867): 87.

16. *Congregationalist,* April 1, 1869, p. 97.

17. *Christian Watchman and Reflector,* July 19, 1862.

18. *Presbyterian,* October 14, 1865, p. 4.

patriotic benevolence, now seemed to threaten excessive materialism. "The intense energy of business," President Theodore D. Woolsey of Yale commented in 1866, "must lead to inequalities of fortune greater than have ever been known before; the power to command capital in large masses must lead to frequent speculation; wealth will spend itself in luxury and pleasure." An age devoted to "lavish expenditure," he warned, would not be congenial to "the culture, the morals, or the religion of the nation." Woolsey much preferred a "slow advance in wealth" to maintain "simplicity of manners" and the "check of necessary economy," but he was certain that America was not entering such a time.[19]

By the end of the decade, one Methodist could venture a jeremiad against the effects of affluence and not fear contradiction:

> Has not our standard of business morality perceptibly fallen within a few years? Have not the pernicious influences of the war period visibly affected our regard for strict business integrity? . . . Prior to the rebellion we were comparatively an economical people, living within our means, and husbanding our individual resources. The war suddenly broke in upon these habits of frugality. The flood-gates of corruption, chicanery, and fraud, were opened wide upon us. We became familiarized to enormous expenditures by the government, and began to increase our cost of maintenance, to indulge in luxuries unthought of before, and, in fact, to live as if we had discovered the philosopher's stone, capable of turning everything into greenbacks. A wild spirit of speculation followed. Men grew weary of following the long and tedious road to wealth, and resorted to the wheel of fortune. . . . Merchants in former years exercised a parental watchfulness over the habits of their clerks, inviting them into their church pews, and encouraging them to cultivate moral and religious associations. Now, however, they are too often indifferent as to their mode of life, and not only encourage, but in many cases instruct them to "cultivate" out-of-town customers, by piloting them through our haunts of sin, and reveling in midnight orgies.[20]

19. Theodore Woolsey, "The New Era," *New Englander* 25 (April 1866): 188.
20. "Business Morality," *Ladies' Repository* 29 (March 1869): 227.

The theme was not new in itself; its American antecedents date at least to Cotton Mather's often-repeated aphorism: "Piety begot prosperity, and the offspring devoured the mother." Nevertheless, the need to revive this genre of oration was particularly distressing to an age that had hoped itself done with such things when the guns were stacked.

One highly visible symbol of moral laxity—the traffic in alcoholic beverages—frightened churchmen with the fearsome prospect of an oncoming "deluge of rum."[21] The Protestant clergy were virtually unanimous that total abstinence provided the only moral solution to the evil, but they were divided about the viability of legislative efforts to end the liquor trade. Some were willing, until the public conscience had been sufficiently aroused, to accept excise laws that would restrict consumption. Still, that compromise galled many willing to endorse it, and, as one clergyman noted ruefully, the fact that many conscientious Christians had abandoned statutory prohibition as unworkable constituted "another practical confession of the failure of democratic institutions."[22] The extent of the vice particularly distressed churchmen. Its prevalence among the lower-class immigrants was to be expected, but the usage of fermented beverages was invading the citadel of middle-class Protestantism. The 1868 General Conference drew attention to the dangerous inroads of intemperance among affluent Methodists in the metropolitan area: "The fashion of the world in the circles in which they move is averse to total abstinence; and we regret to learn that some members of our Churches are inclined to conform to these practices—to put wine and dangerous liquors on their tables—and, far worse, to indulge in their use. . . . Our wealth will bring with it the heaviest curse of heaven if it becomes a source of corruption through any complicity with popular sin."[23] The same creeping intemperance frightened the New School Assembly to admonish the denomination in 1869 "to preserve herself from this growing

21. *Congregationalist,* October 29, 1865, p. 166.
22. *Christian Advocate and Journal,* May 3, 1866, p. 140. For an argument in favor of statutory prohibition, consult *Christian Watchman and Reflector,* July 8, 1869.
23. *Journal of the General Conference of the Methodist Episcopal Church,* pp. 625–26.

evil. She possesses the power, if she will exercise it, to purify herself and keep herself pure."[24] The fear among both Presbyterians and Methodists was that this power had been discarded.

The cities were not constant themes of declamation from pulpit and press, but Protestants well recognized that in these population centers festered virtually all the evils they deplored. There the immigrants largely congregated; intemperance was rampant, and the sin of worldliness was fashionable. Proposed solutions to the problem of the city indicate how thoroughly alien the emerging urban reality was to evangelical Protestantism. The *Christian Advocate* believed that the dangers of city life could be alleviated by incorporating the foreign-born underclass into local congregations "till they shall learn to appreciate both the house of God and the better civilization with which they are there brought into contact."[25] Furthermore, this inclusiveness would mitigate the luxuriant softness into which middle-class Christians had fallen and would further "their own spiritual development" by giving them once more a heroic cause for which to sacrifice.[26] The ideal of a congregation where laborer and merchant, rich and poor, gathered together under one roof to worship represented an attempt to transplant the village to metropolis–to repristinate the ethos in which the Protestant vision of a free society of disciplined individuals could best thrive. If that failed, the editor was prepared to disperse the city. He suggested that all homeless children in New York should be resettled in the countryside or small towns. One Presbyterian pressed the proposal to its logical conclusion and called for the removal of unemployed adults to farms, confident that this action would preserve the coming generation from the "seductions" inevitable in the city.[27] One cannot avoid the distinct feeling of inauthenticity in such programs. Fearful of losing their hegemony in the Republic and uncertain of the ability of the nation to assimilate its newest immigrants, Protestants yet proposed to scatter them into every corner of the land. These self-contradictory proposals, however,

24. *Minutes of the General Assembly of the Presbyterian Church in the United States of America, New School* (1869), 15: 307.
25. *Christian Advocate and Journal,* January 21, 1869, p. 20.
26. Ibid., September 10, 1868, p. 292.
27. *Presbyterian,* February 1, 1868, p. 4.

were not so much an indication of hypocrisy as they were a testimony to the woefully inadequate social theories that the churches carried into what President Woolsey called "the new era."

Amid these challenges to the Protestant dream of a Christian America, internal discord erupted within the last bastion of refuge. Although the woman's movement was still in relative adolescence, the arguments for sexual equality were now raised at a greater tempo. The Civil War had taken the various local benevolent associations for women and welded them into a philanthropic enterprise with national consciousness. Furthermore, women like Clara Barton, Dorothea Dix, and Mary Livermore had performed devoted service that made them heroines to women and men alike. Once exposed to these vistas, many women were not prepared to return contentedly to the hearth; and from this general consciousness raising emerged within the women's movement a new leadership, thoroughly ladylike in image. To be sure, women like the radical Elizabeth Cady Stanton and the free-love advocates Victoria Woodhull and her sister Tennessee Clafflin helped continue the aura of disrepute, but the torch was clearly passing to women of unimpeachable respectability, like Mary Livermore, Julia Ward Howe, and in the 1870s, to the most effective proponent of all, Frances Willard of the Women's Christian Temperance Union.[28] The new character of feminism began to win to the cause a few liberal Protestants who saw in women's suffrage a means of elevating the moral tone of society. The majority of churchmen, still suspicious of the phenomenon, preferred to ignore the issue entirely or to smile it away patronizingly "as among the harmless vagaries of a class of eccentric thinkers whom it is not always wise to oppose seriously"; but the clergy could not long sustain contemptuous laughter once they discerned that the "eccentric thinkers" were no longer representative of the rank and file.[29] Going to a meeting of the Ohio State Woman's Suffrage Convention, the editor of the *Ladies' Repository* was prepared to ridicule the entire affair but was compelled in spite of himself to praise "the order, dignity, delicacy and real womanliness that characterized all

28. O'Neill, *The Woman Movement,* pp. 24–29. See also Mary Earhart, *Frances Willard: From Prayers to Politics,* and Aileen S. Kraditor, ed., *Up from the Pedestal: Selected Writings in the History of American Feminism.*
29. *Christian Advocate and Journal,* December 27, 1866, p. 412.

the proceedings."[30] If the women's movement could not be chuckled into oblivion, the case had to be met squarely, and one Baptist argued bluntly that the movement represented an assault upon "the order of heaven and common sense." Proposing to send women into the political strife of the nation, feminists had sketched a program fatal to woman's role as wife and mother upon which depended "the purity, integrity, strength and moral power of our social compact."[31] Only if woman, said Robert M. Hatfield, remained a "power behind the throne greater than the throne" could the national order be preserved.[32] As the editor of the *Ladies Repository* said after his visit to the suffrage convention, expansion of the feminine sphere beyond the home would not "gain the Eden that the speakers painted in such glowing terms" but would "lose the little of Paradise that had been saved from the Eden of old."[33]

The suggestion that the home was an Edenic garden recurred frequently and suggests that the women's movement was a threat because it endangered the last remnant of solid ground in a world convulsed by shifting terrain. Walter Houghton has written of the glorification of domesticity and woman's role: "It [the home] was a place apart, a walled garden, in which certain virtues too easily crushed by modern life could be preserved, and certain desires of the heart too much thwarted be fulfilled."[34] When Protestants saw the threat of Romanism, a tide of immigrants with alien ways of life, the first signs of urban decay, class stratification, rampant vice, and gross materialism, it is not surprising that they protected their walled gardens with such tenacity: they were under attack in their most precious stronghold.

Nevertheless, there was not a prevalence of a defeatist mentality. References to various dangers were precisely that–acknowledgments of potential threat, not confessions of hopelessness. Nor had the specters achieved in 1869 the terrifying proportions they would assume by the early 1880s. Clerical spokesmen still enunciated their

30. "Editor's Table," *Ladies' Repository* 29 (November 1869): 398.
31. *Christian Watchman and Reflector,* October 14, 1869.
32. *Independent,* July 8, 1869, p. 1.
33. "Editor's Table," *Ladies' Repository* 29 (November 1869): 399.
34. Walter E. Houghton, *The Victorian Frame of Mind, 1830–1870,* p. 343.

fear with sufficient frequency to warrant the assertion that they
knew their vision of American destiny was in question. The dilemma
they faced contained elements of profound irony. "The civilization
which Christianity creates and promotes," the Old School Assembly
noted in 1869, "in turn seeks to hinder and overthrow the sacred
power to which it owes its existence and vigor."[35] Taken at face
value, that declaration may well claim too much for the Protestant
tradition; but interpreted loosely, it is profoundly suggestive, for
the churches had inadvertently helped to facilitate the emerging
spiritual crisis. Clergy had taught their people to expect religious
fulfillment in the events of this world, and the laity had mastered
the lesson so well that the sacral trappings of the temporal began
to wear away. Protestants, for example, had hailed democracy,
material progress, and other modern developments as signs of the
Kingdom; for many, these goals were now deemed acceptable in
their own right and needed no further religious legitimation.[36]
Moreover, faith in America's mission and its recent dramatic vindication had scarcely encouraged mature reflection or sober hopes.
Awaiting a future immeasurably grand, Protestants were almost
fated to experience a painful dissonance between hope and reality.

### THE CONTINUING QUEST FOR A CHRISTIAN AMERICA

The churches met doubts by reaffirming more vigorously the
necessary dependence of American culture upon evangelical Christianity. In a sermon discussing national destiny at the commemora-
tion of the fiftieth anniversary of the Methodist Missionary Society,
the Reverend Cyrus Foss dreamed of "the white wings of friendly
commerce" that would be servant of the Gospel during "the long
millennial age" shortly to arrive.[37] This "friendly commerce"
could be taken as representative of that larger hope that all the
phenomena of the modern world—scientific advance, industrialism,
political liberty, affluence—could be retained, in spite of their

35. *Minutes of the General Assembly of the Presbyterian Church in the
United States of America, Old School* (1869), 18: 951.
36. For a development of this theme as a general principle for the interpretation of religion in America, see Clebsch, *From Sacred to Profane America.*
37. Published in *Christian Advocate and Journal*, January 28, 1869, pp.
26–27.

occasional unruliness, as handmaidens of Christian civilization. The Reverend S. P. Hickok of Amherst, Massachusetts, told the graduating seniors of Union College in 1868 that the "new heavens and new earth" whose advent they were witnessing would not be an order in which progress dissolved into selfish materialism or secularization. The coming era promised "a spiritual age . . . in which the rational shall rule the sensual, and holiness shall be sought rather than happiness."[38] In an essay written the same year, Horace Bushnell predicted that material prosperity in collusion with scientific advance was about to write "a new grand chapter" in the closing story of the New Jerusalem's descent to earth; and Albert Barnes grounded his faith in the future upon the conviction that the forces of secular progress in America had "an essential connection with Christianity. They become incorporated with it. They go with it. They carry Christianity with themselves wherever they go."[39] These were the authentic voices of a generation that had dared to believe that its national history was also a sacred history of redemption.

The presence of countervailing trends, however, deepened the awareness that this Christian civilization was not self-sustaining, and calls for renewed evangelization were in part attempts to forestall the possible collapse of the whole enterprise. The shadow of forces hostile to Christian America was a primary motivation to the reunion of the two branches of the Presbyterian Church in 1870. The New School Assembly warned in 1868: "Six millions of emigrants representing various religions and nationalities, have arrived on our shores within the last thirty years; and four millions of slaves, recently enfranchised, demand Christian education." Among these as well as among the native-born "anti-Christian forces—Romanism, Ecclesiasticism, Rationalism, Infidelity, Materialism, and Paganism itself— assuming new vitality, are struggling for the ascendancy." The herculean task before Protestantism was to create "one new American sentiment" among these "incongruous and antagonistic nationalities thrown up on our shores." To master these formidable challenges, denominations should pool their resources where possible. "Chris-

38. S. P. Hickok, "Humanity Progressing to Perfection," *American Presbyterian and Theological Review,* n.s. 6 (October 1868): 545.
39. Bushnell, *Building Eras in Religion,* pp. 21, 31; Barnes, *Life at Threescore and Ten,* pp. 130–31.

tian forces should be combined and deployed according to the new movements of their adversaries," the Assembly insisted. "It is not time for small or weak detachments, which may easily be defeated in detail. . . . The time has come when minor motives should be merged in the magnanimous purpose, inspired both by patriotism and religion, to Christianize the whole country."[40] Such pronouncements still exuded the optimistic faith that the battle would be won, but it was the confidence of the wary who know their supply lines to be vulnerable to attack.

Toward the close of the decade, the Reverend Joseph P. Thompson saw through the presses two articles that summarized the questions and anxieties of the churches. Thompson feared that in spite of the recent bloody expiation, Americans had not become one fully unified folk. Although the "war-baptism upon the brow of the Celt, or Saxon, of German, Gaul, or African" had temporarily made these one people, this enforced discipline was not proving a sufficient cord of unity. The Civil War had apparently set in motion an "almost preternatural, impulse to all mental and material activities"; and these uncontrolled explosions of energy were rapidly dissipating the national "life power." Democratic institutions nurtured a contentious people for whom equality meant general mediocrity "of intelligence and virtue" or common materialistic greed. Oblivious to these dangers, politicians encouraged the continued influx of the "crudest" immigrants who were fast becoming "a cause of disintegration within the heart of the state."[41] The new Israel needed to recall itself not merely for a season of bloodshed but, more permanently, to the discipline, order, and unity that made republicanism possible. As William James later argued in a different context, America's salvation from the fragmenting effects of affluence, democracy, and pluralism required a moral equivalent to war.

Without a higher concord than shared desire for personal aggrandizement, liberty was dangerous to order and sterile of purpose. Thompson urged Americans to be shut of the notion that the expansion of freedom was the solution of freedom's ills. This, he said, "is

40. *Minutes of the General Assembly of the Presbyterian Church in the United States of America, New School* (1868), 15: 28–30.

41. Joseph P. Thompson, "The Theocratic Principle; or, Religion the Bond of the Republic," *Home Missionary* 41 (August 1868): 85, 88; "How to Build a Nation," *New Englander* 28 (January 1869): 29, 30, 43.

like issuing bogus stock to cover the bankruptcy of the old." Instead, his fellow countrymen must accept fundamental restraints
upon the lust for democracy, wrongly understood. Against financial
interests clamoring for more foreigners to exploit America's resources, Protestants should caution that immigration was beneficial
only if first were secured one "race-stock sufficiently positive and
vigorous to assimilate all foreign elements into its own individu-
ality." Those enamored with economic mobility should be reminded
that labor was not "a bondage to be escaped" by achieving more pay
for less work, and the cracker-barrel democrats seeking equality via
the common denominator of mediocrity had to learn reverence for
the natural moral and intellectual aristocracy of the Republic.

> After the common school has graduated its millions in the
> rudiments of knowledge, these must yet be educated by minds
> trained in the highest forms of thought and the noblest views
> of truth. . . . Educated mind [must] solve for the nation its dis-
> turbing problems of finance and trade by guiding the people to
> sound notions of political economy; so must the men of wisdom
> guard the State by causing to be understood the principles of
> ethics by which alone the life of a nation can be maintained.[42]

What wise men would do for the ignorant, woman must do for the
whole of society. By maintaining in the homes of America a spiritual
influence unsullied by the contests of the male-dominated world,
she would exert "a conservative, elevating, purifying power . . . of
more value to the Republic than all the balances of the Constitution." Finally, the rapidity of social transformation should be
slowed "by a painstaking regard for the past, wrought into the
habits of the people." A sane future for America was assured "by
histories, by orations, and by monuments, by sacred graves worthy
of national pilgrimages, by memorial parks and statues, by storied
pictures in public halls, by legends and mottoes, by commemorative
services and martyr-days." Thus Americans could "keep ever bright
the links of historic continuity that preserve the nation through all
changes and all ages, one."[43]

42. "The Theocratic Principle," p. 90; "How to Build a Nation," pp. 27,
35, 45.
43. "How to Build a Nation," pp. 31, 40, 44.

Like Elisha Mulford who shortly gave classic expression to this longing, many Protestants were anxious to teach their fellow citizens that the nation was "not a confused collection of separate atoms, as grains of sand in a heap" but was rather a living entity with "unity and growth and identity of structure."[44] Such assertions were part of a search for an integrating center to American democracy, and they betokened no little apprehension about the future of the Republic. Lurking in such pronouncements was fear, as John Sproat has said of the liberal reformers of the Gilded Age, "that the American people as a whole were unworthy of self-government."[45] The United States, in short, had yet to realize that inner cohesion and loyalty which would enable an organic society to flourish amid free institutions.

The imposition of unity upon American life was an awesome task. Thompson wrote:

> We stand before a future, vast, momentous, appalling–big with opportunitity, with possibility, with destiny! The millions will come, are coming, are even at the door. The cities will rise, are rising, as by enchantment in a night. The railways will be built; already the tramp of the buffalo gives place to the thunder of the train, and the whoop of the savage to the whistle of steam. . . . But all these constituents of material greatness, whose bare statistics puzzle the brain, will bring with them elements of corruption and disintegration which must be counteracted by a vitalizing moral principle.[46]

His description of the American future–as both "appalling" and "big with opportunity"–was significant. Wealth, the cities, the newest Americans–these might be either blessings or curses, depending on the manner in which the challenge was met. One need not marvel at the disorienting impact of the new era into which Protestants were entering. They had just completed a struggle to secure God's order, had seemingly won their Armageddon, and already the forces of

44. Elisha Mulford, *The Nation: The Foundations of Civil Order and Political Life in the United States*, p. 9.

45. John G. Sproat, *"The Best Men": Liberal Reformers in the Gilded Age*, p. 271.

46. "The Theocratic Principle," p. 96.

disorder stood at the gate. With the expectation of assured success the legacy of their national experience, churchmen could only push forward once more in the weary, anxious hope that their Gospel could scatter the darkness. But the uncertainties remained. In the midst of its usual cheery observations after the triumph of Radical Reconstruction and the inauguration of President Grant, the *Independent* ruminated in a moment of depression: "Both President and Congress ought to unite in advertising a joint proposal: 'Wanted−A Moral Purpose.'"[47] That rubric might have stood as the masthead over the chapter of American history then opening.

47. *Independent,* March 25, 1869, p. 4.

# Epilogue

## American Protestantism in the Gilded Age

Robert H. Weibe has written that "America in the late nineteenth century was a society without a core," and the disunity of various aspects of national life confirms the accuracy of his judgment.[1] Although historians once tagged the postbellum period as a time of Republican ascendancy, the two major parties stood at virtual stalemate—Democrats actually winning a plurality of popular votes in more than half the presidential elections from 1868 through 1892. The inertia created by the absence of a dominant political majority was heightened by the lack of internal party cohesion; and the names *Democrat* and *Republican* were often little more than labels, trotted out at four-year intervals to unite hostile factions and virtually independent state parties. Giant corporations and the railroads may have appeared to aggrieved outsiders as monolithic entities, but they were often jerry-built aggregations of differing economic interests that were neither efficiently centralized nor streamlined. The government of large cities broke down as immigration destroyed the identity of old neighborhoods, and the efforts of well-meaning reformers inadvertently furthered the splintering process by undermining what little order the political machine had created. Many among the laboring classes and the farm population rose in anguished protest against the loss of self-mastery to the impersonal banks, railroads, and industry; and these people in turn, as striker or populist, symbolized to the middle-class American the terrifying forces disturbing his life. The United States had become, in Wiebe's apt phrase, a "distended society," and Henry Adams

1. Robert H. Wiebe, *The Search for Order, 1877–1920*, p. 12. Among the general works on the period from 1865 to 1900, see H. Wayne Morgan, ed., *The Gilded Age*, and Ari Hoogenboom and Olive Hoogenboom, eds., *The Gilded Age*.

provided another classic metaphor for the era: America was exemplifying the principle of entropy as its energies were dissipated from the center.[2]

In the midst of urban jungles and other dislocations, traditional religious beliefs fell upon evil days. Darwin's evolutionary hypothesis discounted the accuracy of Genesis and raised disturbing questions about the moral order of the cosmos. Formerly the rational handiwork of a benevolent God, the universe now seemed to dissolve into random chaos whose only law was the victory of the strongest; and man, the unique centerpiece of creation, was reduced to one of the warring species that had mucked its way out of the primeval slime. To their horror, the Protestant rank and file also learned the results of biblical criticism—that perhaps Moses did not write the Pentateuch, that accounts of miracle were myth, in short, that the premise of a verbally inerrant Bible had come under severe attack. Meanwhile liberalism smoothed the edges of orthodoxy, the comparative study of religions undercut Christianity's claim to uniqueness, and the new historical theology rejected the idea of a changeless faith once delivered to the saints. These trends did not, of course, suddenly erupt from nowhere, but they did intrude upon American thought more forcefully and painfully after 1870. Among the numerous signs that evangelical innocence had sustained a severe wound were religious debates in popular papers, much-publicized heresy trials, and a newly fashionable skepticism typified by the great agnostic Robert G. Ingersoll.[3]

2. Wiebe, *Search for Order*, p. 11. For an introduction to Adams's thought, consult William H. Jordy, *Henry Adams, Scientific Historian*.

3. For a general introduction to these issues, see Paul A. Carter, *The Spiritual Crisis of the Gilded Age;* D. H. Meyer, "American Intellectuals and the Victorian Crisis of Faith," *American Quarterly* 27 (December 1975): 585–603; and Arthur M. Schlesinger, "A Critical Period in American Religion, 1875–1900," *Proceedings of the Massachusetts Historical Society* 24 (June 1933): 523–48. The impact of Darwinian thought upon American religion is surveyed briefly in Bert James Lowenberg, "Darwinism comes to America, 1859–1900," *Mississippi Valley Historical Review* 28 (December 1940): 339–68, and in Paul F. Boller, Jr., *American Thought in Transition: The Impact of Evolutionary Naturalism, 1865-1900*, pp. 22–46. Although devoted almost exclusively to Great Britain, Gertrude Himmelfarb, *Darwin and the Darwinian Revolution*, is of inestimable value in comprehending the

Confused or angry, various movements registered their dissent against a discordant age. Charles T. Russell and his Jehovah's Witnesses waged a running battle against what they believed to be a decadent civilization. Certain that the world was rapidly sliding to the doom foretold in Scripture, they denounced the apostasy of Protestantism and flailed business and government with more than Marxist fervor. Another form of radical adventism appeared within the major churches. In 1876 clergy from several denominations organized annual meetings for Bible study—and later held two important conferences to examine the prophecies. At these gatherings was advanced a particular variant of premillennial theory known as dispensationalism, which constituted a stark repudiation of the millennial tradition studied in this book. The dispensationalists taught that the labor of the saints could in no way create the Kingdom of God on earth; indeed, their schemes reduced the church to a parenthesis within history, and history was rapidly hurtling toward its cataclysmic denouement. Closely tied to belief in the literal infallibility of the Bible, this viewpoint represented a self-conscious effort to create a bulwark against the encroachment of modern ideas. Other Christians, drawn mainly from the Methodist tradition, grew alarmed at the decorous worldliness of the churches; and renewing Wesley's pleas for perfect sanctification, many of them eventually broke away to form a variety of conservative holiness sects. Still others turned outside Protestantism to fill their needs; and for them theosophy, spiritualism, or Christian Science provided peace, harmony, and a sense of oneness with an apparently hostile universe.[4] The popularity of these diverse movements in the late

---

issues at stake in the evolutionary controversy. Various aspects of Protestant liberalism are analyzed in Sydney E. Ahlstrom, *The American Protestant Encounter with World Religions;* Kenneth Cauthen, *The Impact of American Religious Liberalism;* and William R. Hutchison, *The Modernist Impulse in American Protestantism.* On free thought, see Stow Persons, *Free Religion, An American Faith,* and Orvin Larson, *American Infidel: Robert G. Ingersoll, A Biography.*

4. On these various movements, see Kraus, *Dispensationalism in America;* Frederick E. Mayer, *Jehovah's Witnesses;* Donald B. Meyer, *The Positive Thinkers: A Study of the Quest for Health, Wealth, and Personal Power from Mary Baker Eddy to Norman Vincent Peale;* Sandeen, *Roots of Fundamentalism;* and Timothy L. Smith, *Called Unto Holiness; The Story of the Nazarenes: The Formative Years.*

nineteenth century offers striking testimony to the inability of mainline evangelicalism to alleviate the agony of numerous troubled souls and betokens what Paul Carter has styled "the spiritual crisis of the Gilded Age."

Yet the postwar period could also present a confident, even smug, countenance, and this image was at least superficially the predominant one. The age of Darwin was also the age of "Lemonade Lucy" Hayes's hymn sings and nonalcoholic soirées in the White House. It was also a time of sentimental gospel tunes dripping with "blessed assurance"—a comforting message reiterated in popular religious novels like Lew Wallace's *Ben Hur* or in the packed revival meetings of Dwight Moody and Ira Sankey. For many, the outward growth, prestige, and affluence of Protestantism seemed adequate refutation of the skeptics. When Ingersoll predicted the imminent collapse of Christianity, former Chaplain Charles McCabe sent him a telegraph pointing to statistics: "Dear Robert: All hail the power of Jesus' name—we are building more than one Methodist Church for every day in the year, and propose to make it two a day."[5] Church extension was only one of the vigorous demonstrations that hope of building the Kingdom of God in America still lived. Through the Women's Christian Temperance Union and later the Anti-Saloon League, Protestants renewed their effort to dry up every drop of alcohol in the land. The Social Gospel, in spite of its minority status in the churches, offered a significant new way to achieve the old goal of a Christian republic. During the last two decades of the century, the foreign missionary endeavor burgeoned into a mighty crusade, and the "evangelization of the world in this generation" stirred the campuses as profoundly, if not so disruptively, as antiwar protests or civil-rights marches have done more recently. Though this impulse was in some quarters associated exclusively with saving souls, the movement in general retained a close identification with belief in

5. McCabe is quoted in Winthrop S. Hudson, *American Protestantism*, p. 126. Information on popular novels and music can be found in Paul Carter, *The Spiritual Crisis of the Gilded Age*, pp. 275–88; Morgan, ed., *Gilded Age*, pp. 275–88; Henry Nash Smith, ed., *Popular Culture and Industrialism, 1865-1890*, pp. 505–19; and Willard Thorp, "The Religious Novel as Best Seller in America," in *Religious Perspectives in American Culture*, vol. 2 of *Religion in American Life*, ed. James Ward Smith and A. Leland Jamison, pp. 195–242.

the United States' onward march to save the world. That commitment to global mission played an important role in the jingoism of
the Spanish-American War, most Protestants suppressing initial
doubts to thump the drums for war and frequently for imperialism.
Thus its severe difficulties notwithstanding, the Gilded Age continued to hear a chorus of hopeful voices, and faith in the redeemer
nation's destiny was far from moribund.[6]

These expressions of confident purpose, however, were repeated
so frequently and so loudly that one detects a nervous effort at
self-reassurance. Or in Owen Chadwick's metaphor, Protestants
believed themselves safe but heard wolves in the underbrush and
built their protective hedges a little higher.[7] The extent to which
nostalgia and solace tinged popular piety testified inadvertently to
deeply felt anxieties. Religious novels, for example, often portrayed
the faith of a previous small-town generation whose familiar virtues
contrasted implicitly with the present disorder of sprawling cities.
Fiction also dwelt at length upon bereavement and personal immor-
tality, writers sometimes speculating with immodest precision
about the details of the future state. Not to appreciate the doubts
half-concealed in this morbid curiosity is to miss an important part
of the inner crisis of the Gilded Age. Similarly, hymns spoke of
languor and promised release as Christians retreated to a "sweet
hour of prayer, that calls me from a world of care" or longed for
"the sweet by and by."[8] Even in its activistic mode, Kingdom-
building zeal scarcely hid an awareness that enemies were fast
closing on the model republic, and it is significant that the mania

6. On the Social Gospel, see Charles Howard Hopkins, *The Rise of the
Social Gospel in American Protestantism, 1865–1915.* Also useful are Aaron I.
Abell, *The Urban Impact on American Protestantism, 1865–1900,* and Henry
F. May, *Protestant Churches and Industrial America.* The temperance move-
ment receives treatment in Earhart, *Frances Willard,* and Joseph R. Gusfield,
*Symbolic Crusade: Status Politics and the American Temperance Movement.*
The missionary spirit and its connection with imperialism are considered in
Kenneth M. MacKenzie, *The Robe and the Sword: The Methodist Church and
the Rise of Imperialism,* and Paul A. Varg, *Missionaries, Chinese and Diplo-
mats.* See also William A. Karraker, "The American Churches and the Spanish-
American War" (Ph.D. diss., University of Chicago, 1940).

7. Chadwick, *Victorian Church,* 1: 527.

8. On hymnology and novels, see the works cited in note 5 above.

for crusading was accompanied by a reawakened nativism, self-consciously racist and anxious to purge the land of un-American— that is, non-Protestant—practices.[9] Josiah Strong's classic *Our Country* (1886) demonstrated the integral relationship between doubt and confident chauvinism in the religious thought of the Gilded Age. His oft-quoted prediction that the Anglo-Saxons of the United States "will move down upon Mexico, down upon Central and South America, out upon the islands of the sea, over upon Africa and beyond" comes after more than one hundred pages of warnings that immigration, Roman Catholicism, Mormonism, intemperance, the cities, and socialism constituted horrendous dangers to the national life.[10] His jingoism was not a serene confidence in the unchallenged greatness of the Republic but a proposed remedy to counteract serious ills. The subtitle of his book captured the interdependence of the two themes succinctly—*Our Country: Its Possible Future and Its Present Crisis.* Faced with evidence disconfirming the expected glory, churchmen of Strong's persuasion retreated into shrill cries for redoubled sacrifice to salvage the threatened destiny.[11]

No one better exemplified the divided spirit of American Protestantism than Dwight L. Moody. A friend of dispensationalists and theological liberals alike, the great evangelist managed to absorb "the shock of warring parties in his own expansive personality," and his influence upon religious life was an ambiguous one.[12] On one hand, he was an activist in the tradition of the old united front, for he aimed at bringing together into one evangelical coalition Protestants of diverse persuasions. Closely identified with the YMCA during much of his career, he also exercised a decisive influence upon the Student Volunteer Movement for Foreign Missions,

9. This new outburst of nativism is discussed in Higham, *Strangers in the Land.*
10. Josiah Strong, *Our Country: Its Possible Future and Its Present Crisis,* ed. Jurgen Herbst, p. 214. His catalog of perils is discussed on pp. 41–186.
11. The thesis that disconfirmation of a belief system may, under certain circumstances, lead to a renewed commitment and proselytization is suggestively analyzed in Leon Festinger, Henry W. Riecken, and Stanley Schacter, *When Prophecy Fails.* This theory of "cognitive dissonance" has helped to form my interpretation of Gilded Age Protestantism.
12. Marty, *Righteous Empire,* pp. 180–81.

through which rose to prominence such great architects of the ecumenical movement as John R. Mott, Robert E. Speer, and Sherwood Eddy. Yet a strong note of reaction and unmitigated escapism was also apparent in Moody. Although he helped pioneer mass urban evangelism, his meetings did more to revive the ethos of his own village childhood than to confront the reality of the city. His sermons seldom alluded to the evils of metropolis, and his examples of piety were more often than not set in the idyllic context of a farm or a small town. It is little wonder that his appeal was largely restricted to the middle class, many of whom were in spirit, if not in fact, aliens in the midst of Babylon's satanic mills. Furthermore, Moody explicitly rejected the hope of the church's building the Kingdom of God on earth. A moderate premillennialist, he often preached that the world could be saved only after the Second Coming and urged Christians to concentrate on saving *individual* souls from judgment. "I look on this world as a wrecked vessel," he observed. "God has given me a life-boat and said to me, 'Moody, save all you can.'"[13]

These profound contrasts between hope and fear, crusades and doubts, give the Gilded Age what Sydney Ahlstrom calls "a strange formlessness."[14] This disorder was more extensive than other difficulties Protestantism had faced. Although serious problems threatened their hopes during the antebellum period, slavery had been the paramount conundrum vexing the religious community. In spite of its intractability, this dilemma was at least plainly recognizable, and most churchmen could share, no matter how severe their differences, the conviction that a common evangelical faith was shaping the destiny of the redeemer nation. In the postwar era, social problems were so complex and so diverse that few could delineate the issues with precision. Moreover, evangelical control of American life receded as immigrant groups gained greater power and as the churches confronted internal dissent, nagging uncertainty, and growing secularism. Amid these overpowering and barely understood forces, it was not surprising that Protestant response often lurched

13. James F. Findlay, Jr., *Dwight L. Moody: American Evangelist, 1837–1899*, p. 353 and passim. Also helpful is William G. McLoughlin, *Modern Revivalism: Charles Grandison Finney to Billy Graham*, pp. 217–81.
14. Ahlstrom, *Religious History of the American People*, p. 733.

from crusading to escapism. Prolonged stress demands relief in psychic withdrawal or in a cathartic burst of activity, and frequently the two moods oscillate. To assess the temper of the Gilded Age in this fashion is to perceive that disillusionment and strident reaffirmation were the Janus faces revealing an unprecedented challenge to a religious self-identity no longer able to integrate the facts of its life.

This reckoning would have come whether or not Americans had fought a civil war. Urbanization, industrialism, pluralism, and the various modes of scientific thought had unleashed their power against traditional dogmas before Sumter. Together these changes represented a long-term crisis of modernity afflicting Western civilization; but the nation's domestic turmoil had helped distract Americans from such problems and postponed the moment of full impact until accumulated forces descended with the strength of a drop-forger. Moreover, the ideology by which the Protestant majority had interpreted the war ill prepared them for the realities ahead. Cast as an apocalyptic struggle, the Civil War fostered the hope that the United States could secure a final resolution of its problems and a decisive vindication of its destiny. Slavery providentially ended, free institutions would function harmoniously, and the American people, at last one folk, would possess the internal cohesion and loyalty to make democracy truly viable. In conjunction with other simplistic notions about society and reform, such expectations promised a national future incomparably grand. Yet after Armageddon, the United States continued to encounter new problems. Reconstruction petered out inconclusively, and evangelical hopes for a unified Protestant republic went aground upon the divisive intellectual and social forces of the Gilded Age. Faced with corroboration that cherished dreams had not yet been realized, Protestants alternated between disillusionment and frantic activism. What sermons and press had taught them to expect simply was not happening.

This study has repeatedly emphasized the churches' faith in the United States as a new Israel, a nation set apart from all others for a special mission. Unless Americans could attain a unique status and a higher righteousness, they believed their corporate life meant nothing. The choice lay between dizzying grandeur or abysmal failure; no third option was available. Although this superhuman aspiration contributed admirable efforts at reform and self-criticism, it also tempted citizens to exaggerate their national achievement to measure up to the expected standard, and it left them especially susceptible to radical disillusionment. Given the religious commitments of the mid-nineteenth century, one perhaps cannot expect that Protestants would have acted otherwise; but had they been able to settle for a less exalted conception of the United States, they might not have been so easily driven into an irresponsible escape from social ills or into often futile crusades during the years from 1865 to 1900. Without question, the denominations would have maintained greater fidelity to the classic Christian tradition if they had claimed less for the Republic, and the nation itself would probably have been better for their reticence.

# Bibliography

*Primary Sources*

DENOMINATIONAL MINUTES

*Journal of the General Conference of the Methodist Episcopal Church, Held in Chicago, Ill., 1868.* New York: Carlton and Lanahan, 1868.

*Minutes of the General Assembly of the Presbyterian Church in the United States of America, New School.* New York: Presbyterian Publication Committee, 1860–69.

*Minutes of the General Assembly of the Presbyterian Church in the United States of America, Old School.* Philadelphia: Presbyterian Board of Publication, 1860–69.

PERIODICALS

*African Repository.* Washington, D.C. The monthly publication of the American Colonization Society.

*American Missionary.* New York. The monthly voice of the American Missionary Association.

*American Presbyterian and Theological Review.* New York. A quarterly espousing the moderate New School position and largely dominated by Union Seminary faculty.

*American Theological Review.* New York. Became *American Presbyterian and Theological Review* in 1863.

*Biblical Repertory and Princeton Review.* Philadelphia. The quarterly journal of Princeton Seminary and voice of Old School Presbyterianism.

*Bibliotheca Sacra.* Boston. A Congregational quarterly devoted largely to technical biblical and theological studies with occasional pieces on contemporary themes.

*Christian Advocate and Journal.* New York. The leading weekly of the Methodist Episcopal Church.

*Christian Review.* Boston. Baptist quarterly.

*Christian Watchman and Reflector.* Boston. Baptist weekly.

*Congregationalist.* Boston. Weekly.

*Continental Monthly.* Boston. A literary magazine.

*Home Missionary.* New York. Monthly publication of the American Home Missions Society.

*Independent.* New York. The leading religious weekly of the nation; interdenominational.

*Ladies' Repository.* Cincinnati. A monthly ladies' magazine published by the Methodist church.

*Methodist Quarterly Review.* New York.

*Missionary Magazine.* Boston. A monthly publication of the American Baptist Missionary Union.

*National Preacher.* New York. A monthly journal devoted to publishing sermons from clergy of the various evangelical denominations.

*New Englander.* New Haven. Quarterly journal espousing the religious views of the Yale faculty and Connecticut Congregationalism.

*Presbyterian.* Philadelphia. Weekly voice of Old School Presbyterianism.

### SERMONS, ADDRESSES, AND PAMPHLETS

Atterbury, John G. *God in Civil Government,* "A Discourse Preached in the First Presbyterian Church, New Albany, Nov. 27, 1862." New Albany: Geo. R. Beach, 1862.

Barnes, Albert. *The Love of Country,* "A Sermon Delivered in the First Presbyterian Church, Philadelphia. April 28, 1861." Philadelphia: C. Sherman and Son, 1861.

Bassett, George W. *A Discourse on the Wickedness and Folly of the Present War,* "Delivered in the Court House at Ottawa, Ill., on Sabbath, Aug. 11, 1861." N.d., n.p.

Beecher, Henry Ward. *Patriotic Addresses.* New York: Fords, Howard, and Hulbert, 1887.

Beman, N. S. *Thanksgiving in the Times of Civil War,* "A Discourse Preached in the First Presbyterian Church, Troy, New York, Nov. 28th, 1861." Troy: A. W. Scribner and Co., 1861.

Bentley, Edward W. *The Lord Our National God,* "A Sermon Preached Before the United Congregations of the Methodist Episcopal and Reformed Dutch Churches, in the M.E. Church, Ellenville, N.Y., Thursday, November 29th, 1860." New York: John A. Gray, 1860.

*The Bible on the Present Crisis.* New York: Sinclair Tousey, 1863.

Bingham, Joel F. *Great Providences Toward the Loyal Part of This Nation,* "A Discourse Delivered at a United Service of the Seven

Presbyterian Congregations of Buffalo, November 24, 1864."
Buffalo, N.Y.: Breed, Butler and Co., 1864.

———. *The Hour of Patriotism,* "A Discourse Delivered at the United
Service of the First, Lafayette Street, North, and Westminster
Presbyterian Churches, Buffalo, Nov. 27, 1862." Buffalo, N.Y.:
Franklin, 1862.

———. *National Disappointment,* "A Discourse Occasioned by the
Assassination of President Lincoln." Buffalo, N.Y.: Breed, Butler,
and Co., 1865.

Bittinger, J. B. *A Sermon Preached before the Presbyterian Churches
of Cleveland.* Cleveland: E. Cowles and Co., 1861.

Blake, Mortimer. *The Issues of the Rebellion,* "A Sermon Preached
Before the Taunton and Raynham Volunteers." Taunton: Republican Office, 1861.

Boardman, Henry A. *Thanksgiving in War,* "A Sermon, Preached in
the Tenth Presbyterian Church, Philadelphia, on the 28th Day of
November, 1861." Philadelphia: C. Sherman and Son, 1861.

———. *What Christianity Demands of Us at the Present Crisis,* "A
Sermon Preached on Thanksgiving Day, Nov. 29, 1860." Philadelphia: J. B. Lippincott and Co., 1860.

Bouton, Nathaniel. *Days of Adversity,* "A New Year's Sermon,
Preached in Concord, N.H., January 6, 1861." Concord: P. B.
Cogswell, 1861.

Bushnell, Horace. *Barbarism the First Danger.* New York: William
Osborn for the American Home Missionary Society, 1847.

———. *Building Eras in Religion.* New York: Charles Scribner's Sons,
1881.

———. *The Census and Slavery,* "A Thanksgiving Discourse, Delivered
in the Chapel at Clifton Springs, N.Y., November 29, 1860."
Hartford: Lucius E. Hunt, 1860.

———. *The Northern Iron,* "A Discourse Delivered in the North
Church, Hartford, on the Annual State Fast, April 14, 1854."
Hartford: Edwin Hunt and Son, 1854.

———. *Reverses Needed,* "A Discourse Delivered on the Sunday
after the Disaster of Bull Run, in the North Church, Hartford."
Hartford: L. E. Hunt, 1861.

———. *Work and Play; or Literary Varieties.* New York: Charles
Scribner, 1864.

Canfield, Sherman. *The American Crisis,* "A Discourse Delivered on
the Day of National Thanksgiving, November 24th, 1864." Syracuse: Journal Book and Job Office, 1865.

*Christ in the Army: A Selection of Sketches of the Work of the U.S.* *Christian Commission.* Philadelphia: J. B. Rodgers for the Ladies Christian Commission, 1865.

Clark, Frederick G. *Gold in the Fire: Our National Position,* "A Sermon Preached in the West Twenty-third Street Presbyterian Church, City of New York, on Thanksgiving Day, Nov. 27th, 1862." New York: John H. Duychinck, 1862.

Cleaveland, Elisha P. *Our Duty in Regard to the Rebellion,* "A Fast Day Sermon, Preached in the Third Congregational Church, New Haven, April 3, 1863." New Haven: Thomas H. Pease, 1863.

Corning, James Leonard. *Religion and Politics!* Milwaukee: Strickland and Co., 1860.

Darling, Henry. *Chastened, but Not Killed,* "A Discourse Delivered on the Day of the National Fast, August 4th, 1864." Albany: Van Benthuysen, 1864.

Dexter, Henry Martyn. *What Ought to Be Done with the Freedmen and with the Rebels?* "A Sermon Preached in the Berkeley Street Church, Boston, on Sunday, April 23, 1865." Boston: Nichols and Noyes, 1865.

Duffield, George, Jr. *The God of Our Fathers,* "An Historical Sermon Preached in the Coates' Street Presbyterian Church, Philadelphia, on Fast Day, January 4, 1861." Philadelphia: T. B. Pugh, 1861.

———. *The Great Rebellion Thus Far a Failure,* "A Thanksgiving Sermon Preached in the Presbyterian Church, Adrian, Michigan, November 28th, 1861." Adrian: S. P. Jermain and Co., 1861.

Dwight, William T. *The Nationality of a People, Its Vital Element,* "An Oration Delivered in the New City Hall Before the City Government, and Citizens, of Portland, July 4, 1861." Portland, Maine: N. A. Foster, 1861.

Dwinell, Israel E. *Hope for Our Country,* "A Sermon, Preached in the South Church, Salem, October 19, 1862." Salem: Charles W. Swasey, 1862.

Eddy, Daniel C. *Our Country: Its Pride and Its Peril,* "A Discourse Delivered in Harvard Street Baptist Church, Boston, August 11, 1861, on the Return of the Pastor from Syria." Boston: John M. Hewes, 1861.

———. *The Union, the Constitution and the Laws,* "A Discourse Delivered in the Tabernacle Church, Philadelphia, before the First and Tabernacle Baptist Congregations, on the National Fast Day, April 30th, 1863." Philadelphia: American Baptist Publication Society, 1863.

Eddy, Zachary. *A Discourse on the War*, "Preached to the North-ampton Volunteers Sunday Evening, April 28, 1861." Northampton, Mass.: Trumbull and Gere, 1861.

——. *Secession:—Shall It Be Peace or War?* "A Fast Day Sermon Delivered in the First Church, Northampton, April 4, 1861." Northampton, Mass.: Trumbull and Gere, 1861.

Eells, W. W. *How and Why We Give Thanks*, "A Thanksgiving Sermon Preached in the First Presbyterian Church, Pittsburgh, on Thursday, November 26th, 1863." Pittsburgh: W. S. Haven, 1864.

Eggleston, Nathaniel H. *Reasons for Thanksgiving*, "A Discourse to the Congregational Church and Society in Stockbridge, Mass., on the Day of Annual Thanksgiving, November 21, 1861." Pittsfield, Mass.: Henry Chickering, 1861.

Fish, Henry Clay. *The Duty of the Hour: or, Lessons from Our Reverses*. New York: Sheldon and Co., 1862.

——. *The Valley of Achor a Door of Hope; or the Grand Issues of the War*, "A Discourse Delivered on Thanksgiving Day, November 26, 1863." New York: Sheldon and Co., 1863.

Fisher, George P. *Thoughts Proper to the Present Crisis*, "A Sermon Preached in the Chapel of Yale College, on Fast Day, January 4, 1861." New Haven: Tuttle, Morehouse and Taylor, 1861.

Foss, Cyrus D. *Songs in the Night*. New York: N. Tibbals and Co., 1861.

Gaylord, William L. *The Soldier God's Minister*, "A Discourse Delivered in the Congregational Church, Fitzwilliam, N.H., Sabbath Afternoon, October 5, 1862, on the Occasion of the Departure of a Company of Volunteers for the Seat of War." Fitchburg, Mass.: Rollston, 1862.

Goodell, C. L. *Thanksgiving Sermon*, "Preached at the Union Service of the First and South Congregational Churches, New Britain, Conn., November 26, 1863." Hartford: Case, Lockwood and Company, 1863.

Goodrich, William H. *A Sermon on the Christian Necessity of War*. Cleveland: Fairbanks, Benedict and Co., 1861.

Gordon, Adoniram Judson. *The Chosen Fast*, "A Discourse Preached at a United Service Held at the Baptist Church, in Jamaica Plain, on the Occasion of the State Fast, Thursday, April 13th, 1865." Boston: N. P. Kemp, 1865.

Hall, Nathaniel. *The Moral Significance of the Contrasts Between Slavery and Freedom*, "A Discourse Preached in the First Church, Dorchester, May 10, 1864." Boston: Walker, Wise and Company, 1864.

Hamilton, D. H. *An Oration Before the Alumni of Union College.* Jacksonville: Journal Book and Job Print, 1863.

Harris, Samuel. *Our Country's Claim,* "Oration at the Citizens' Celebration of the Eighty-fifth Anniversary of the Declaration of Independence." Bangor, Maine: Wheeler and Lynde, 1861.

Haven, Gilbert. *National Sermons.* Boston: Lee and Shepherd, 1869.

Hibbard, F. G., ed. *Works of Rev. Leonidas Hamline, D.D.: Sermons.* Cincinnati: Hitchcock and Walden, 1869.

Hough, J. W. *Our Country's Mission, or the Present Suffering of the Nation Justified by Its Future Glory,* "A Discourse Preached at Williston, Vermont, on the Day of the National Fast, August 4th, 1864." Burlington, Vt.: Free Press, 1864.

Hovey, Horace. *Freedom's Banner,* "A Sermon Preached to the Coldwater Light Artillery and the Coldwater Zouave Cadets, April 28th, 1861." Coldwater, Mich.: 1861.

Humphrey, Heman. *Our Nation,* "A Discourse Delivered at Pittsfield, Mass., January 4, 1861." Pittsfield: Henry Chickering, 1861.

Ide, George. *Battle Echoes, or, Lessons From the War.* Boston: Gould and Lincoln, 1866.

Kimball, Henry. *The Ship of State Bound for Tarshish,* "A Sermon Preached in the First Congregational Church in Sandwich, November 21, 1861." Boston: Geo. C. Rand and Avery, 1861.

Kirk, Edward Norris. *A Sermon Preached Before the American Missionary Association.* New York: American Missionary Association, 1865.

Lanphear, O. T. *Peace by Power,* "A Discourse Preached in the College Street Church, New Haven, Sabbath Evening, Oct. 9, 1864." New Haven: J. H. Benham, 1864.

Leeds, S. P. *Thy Kingdom Come: Thy Will Be Done,* "A Discourse Delivered on the National Fast, Sept. 26, 1861, in the Congregational Church at Dartmouth College." Windsor, Vt.: Bishop and Tracy, 1861.

Lord, J. C. *On the Character and Influence of Washington,* "Delivered Before the Union Continentals of Buffalo, on Sabbath, February 22nd, 1863." Buffalo, N.Y.: A. M. Clapp and Co., 1863.

Magie, David. *A Discourse Delivered in the Second Presbyterian Church.* New York: Francis Hart and Co., 1863.

March, Daniel. *Steadfastness and Preparation in the Day of Adversity,* "A Sermon Preached in the Clinton Street Presbyterian Church, Philadelphia, September 14th, 1862." Philadelphia: C. Sherman and Son, 1862.

Marshall, James. *The Nation's Changes,* "A Discourse Delivered in the Chesapeake General Hospital, Near Fort Monroe, Va., on the Day of the National Thanksgiving, Nov. 26th, 1863." Baltimore: John F. Wiley, 1863.

———. *The Nation's Inquiry,* "A Discourse Delivered in the Chesapeake General Hospital, Near Fort Monroe, Va., on the Day of the National Fast, April 30, 1863." Philadelphia: King and Baird, 1863.

Nadal, B. H. *The War in the Light of Divine Providence.* New Haven: Tuttle, Morehouse and Taylor, 1863.

Nichols, Starr H. *Our Sins and Our Repentance,* "Preached September 26, 1861." Mansfield, Ohio: Pritchard, 1861.

Niles, William A. *Our Country's Peril and Hope,* "A Sermon Delivered on Occasion of the National Fast, January 4th, 1861, in the Presbyterian Church, Corning, N.Y." Corning: E. E. Robinson, 1861.

Ottman, S. *God Always for the Right, and Against Wrong,* "A Discourse Delivered on the Occasion of Our National Fast, January 4, 1861, to the Presbyterian Church at Pultney, N.Y." Pennyan, N.Y.: S. C. Cleveland, n.d.

Paine, Levi. *Political Lessons of the Rebellion,* "A Sermon Delivered at Farmington, Connecticut, on Fast Day, April 18, 1862." Farmington: Samuel Cowles, 1862.

Palmer, Ray. *The Opening Future: or the Results of the Present War,* "A Thanksgiving Discourse, November 26th, 1863." Albany: J. Munsell, 1863.

Peck, George. *Our Country: Its Trial and Triumph.* New York: Carlton and Porter, 1865.

Perrin, Lavalette. *The Claims of Caesar,* "A Sermon Preached in the Center Church, New Britain, May 19, 1861." Hartford: Case, Lockwood and Company, 1861.

Phelps, S. D. *National Symptoms,* "A Discourse Preached in the First Baptist Church, New Haven, on the Day of the Annual State Fast, April 18, 1862." New Haven: Thomas H. Pease, 1862.

Post, Henry A. *Sermon Preached in the Presbyterian Church, Warrenburgh.* Albany: Weed, Parsons and Company, 1861.

Post, Truman M. *Palingenesy: National Regeneration.* St. Louis: George Knapp and Co., 1864.

Prentiss, George L. *The Free Christian State and the Present Struggle,* "An Address Delivered Before the Association of the Alumni of Bowdoin College." New York: W. H. Bidwell, 1861.

Rankin, J. E. *The Battle Not Man's, But God's,* "A Discourse Delivered Before the United Congregational Churches in Lowell on the Day of National Thanksgiving, August 6th, 1863." Lowell, Mass.: Stone and Huse, 1863.

Smith, Henry. *God in the War,* "A Discourse Preached in Behalf of the U.S. Christian Commission on the Day of National Thanksgiving, August 6th, 1863." 3d ed. Buffalo, N.Y.: Wheeler, Matthews and Warren, 1863.

Smith, Moses. *God's Honor Man's Ultimate Success,* "A Sermon Preached on Sunday, September 27th, 1863." New Haven: Thomas J. Stafford, 1863.

Spear, Samuel T. *The Nation's Blessing in Trial,* "A Sermon Preached in the South Presbyterian Church of Brooklyn." Brooklyn: Wm. W. Rose, 1862.

———. *Two Sermons for the Times.* New York: Nathan Lane and Co., 1861.

Sprague, William B. *Glorifying God in the Fires,* "A Discourse Delivered in the Second Presbyterian Church, Albany, November 28, 1861, the Day of the Annual Thanksgiving, in the State of New York." Albany: C. Van Benthuysen, 1861.

Spring, Gardiner. *State Thanksgiving During the Rebellion,* "A Sermon Preached November 28, 1861." New York: Harper and Brothers, 1862.

Stearns, William A. *Necessities of the War and the Conditions of Success in It,* "A Sermon Preached in the Village Church before the College and United Congregations of the Town of Amherst, Mass." Amherst: Henry A. March, 1861.

Stone, A. L. *The Divineness of Human Government,* "A Discourse Delivered in the Park Street Church." Boston: Henry Hoyt, 1861.

———. *Emancipation,* "A Discourse Delivered in Park Street Church, on Fast Day Morning, April 3, 1862." Boston: Henry Hoyt, 1862.

Sunderland, Byron. *The Crisis of the Times,* "A Sermon Preached in the First Presbyterian Church, Washington, D.C., on the Evening of the National Fast, Thursday, April 30, 1863." Washington, D.C.: National Banner Press, 1863.

Tappan, Lewis. *The War: Its Cause and Remedy; Immediate Emancipation: The Only Wise and Safe Mode.* In vol. 1 of *Union Pamphlets of the Civil War.* 2 vols. Edited by Frank Freidel. Cambridge: Belknap Press of the Harvard University Press, 1967.

Tarbox, Increase N. *The Curse; or, The Position in the World's History Occupied by the Race of Ham.* Boston: American Tract Society, 1864.

Thome, James. *The Future of the Freed People*. Cincinnati: American Reform Tract and Book Society, 1863.

Thompson, Joseph P. *The President's Fast*, "Preached in the Broadway Tabernacle Church, January 4, 1861." New York: Thomas Holman, 1861.

——. *The Psalter and the Sword*, "A Sermon Preached in the Broadway Tabernacle Church, on Thanksgiving Day, November 7, 1862." New York: L. S. Harrison, 1863.

Thompson, M. L. P. *Discourses*, "Preached in the Second Presbyterian Church, Cincinnati, Ohio, September 26 and November 28, 1861." Cincinnati: Gazette Company, 1861.

Van Dyke, Henry J. *The Character and Influence of Abolitionism*, "A Sermon Preached in the First Presbyterian Church, Brooklyn, on Sabbath Evening December 9th, 1860." New York: D. Appleton and Company, 1860.

——. *The Spirituality and Independence of the Church*. New York, 1864.

Vincent, Marvin R. *Our National Discipline*, "A Thanksgiving Sermon, Preached in the First Presbyterian Church, Troy, N.Y., Nov. 26, 1863." Troy: A. W. Scribner, 1863.

Walker, George Leon. *The Offered National Regeneration*, "A Sermon Preached in the State Street Church, Portland, on the Occasion of the National Fast, September 26, 1861." Portland, Maine: Little, Bro., and Co., 1861.

Webb, Edwin. *Memorial Sermons*. Boston: Geo. C. Rand and Avery, 1865.

West, Nathaniel, Jr. *Establishment in National Righteousness*, "A Sermon Preached in the Second Presbyterian Church, Brooklyn, N.Y." New York: John F. Trow, 1861.

Williams, Lester, Jr. *Freedom of Speech and the Union*, "A Discourse Delivered December 30, 1860, at Holden, Mass." Worcester, Mass.: Charles Hamilton, n.d.

Willson, Edmund B. *Reasons for Thanksgiving*, "A Sermon Preached in the North Church, Salem, April 20, 1862." Salem, Mass.: Observer, 1862.

Wilson, James P. *Our National Fast*, "A Sermon Preached in the South Park Presbyterian Church, January 4th, 1861." Newark, N.J.: A. Stephen Holbrook, 1861.

OTHER CONTEMPORARY SOURCES

Adams, Charles Francis, ed. *The Works of John Adams*. 10 vols. Boston: Charles C. Little and James Brown, 1851.

Bacon, Leonard. *Slavery Discussed in Occasional Essays, from 1833 to 1846.* New York: Baker and Scribner, 1846.

Baird, Robert. *Religion in America.* Edited by Henry Warner Bowden. New York: Harper & Row, 1970.

Bangs, Heman. *The Autobiography and Journal of Rev. Heman Bangs.* New York: N. Tibbals and Son, 1872.

Barnes, Albert. *Life at Threescore and Ten.* New York: American Tract Society, 1871.

Beecher, Edward. *Narrative of Riots at Alton in Connection with the Death of Rev. Elijah P. Lovejoy.* Alton: George Holton, 1838.

Beecher, Lyman. *The Autobiography of Lyman Beecher.* Edited by Barbara M. Cross. 2 vols. Cambridge: Belknap Press of the Harvard University Press, 1961.

Boynton, Charles Brandon. *History of the Great Western Sanitary Fair.* Cincinnati: C. F. Vent and Co., 1864.

Brockett, Linus P. *The Philanthropic Results of the War in America.* New York: Sheldon and Co., 1864.

———, and Vaughn, Mary C. *Woman's Work in the Civil War: A Record of Heroism, Patriotism and Patience.* Philadelphia: Zeigler, McCurdy and Co., 1867.

Cogswell, William. *The Harbinger of the Millennium.* Boston: Peirce and Parker, 1833.

Crèvecoeur, J. Hector St. John de. *Letters from an American Farmer and Sketches of Eighteenth Century America.* New American Library, 1963.

Crooks, George R. *The Life of Bishop Matthew Simpson.* New York: Harper and Brothers, 1891.

Dow, Lorenzo. *History of Cosmopolite: or the Writings of Rev. Lorenzo Dow.* Philadelphia: Jas. B. Smith and Co., 1859.

Edwards, Jonathan. *A History of the Work of Redemption.* New York: American Tract Society, 1838.

Emerson, Joseph. *Lectures on the Millennium.* Boston: Samuel T. Armstrong, 1818.

Finney, Charles Grandison. *Lectures on Revivals of Religion.* Edited by William G. McLoughlin. Cambridge: Belknap Press of the Harvard University Press, 1960.

Fish Henry C. *Primitive Piety Revived, or the Aggressive Power of the Christian Church.* Boston: Congregational Board of Publication, 1855.

French, Austa M. *Slavery in South Carolina.* New York: Winchell M. French, 1862.

Fuller, Richard and Wayland, Francis. *Domestic Slavery Considered as a Scriptural Institution.* New York: Lewis Colby and Co., 1847.

Gordon, Ernest B. *Adoniram Judson Gordon.* New York: Fleming H. Revell, 1896.

Grierson, Francis. *The Valley of Shadows: Recollections of the Lincoln Country, 1858–1863.* Boston and New York: Houghton Mifflin Company, 1909.

Hamilton, Alexander; Madison, James; and Jay, John. *The Federalist Papers.* New York: New American Library, 1961.

Helper, Hinton Rowan. *The Impending Crisis.* New York: Burdick Brothers, 1857.

———. *Nojoque: Question for a Continent.* New York: G. W. Carleton and Co., 1867.

Hodge, Archibald Alexander. *The Life of Charles Hodge, D.D., L.L.D.* New York: Charles Scribner's Sons, 1880.

Hopkins, Samuel. *A Treatise on the Millennium.* Boston: Isaiah Thomas and Ebenezer T. Andrews, 1793.

———. *The Works of Samuel Hopkins.* 3 vols. Boston: Doctrinal Tract and Book Society, 1852.

Howe, Julia Ward. *Reminiscences, 1819–1899.* Afro-American Studies. New York: New American Library, 1969.

Johnson, Edward. *Wonder-Working Providence.* Edited by J. Franklin Jameson. New York: Charles Scribner's Sons, 1910.

Marlay, John F. *The Life of Rev. Thomas A. Morris, D.D.* Cincinnati: Hitchcock and Walden, 1875.

Matlack, Lucius. *Antislavery Struggle and Triumph in the Methodist Episcopal Church.* New York: Phillips and Hunt, 1881.

Mears, David O. *Life of Edward Norris Kirk, D.D.* Boston: Lockwood, Brooks, and Company, 1877.

Moss, Lemuel. *Annals of the United States Christian Commission.* Philadelphia: J. B. Lippincott and Co., 1868.

Mulford, Elisha. *The Nation: The Foundations of Civil Order and Political Life in the United States.* New York: Hurd and Houghton, 1870.

Palmer, Benjamin M. *The Life and Letters of James Henley Thornwell.* Richmond: Whittel and Sheperson, 1875.

Palmer, Walter C. *Life and Letters of Leonidas L. Hamline, D.D.* New York: Carlton and Porter, 1866.

Peck, George. *The Life and Times of George Peck, D.D.* New York: Nelson and Phillips, 1874.

Post, Truman A. *Truman Marcellus Post, D.D.* Boston: Congregational Sunday-School and Publishing Society, 1891.

*Presbyterian Reunion: A Memorial Volume.* New York: DeWitt C. Lent and Company, 1870.

Read, Hollis. *The Coming Crisis of the World, or the Great Battle and the Golden Age.* Columbus: Follett, Foster and Company, 1861.

———. *The Negro Problem Solved.* New York: A. A. Constantine, 1864.

*The Sanitary Commission of the United States Army: A Succinct Narrative of Its Works and Purposes.* New York: 1864.

Schaff, Philip. *America: A Sketch of Its Political, Social, and Religious Character.* Edited by Perry Miller. Cambridge: Belknap Press of the Harvard University Press, 1961.

Smith, Edward P. *Incidents of the United States Christian Commission.* Philadelphia: J. B. Lippincott and Co., 1869.

Stearns, Lewis F. *Henry Boynton Smith.* New York: Houghton Mifflin and Co., 1892.

Stowe, Harriet Beecher. *Poganuc People: Their Loves and Their Lives.* New York: Fords, Howard and Hulbert, 1878.

———. *Uncle Tom's Cabin.* New York: New American Library, 1966.

Strong, Josiah. *Our Country: Its Possible Future and Its Present Crisis.* Edited by Jurgen Herbst. Cambridge: Belknap Press of the Harvard University Press, 1963.

Thompson, Robert Ellis, ed. *The Life of George H. Stuart.* Philadelphia: J. M. Stoddart and Co., 1890.

Tourgée, Albion. *A Fool's Errand.* New York: Fords, Howard and Hulbert, 1880.

Wayland, Francis. *The Elements of Moral Science.* Boston: Gould, Kendell, and Lincoln, 1849.

Wayland, Francis, Jr., and Wayland, H. L. *A Memoir of the Life and Labors of Francis Wayland, D.D., L.L.D.* 2 vols. New York: Sheldon and Company, 1867.

### Secondary Sources

Aaron, Daniel. *The Unwritten War: American Writers and the Civil War.* New York: Alfred A. Knopf, 1973.

Abell, Aaron I. *The Urban Impact on American Protestantism, 1865–1900.* Cambridge: Harvard University Press, 1943.

Ahlstrom, Sydney E. *The American Protestant Encounter with World Religions.* Beloit, Wis.: Beloit College, 1962.

———. *A Religious History of the American People.* New Haven: Yale University Press, 1972.

Albrecht, Robert M. "The Theological Response of the Transcendentalists to the Civil War." *New England Quarterly* 38 (March 1965): 21–34.

Bailyn, Bernard. *The Ideological Origins of the American Revolution.* Cambridge: Belknap Press of the Harvard University Press, 1967.

Baker, Robert A. *Relations Between Northern and Southern Baptists.* Fort Worth, Tex.: Seminary Hill Press, 1948.

Barnes, Gilbert Hobbs. *The Anti-Slavery Impulse, 1830–1844.* New York: D. Appleton-Century Co., 1933.

Basler, Roy, ed. *Abraham Lincoln: His Speeches and Writings.* Cleveland: World Publishing Company, 1946.

Beam, Christopher M. "Millennialism and American Nationalism, 1740–1800." *Journal of Presbyterian History* 54 (Spring 1976): 182–99.

Beard, Augustus Field. *A Crusade of Brotherhood: A History of the American Missionary Association.* Boston: Pilgrim Press,1909.

Beardsley, Frank Grenville. *A History of American Revivals.* 3d ed. New York: American Tract Society, 1912.

Beitzinger, A. J. *A History of American Political Thought.* New York: Dodd, Mead and Co., 1972.

Bellah, Robert N. "Civil Religion in America," *Daedalus* 96 (Winter 1967): 1–21.

Bertelson, David. *The Lazy South.* New York: Oxford University Press, 1967.

Billington, Ray A. *The Protestant Crusade, 1800–1860: A Study of the Origins of American Nativism.* New York: Macmillan, 1938.

Blassingame, John W. *The Slave Community: Plantation Life in the Antebellum South.* New York: Oxford University Press, 1972.

Bodo, John R. *The Protestant Clergy and Public Issues, 1812–1848.* Princeton: Princeton University Press, 1954.

Boller, Paul F., Jr. *American Thought in Transition: The Impact of Evolutionary Naturalism, 1865–1900.* Chicago: Rand McNally and Co., 1969.

Bremner, Robert H. *American Philanthropy.* Chicago: University of Chicago Press, 1960.

Bridenbaugh, Carl. *Mitre and Sceptre: Transatlantic Faiths, Ideas, Personalities and Politics.* New York: Oxford University Press, 1962.

Brock, Peter. *Radical Pacifists in Antebellum America.* Princeton: Princeton University Press, 1968.

Brock, William R. *An American Crisis: Congress and Reconstruction.* New York: St. Martin's Press, 1963.

———. *Conflict and Transformation: The United States, 1844–1877.* Baltimore: Penguin Books, 1973.

Brown, Ira. "Watchers for the Second Coming: The Millennial Tradition in America." *Mississippi Valley Historical Review* 39 (December 1952): 441–45.

Bucke, Emory Stevens, ed. *The History of American Methodism.* 3 vols. Nashville: Abingdon Press, 1964.

Burns, Edward McNall. *The American Idea of Mission: Concepts of National Purpose and Destiny.* New Brunswick, N.J.: Rutgers University Press, 1957.

Capp, B. S. *The Fifth Monarchy Men: A Study in Seventeenth-century Millenarianism.* Totowa, N.J.: Rowman and Littlefield, 1972.

Carter, Paul A. *The Spiritual Crisis of the Gilded Age.* DeKalb, Ill.: Northern Illinois University Press, 1971.

Cash, Wilbur J. *The Mind of the South.* Garden City, N.Y.: Doubleday and Co., 1954.

Cauthen, Kenneth. *The Impact of American Religious Liberalism.* New York: Harper & Row, 1962.

Chadwick, Owen. *The Victorian Church.* 2 vols. New York: Oxford University Press, 1966.

Cherry, Conrad, ed. *God's New Israel: Religious Interpretations of American Destiny.* Englewood Cliffs, N.J.: Prentice-Hall, 1971.

Clebsch, William A. "American Churches as Traducers of Tradition." *Anglican Theological Review* 52 (January 1971): 21–34.

———. "Christian Interpretations of the Civil War." *Church History* 30 (June 1961): 212–22.

———. *From Sacred to Profane America: The Role of Religion in American History.* New York: Harper & Row, 1968.

Cohn, Norman. *The Pursuit of the Millennium.* New York: Oxford University Press, 1957.

Cole, Charles C., Jr. *The Social Ideas of the Northern Evangelists, 1826–1860.* New York: Columbia University Press, 1954.

Cross, Whitney R. *The Burned-over District: The Social and Intellectual History of Enthusiastic Religion in Western New York, 1800–1850.* Ithaca, N.Y.: Cornell University Press, 1950.

Davidson, James W. "Eschatology in New England: 1700–1763." Ph.D. dissertation, Yale University, 1973.

Davis, David Brion. "The Emergence of Immediatism in British and American Antislavery Thought." *Mississippi Valley Historical Review* 49 (September 1962): 204–30.

——. *The Fear of Conspiracy: Images of Un-American Subversion from the Revolution to the Present.* Ithaca, N.Y.: Cornell University Press, 1971.

——. *The Problem of Slavery in the Age of Revolution, 1770–1823.* Ithaca, N.Y.: Cornell University Press, 1975.

——. *The Problem of Slavery in Western Culture.* Ithaca, N.Y.: Cornell University Press, 1966.

——. *The Slave Power Conspiracy and the Paranoid Style.* Baton Rouge: Louisiana State University Press, 1969.

——. "Some Themes of Countersubversion: An Analysis of Anti-Masonic, Anti-Catholic, and Anti-Mormon Literature." *Mississippi Valley Historical Review* 47 (September 1960): 205–25.

Degler, Carl N. *Neither Black nor White: Slavery and Race Relations in Brazil and the United States.* New York: Macmillan, 1971.

Drake, Richard B. "The American Missionary Association and the Southern Negro, 1861–1888." Ph.D. dissertation, Emory University, 1957.

——. "Freedmen's Aid Societies and Sectional Compromise." *Journal of Southern History* 29 (May 1963): 175–86.

Duberman, Martin, ed. *The Antislavery Vanguard: New Essays on the Abolitionists.* Princeton: Princeton University Press, 1965.

Dunham, Chester A. *The Attitude of the Northern Clergy toward the South, 1860–1865.* Toledo, Ohio: Gray Company, 1942.

Earhart, Mary. *Frances Willard: From Prayers to Politics.* Chicago: University of Chicago Press, 1944.

Elkins, Stanley. *Slavery: A Problem in American Institutional Life.* Chicago: University of Chicago Press, 1959.

Ellis, John Tracy. *American Catholicism.* Garden City, N.Y.: Image Books, Doubleday and Company, 1965.

Ellsworth, Clayton Sumner. "The American Churches and the Mexican War." *American Historical Review* 45 (January 1940): 301–26.

Elsbree, Oliver W. *The Rise of the Missionary Spirit in America.* Williamsport, Pa.: Williamsport Printing and Binding Co., 1928.

Elson, Ruth Miller. *Guardians of Tradition: American Schoolbooks in the Nineteenth Century.* Lincoln: University of Nebraska Press, 1964.

Engelder, Conrad James. "The Churches and Slavery: A Study of the Attitudes Toward Slavery of the Major Protestant Denominations." Ph.D. dissertation, University of Michigan, 1964.

Festinger, Leon; Riecken, Henry W.; and Schacter, Stanley. *When Prophecy Fails.* Minneapolis: University of Minnesota Press, 1956.

Filler, Louis. *The Crusade Against Slavery, 1830–1860.* The New American Nation Series. New York: Harper and Brothers, 1960.

——. "Liberalism, Anti-Slavery and the Founding of the Independent." *New England Quarterly* 27 (September 1954): 291–306.

Findlay, James F., Jr. *Dwight L. Moody: American Evangelist, 1837–1899.* Chicago: University of Chicago Press, 1969.

Fogel, Robert William, and Engerman, Stanley L. *Time on the Cross: The Economics of American Negro Slavery.* Boston: Little, Brown and Company, 1974.

Foster, Charles I. *An Errand of Mercy: The Evangelical United Front, 1790–1837.* Chapel Hill: University of North Carolina Press, 1960.

Francis, Russell E. "Pentecost: 1858." Ph.D. dissertation, University of Pennsylvania, 1948.

Franklin, John Hope. *Reconstruction: After the Civil War.* Chicago: University of Chicago Press, 1961.

Fredrickson, George M. *The Black Image in the White Mind: The Debate on Afro-American Character and Destiny, 1817–1914.* New York: Harper & Row, 1971.

——. *The Inner Civil War: Northern Intellectuals and the Crisis of the Union.* New York: Harper & Row, 1965.

Froom, Le Roy Edwin. *The Prophetic Faith of Our Fathers.* 4 vols. Washington, D.C.: Review and Herald Association Press, 1946–54.

Gabriel, Ralph Henry. *The Course of American Democratic Thought.* New York: Ronald Press, 1940.

Gaustad, Edwin S., ed. *The Rise of Adventism.* New York: Harper & Row, 1974.

Genovese, Eugene D. *Roll, Jordan, Roll: The World the Slaves Made.* New York: Pantheon, 1974.

Geyl, Pieter. "The American Civil War and the Problem of Inevitability." *The New England Quarterly* 24 (June 1951): 147–68.

Goen, C. C. "Jonathan Edwards: A New Departure in Eschatology." *Church History* 28 (March 1959): 25–40.

Goodykoontz, Colin Brummitt. *Home Missions on the American*

*Frontier, with Particular Reference to the American Home Missionary Society.* Caldwell, Idaho: Caxton, 1939.

Gravely, William. *Gilbert Haven, Methodist Abolitionist: A Study in Race, Religion, and Reform, 1850–1900.* Nashville: Abingdon Press, 1973.

Gray, Wood. *The Hidden Civil War: The Story of the Copperheads.* New York: Viking Press, 1942.

Gribbin, William. *The Churches Militant: The War of 1812 and American Religion.* New Haven: Yale University Press, 1973.

Griffin, Clifford S. *Their Brothers' Keepers: Moral Stewardship in the United States, 1800–1865.* New Brunswick, N.J.: Rutgers University Press, 1960.

Gusfield, Joseph R. *Symbolic Crusade: Status Politics and the American Temperance Movement.* Urbana: University of Illinois Press, 1963.

Gutman, Herbert G. *The Black Family in Slavery and Freedom, 1750–1925.* New York: Pantheon, 1976.

——. *Slavery and the Numbers Game: A Critique of Time on the Cross.* Urbana: University of Illinois Press, 1975.

Handy, Robert T. *A Christian America: Protestant Hopes and Historical Realities.* New York: Oxford University Press, 1971.

Hatch, Nathan O. "The Origins of Civil Millennialism in America: New England Clergymen, the War with France, and the Revolution." *William and Mary Quarterly,* 3d ser. 31 (July 1974): 407–30.

Heimert, Alan E. *Religion and the American Mind: From the Great Awakening to the Revolution.* Cambridge: Harvard University Press, 1966.

Higham, John. *Strangers in the Land: Patterns of American Nativism. 1860–1925.* New Brunswick, N.J.: Rutgers University Press, 1963.

Himmelfarb, Gertrude. *Darwin and the Darwinian Revolution.* Garden City, N.Y.: Doubleday and Co., 1959.

Hirshon, Stanley P. *Farewell to the Bloody Shirt: Northern Republicans and the Southern Negro, 1877–1893.* Bloomington: Indiana University Press, 1962.

Hoogenboom, Ari, and Hoogenboom, Olive, eds. *The Gilded Age.* Englewood Cliffs, N.J.: Prentice-Hall, 1967.

Hopkins, Charles Howard. *History of the Y.M.C.A. in North America.* New York: Association Press, 1951.

———. *The Rise of the Social Gospel in American Protestantism, 1865–1915.* New Haven: Yale University Press, 1940.

Houghton, Walter E. *The Victorian Frame of Mind, 1830–1870.* New Haven: Yale University Press, 1957.

Howard, Victor B. "The Anti-Slavery Movement in the Presbyterian Church, 1835–1861." Ph.D. dissertation, Ohio State University, 1961.

Hudson, Winthrop S. *American Protestantism.* Chicago: University of Chicago Press, 1961.

———. *Nationalism and Religion in America: Concepts of American Identity and Mission.* New York: Harper & Row, 1970.

Hutchison, William R. *The Modernist Impulse in American Protestantism.* Cambridge: Harvard University Press, 1976.

Hyman, Harold M., ed. *Heard Round the World.* New York: Alfred A. Knopf, 1969.

———. *A More Perfect Union: The Impact of the Civil War and Reconstruction on the Constitution.* New York: Alfred A. Knopf, 1973.

———. *To Try Men's Souls: Loyalty Tests in American History.* Berkeley and Los Angeles: University of California Press, 1959.

Jenkins, Frank E. *Anglo-Saxon Congregationalism in the South.* Atlanta: Franklin-Turner Company, 1908.

Jordan, Winthrop D. *White over Black: American Attitudes Toward the Negro, 1550–1812.* Chapel Hill: University of North Carolina Press, 1968.

Jordy, William H. *Henry Adams, Scientific Historian.* New Haven: Yale University Press, 1952.

Karraker, William A. "The American Churches and the Spanish-American War." Ph.D. dissertation, University of Chicago, 1940.

Kirby, James E. "Matthew Simpson and the Mission of America." *Church History* 36 (September 1967): 299–307.

Klement, Frank L. *The Copperheads in the Middle West.* Chicago: University of Chicago Press, 1960.

Kohn, Hans. *Nationalism: Its Meaning and History.* Princeton: Van Nostrand, 1965.

Kraditor, Aileen S. *Means and Ends in American Abolitionism: Garrison and His Critics on Strategy and Tactics, 1834–1850.* New York: Random House, 1969.

———, ed. *Up from the Pedestal: Selected Writings in the History of American Feminism.* Chicago: Quadrangle Books, 1968.

Kraus, C. Norman. *Dispensationalism in America: Its Rise and Development.* Richmond: John Knox Press, 1958.

Krout, John Allen. *The Origins of Prohibition.* New York: Alfred A. Knopf, 1925.

Larson, Orvin. *American Infidel: Robert G. Ingersoll, A Biography.* New York: Citadel Press, 1962.

Lewis, R. W. B. *The American Adam: Innocence, Tragedy and Tradition in the Nineteenth Century.* Chicago: University of Chicago Press, 1955.

Little, David. *Religion, Order, and Law: A Study in Pre-Revolutionary England.* New York: Harper & Row, 1969.

Long, Charles. "Civil Rights—Civil Religion: Visible People and Invisible Religion." In *American Civil Religion,* edited by Russell E. Richey and Donald G. Jones. New York: Harper & Row, 1974.

Lowenberg, Bert James. "Darwinism Comes to America, 1859–1900." *Mississippi Valley Historical Review* 28 (December 1940): 339–68.

McFeely, William S. *Yankee Stepfather: General O. O. Howard and the Freedmen.* New Haven: Yale University Press, 1968.

MacKenzie, Kenneth M. *The Robe and the Sword: The Methodist Church and the Rise of Imperialism.* Washington, D.C.: Public Affairs Press, 1961.

MacLear, James F. "New England and the Fifth Monarchy: The Quest for the Millennium in Early American Puritanism." *William and Mary Quarterly,* 3d ser. 32 (April 1975): 223–60.

———. "The Republic and the Millennium." In *The Religion of the Republic,* edited by Elwyn A. Smith. Philadelphia: Fortress Press, 1971.

McKittrick, Eric L. *Andrew Johnson and Reconstruction.* Chicago: University of Chicago Press, 1960.

McLoughlin, William G. *Modern Revivalism: Charles Grandison Finney to Billy Graham.* New York: Ronald Press, 1959.

McPherson, James M. *The Struggle for Equality: Abolitionists and the Negro in the Civil War and Reconstruction.* Princeton: Princeton University Press, 1964.

Marsden, George M. *The Evangelical Mind and the New School Presbyterian Experience: A Case Study of Thought and Theology in Nineteenth Century America.* New Haven: Yale University Press, 1970.

Marty, Martin E. *The Modern Schism: Three Paths to the Secular.* New York: Harper & Row, 1969.

——. *Righteous Empire: The Protestant Experience in America.* New York: Dial Press, 1970.

Marx, Leo. *The Machine in the Garden: Technology and the Pastoral Ideal in America.* New York: Oxford University Press, 1964.

Mathews, Donald G. *Slavery and Methodism: A Chapter in American Morality, 1780–1845.* Princeton: Princeton University Press, 1965.

Maxwell, William Quentin. *Lincoln's Fifth Wheel: The Political History of the United States Sanitary Commission.* New York: Longmans, Green and Co., 1956.

May, Henry F. *The Enlightenment in America.* New York: Oxford University Press, 1976.

——. *Protestant Churches and Industrial America.* New York: Harper & Row, 1949.

Mayer, Frederick E. *Jehovah's Witnesses.* St. Louis: Concordia Publishing House, 1952.

Mead, Sidney E. *The Lively Experiment: The Shaping of Christianity in America.* New York: Harper & Row, 1963.

Meredith, Robert. *The Politics of the Universe: Edward Beecher, Abolition, and Orthodoxy.* Nashville: Vanderbilt University Press, 1968.

Meyer, Donald B. *The Positive Thinkers: A Study of the Quest for Health, Wealth, and Personal Power from Mary Baker Eddy to Norman Vincent Peale.* Garden City, N.Y.: Doubleday and Co., 1965.

Meyer, D. H. "American Intellectuals and the Victorian Crisis of Faith." *American Quarterly* 27 (December 1975): 583–603.

——. *The Instructed Conscience: The Shaping of the American National Ethic.* Philadelphia: University of Pennsylvania Press, 1972.

Meyers, Marvin. *The Jacksonian Persuasion: Politics and Belief.* Stanford: Stanford University Press, 1957.

Miller, Perry. *Errand into the Wilderness.* Cambridge: Belknap Press of the Harvard University Press, 1956.

——. "From the Covenant to the Revival." In *The Shaping of American Religion.* Vol. 1 of *Religion in American Life,* edited by James Ward Smith and A. Leland Jamison. Princeton: Princeton University Press, 1961.

——. *The New England Mind: From Colony to Province.* Boston: Beacon Press, 1961.

———, and Johnson, Thomas H., eds. *The Puritans: A Sourcebook of Their Writings*. 2 vols. New York: Harper & Row, 1963.

Miller, Stuart Creighton. *The Unwelcome Immigrant: The American Image of the Chinese, 1785–1882*. Berkeley: University of California Press, 1969.

Moorhead, James H. "Henry J. Van Dyke, Sr.: Conservative Apostle of a Broad Church." *Journal of Presbyterian History* 50 (Spring 1972): 19–38.

Morgan, Edmund S. "The Puritan Ethic and the American Revolution." *William and Mary Quarterly,* 3d ser. 24 (January 1967): 3–43.

Morgan, H. Wayne, ed. *The Gilded Age*. Rev. ed. Syracuse: Syracuse University Press, 1970.

Morrow, Ralph E. *Northern Methodism and Reconstruction*. East Lansing: Michigan State University Press, 1956.

Murray, Andrew E. *Presbyterians and the Negro—A History*. Philadelphia: Presbyterian Historical Society, 1966.

Nagel, Paul C. *One Nation Indivisible: The Union in American Thought, 1776–1861*. New York: Oxford University Press, 1964.

———. *This Sacred Trust: American Nationality, 1798–1898*. New York: Oxford University Press, 1971.

Nevins, Allan. *The Ordeal of the Union*. 4 vols. New York: Scribner, 1947–50.

Nichols, James Hastings, ed. *The Mercersburg Theology*. New York: Oxford University Press, 1966.

Ninde, Edward S. *The Story of the American Hymn*. New York: Abingdon Press, 1921.

O'Neill, William S. *The Woman Movement: Feminism in the United States*. Chicago: Quadrangle Books, 1969.

Parmelee, Julius M. "Freedmen's Aid Societies, in the South." In vol. 1 of *Negro Education: A Study of the Private and Higher Schools for Colored People in the United States*. 2 vols. Washington, D.C.: Government Printing Office, 1917.

Perry, Lewis: *Radical Abolitionism: Anarchy and the Government of God in Antislavery Thought*. Ithaca, N.Y.: Cornell University Press, 1973.

Persons, Stow. *Free Religion, An American Faith*. New Haven: Yale University Press, 1947.

Peterson, Merrill D. *The Jefferson Image in the American Mind*. New York: Oxford University Press, 1960.

Phillips, Ulrich B. *American Negro Slavery: A Survey of the Supply,*

*Employment and Control of Negro Labor as Determined by the Plantation Regime.* New York: D. Appleton, 1918.

Potter, David M. *The Impending Crisis, 1848–1861.* Edited by Don E. Fehrenbacher. New York: Harper & Row, 1976.

———. *Lincoln and His Party in the Secession Crisis.* New Haven: Yale University Press, 1942.

Pressly, Thomas J. *Americans Interpret Their Civil War.* New York: Free Press by arrangement with Princeton University Press, 1962.

Rice, C. Duncan. *The Rise and Fall of Black Slavery.* New York: Harper & Row, 1975.

Richards, Leonard L. *"Gentlemen of Property and Standing": Anti-Abolition Mobs in Jacksonian America.* New York: Oxford University Press, 1971.

Rose, Willie Lee. *Rehearsal for Reconstruction: The Port Royal Experiment.* Indianapolis: Bobbs-Merrill, 1964.

Sandeen, Ernest L. *The Roots of Fundamentalism: British and American Millenarianism, 1800–1930.* Chicago: University of Chicago Press, 1970.

Scherer, Lester B. *Slavery and the Churches in Early America, 1619–1819.* Grand Rapids, Mich.: Wm. B. Eerdmans, 1975.

Schlesinger, Arthur M. "A Critical Period in American Religion, 1875–1900." *Proceedings of the Massachusetts Historical Society* 24 (June 1933): 523–48.

Schneider, Herbert W. *A History of American Philosophy.* 2d ed. New York: Columbia University Press, 1963.

Schwartz, Hillel. "The End of the Beginning: Millenarian Studies, 1969–1975." *Religious Studies Review* 2 (July 1976): 1–15.

Silver, James W. *Confederate Morale and Church Propaganda.* Tuscaloosa, Ala.: Confederate Publishing Company, 1957.

Smith, David E. "Millenarian Scholarship in America." *American Quarterly* 17 (Fall 1965): 535–49.

Smith, Henry Nash, ed. *Popular Culture and Industrialism, 1865–1900.* Garden City, N.Y.: Doubleday and Co., 1967.

———. *Virgin Land: The American West as Symbol and Myth.* Cambridge: Harvard University Press, 1950.

Smith, Hilrie Shelton. *In His Image, But . . . Racism in Southern Religion, 1780–1910.* Durham: Duke University Press, 1972.

Smith, Page. *A New Age Now Begins: A Peoples's History of the American Revolution.* 2 vols. New York: McGraw-Hill, 1976.

Smith, Timothy L. *Called Unto Holiness; The Story of the Naza-*

*renes: The Formative Years.* Kansas City, Mo.: Nazarene Publishing House, 1962.

————. *Revivalism and Social Reform: American Protestantism on the Eve of the Civil War.* Nashville: Abingdon Press, 1957.

Spicer, Carl L. "The Great Awakening of 1857 and 1858." Ph.D. dissertation, Ohio State University, 1935.

Sproat, John G. *"The Best Men": Liberal Reformers in the Gilded Age.* New York: Oxford University Press, 1968.

Stampp, Kenneth M. *The Era of Reconstruction, 1865–1877.* New York: Alfred A. Knopf, 1967.

————. *And the War Came: The North and the Secession Crisis, 1860–1861.* Baton Rouge: Louisiana State University Press, 1950.

Staudenraus, P. J. *The African Colonization Movement, 1816–1865.* New York: Columbia University Press, 1961.

Strout, Cushing. *The American Image of the Old World.* New York: Harper & Row, 1963.

————. *The New Heavens and the New Earth: Political Religion in America.* New York: Harper & Row, 1974.

Swaney, Charles Baumer. *Episcopal Methodism and Slavery: With Sidelights on Ecclesiastical Politics.* New York: Negro Universities Press, 1969.

Sweet, William Warren. *The Methodist Episcopal Church and the Civil War.* Cincinnati: Methodist Book Concern Press, 1912.

Taylor, William R. *Cavalier and Yankee: The Old South and American National Character.* New York: George Braziller, 1961.

Thompson, Ernest Trice. *Presbyterians in the South.* 3 vols. Richmond: John Knox Press, 1963–73.

Thorp, Willard. "The Religious Novel as Best Seller in America" in *Religious Perspectives in American Culture.* Vol. 2 of *Religion in American Life,* edited by James Ward Smith and A. Leland Jamison. Princeton: Princeton University Press, 1961.

Thrupp, Sylvia L., ed. *Millennial Dreams in Action.* New York: Schocken, 1970.

Toon, Peter, ed. *Puritans, the Millennium and the Future of Israel: Puritan Eschatology, 1600–60.* London: J. Clarke and Co., 1970.

Torbet, Robert G. *A History of the Baptists.* Rev. ed. Valley Forge, Chicago, and Los Angeles: Judson Press, 1963.

Trachtenberg, Alan, ed. *Democratic Vistas, 1860–1880.* New York: George Braziller, 1970.

Troeltsch, Ernst. *The Social Teachings of the Christian Churches.* 2 vols. New York: Harper & Row, 1960.

Tuveson, Ernest Lee. *Millennium and Utopia: A Study in the Background of the Idea of Progress.* Berkeley: University of California Press, 1949.

——. *Redeemer Nation: The Idea of America's Millennial Role.* Chicago: University of Chicago Press, 1968.

Van der Meer, F. *Augustine the Bishop: Church and Society at the Dawn of the Middle Ages.* New York: Harper & Row, 1965.

Vander Velde, Lewis G. *The Presbyterian Churches and the Federal Union, 1861–1869.* Harvard Historical Studies, vol. 33. Cambridge: Harvard University Press, 1932.

Varg, Paul A. *Missionaries, Chinese and Diplomats.* Princeton: Princeton University Press, 1958.

Voegeli, V. Jacque. *Free But Not Equal: The Midwest and the Negro During the Civil War.* Chicago: University of Chicago Press, 1967.

Walker, Williston. *A History of the Congregational Churches in the United States.* Boston: Pilgrim Press, 1894.

Walzer, Michael. *The Revolution of the Saints: A Study in the Origins of Radical Politics.* Cambridge: Harvard University Press, 1965.

Wiebe, Robert H. *The Search for Order, 1877–1920.* New York: Hill and Wang, 1967.

Williams, George Hunston. *Wilderness and Paradise in Christian Thought.* New York: Harper & Row, 1962.

Wilson, Edmund. *Patriotic Gore: Studies in the Literature of the American Civil War.* New York: Oxford University Press, 1962.

Wilson, John F. *Pulpit in Parliament: Puritanism During the English Civil Wars, 1640–1648.* Princeton: Princeton University Press, 1969.

Wolf, William J. *The Almost Chosen People.* Garden City, N.Y.: Doubleday and Co., 1959.

Wood, Gordon S. *The Creation of the American Republic, 1776–1787.* Chapel Hill: University of North Carolina Press, 1969.

Woodward, C. Vann. *Origins of the New South, 1877–1913.* University, La.: University of Louisiana Press, 1951.

——. "The Southern Ethic in a Puritan World." *William and Mary Quarterly,* 3d ser. 25 (July 1968): 343–70.

——. *The Strange Career of Jim Crow.* 2d rev. ed. New York: Oxford University Press, 1966.

Wyatt-Brown, Bertram. *Lewis Tappan and the Evangelical War Against Slavery.* Cleveland: Case Western Reserve University Press, 1969.

York, Robert M. *George B. Cheever, Religious and Social Reformer, 1807–1890.* University of Maine Studies, second series, no. 69. Orono: University of Maine Press, 1955.

Zilversmit, Arthur. *The First Emancipation: The Abolition of Slavery in the North.* Chicago: University of Chicago Press, 1967.

Zoellner, Robert H. "Negro Colonization: The Climate of Opinion Surrounding Lincoln, 1860–65." *Mid-America* 42 (July 1960): 131–50.

# Index

Abolitionism: and religious beliefs, 12*n*–13*n*, 17–18; clerical view of, 25; rhetoric of, 28–29, 30–31; and Protestant teachings, 83, 85; opposition to, 87–90, 91; and gag rule, 90; and military argument, 100–101; and colonization, 104–05; Presbyterian support for, 127

Adams, Henry, 236

Adams, John, 5

Adams, John Quincy, 97

Adams, William, 158, 190

Afro-Americans. *See* Blacks

Ahlstrom, Sydney, 242

Alden, Edmund K., 198

Amendments, constitutional, 83; Thirteenth, 179, 182; Fourteenth, 184; Fifteenth, 187, 189, 192

American Anti-Slavery Society, 17–18

American Board of Commissioners for Foreign Missions, 17, 93

American and Foreign Christian Union, 221

American Home Missionary Society, 197, 203, 214

*American Missionary,* 114–15, 196, 211–12, 221

American Missionary Association (AMA): founding of, 17; activity during war, 68, 117; on Reconstruction, 113, 123, 183; and land reform, 195–96; campaign in South, 197, 205–06, 215

*American Presbyterian and Theological Review,* 48, 62–63

*American Theological Review,* 19

American Tract Society, 17, 40, 59, 93, 124. *See also* Tract societies

Amnesty, 179, 180–81, 182

Anti-Catholicism, 7; of postwar era, 220–22, 224. *See also* Roman Catholicism

Archibald, R. T., 109

Aristocracy: of North vs. South, 39; Protestant view of, 75, 115, 121, 164

Arnold, S. G., 160

Atterbury, John G., 134

Backus, J. S., 199

Bacon, Leonard, 88, 180, 181

Baird, Robert, 11

Bancroft, George, 132*n*

Bangs, Heman, 27

Baptist Home Missionary Society, American, 199, 213, 214

Baptist Missionary Union, American, 198–99

Baptists: evangelism of, 11, 17, 71; press, 37, 43, 56, 98, 103, 147; on preservation of union, 39, 156; and slavery issue, 48, 86, 88, 93, 98, 109; North vs. South, 199; postwar reunification of, 213; and women's movement, 229

Barnes, Albert, 41, 218, 231

Barton, Clara, 228

Bassett, George W., 142, 143

Baxter, Michael, 57

Beecher, Edward, 12–13, 90–91

Beecher, Henry Ward, 56, 79, 93, 97–98, 179

Beecher, Lyman, 10

Bellows, Henry W., 66

Benevolent societies, 7; during antebellum period, 16–17; activity during war, 65–69; for women, 228

Benezet, Anthony, 85
Bentley, Edward, 28
Bible societies, 7, 17, 68, 80
Bingham, Joel, 56, 146, 164, 165, 175
Bittenger, J. B., 159
Blacks: organizations aiding, 67–68; postwar problems of, 191–93; Northern view of, 200, 206; education for, 201, 205. *See also* Freedmen
Blyden, E. W., 106
Boardman, Henry, 24, 37, 146, 147
Booth, Robert R., 199
Bourne, George, 87
Brockett, Linus P., 68
Brown, John, 19, 93
Buchanan, James, 23, 94
Burns, Edward McNall, 43
Bushnell, Horace, 7, 29, 93, 139, 140, 141, 147, 153–54, 161, 169, 170, 231
Butler, Henry, 180

Campbell, S. M., 223
Canfield, Sherman, 52, 111
Chadwick, Owen, 219
Chamberlayne, Israel, 92
Chinese laborers, perceived threat of, 222
*Christian Advocate and Journal,* 12, 39–40, 54, 64, 65, 72–73, 104, 108, 110, 131, 156, 160, 187–88, 202, 209–27 passim
*Christian Intelligencer* (Dutch Reformed Church), 57
*Christian Review* (Baptist), 37, 43, 56, 98, 103, 143
*Christian Watchman and Reflector,* 32, 34, 38–39, 74–75, 98, 100, 116, 121, 190, 214
Cities, perceived threat of, 234, 241
Civil rights: threat to, 150–53, 159; postwar policy, 182–84; and vote, 191

Civil War: beginning of, 23, 35–36; jeremiadic interpretation of, 43–49; historical purpose of, 50; millennial significance of, 54, 55, 61; in world history, 56–65; philanthropy during, 68–69; revivalist fervor during, 70, 71–71; debate over purpose of, 97–98; colonization policy during, 104–09; vernacular of, 146, 157; and melting pot concept, 166
Clafflin, Tennessee, 228
Clark, Davis W., 20, 215
Clark, Frederick G., 96, 109–10
Clark, Walter D., 42, 77
Clay, Henry, 105
Clebsch, William, 80
Clergy: endorsement of revivalism by, 20; response to secession, 25; on disunion, 33; and preservation of union, 35, 36, 37, 144; patriotism of, 41; revivalist fervor of, 71–72; colonization schemes of, 106–09; Confederate, 110; and national policy, 128; view of democracy, 130; on Republican institutions, 131; postwar attitudes of, 179–180, 181, 216; and Freedmen's Bureau, 194; on impartial suffrage, 196; Southern attitudes toward, 204; view of President Grant, 211–12; and freedmen, 215; nativism of, 223; and temperance movement, 226; and American destiny, 229. *See also* Protestantism
Cogswell, William, 8
Colonization policy, 90, 104–09
Colonization Society, 87, 105, 106
Confederacy: strength of, 27; and emancipation, 101; government of, 143; and postwar policy, 178; as successor to Israel, 110. *See also* Reconstruction
*Congregationalist,* 184, 191, 193–94,

202, 210; anti-Catholic 219, 224
Congregationalists: and Plan of
Union, 17n; on American destiny,
32-33; and slavery issue, 82, 86,
88, 93, 99; on democracy,
133-34, 138
Conservatives: and secession, 27;
and disunion, 41; and abolitionists,
88
Copperheads, 151-52, 153, 155
Corning, James L., 52
Coxe, Arthur C., 74
Crane, J. Townley, 26
Crittenden proposal, 23, 32, 33
Crooks, George R., 213
Crusade, Civil War as, 55, 80, 244
Cumming, John, 57
Curry, Daniel, 104, 216-17

Darby, John Nelson, 57
Darwin, Charles, 237
Davis, Jefferson, 35
Democracy: and role of religion, 11;
Protestant view of, 12, 130-31,
133-46; vs. aristocracy, 39-40,
75-76; predictions for, 73, 74;
Jeffersonian, 135-36, 139, 143;
Jacksonian, 138; individualistic,
162. See also Government
Democratic party, peace faction of,
101, 127, 151-52, 153, 155; in
postwar period, 236. See also
Political parties
Dexter, Henry M., 122
Dispensationalism, 238, 241
Disunionists, 26, 33, 35
Dix, Dorothea, 228
Doolittle, J. R., 69
Douglas, Stephen, 105
Dow, Lorenzo, 10
Dred Scott decision, 19, 91, 144
Duffield, George Jr., 21, 47, 97
Dunham, Chester A., 91, 180
Dutch Reformed Church, 20, 57;
press, 54

Dwight, William T., 39
Dwinnell, Israel, 78

Ecumenical movement, 242
Eddy, Daniel C., 40, 64
Eddy, Sherwood, 242
Eddy, Zachary, 34, 41
Edwards, Jonathan, 4-5, 9
Eells, W. W., 55, 103
Eggleston, Nathaniel, 47, 109
Emancipation: arguments for, 82,
98-101, 114-16; manumission
laws, 85, 87; gradualist philosophy
for, 87-89, 92; military expediency
of, 97, 100-01; reaction of Prot-
estant clergy to, 103; AMA on, 183
Emancipation Proclamation, 96, 112
Emerson, Ralph Waldo, 132n
Engerman, Stanley L., 94
England: millenarianism in, 57;
attitudes toward, 75, 167
Escapism, 242, 243, 244
Eschatology, biblical: Amos, 8;
Malachi, 19; Daniel, 58, 62;
Ezekiel, 59; Revelation, 58, 59,
62, 63, 78; Joel, 60; Isaiah, 106;
Psalm II, 128
Evangelical united front, 7;
disintegration of, 16-17; later
attitudes toward, 50; during
Civil War, 66
Evangelism: role of, 11-12; and
military power, 80-81; and
slavery issue, 84; in postwar
South, 196-217; world, 198-200;
postwar call for, 230, 237; and
immigration, 242. See also
Revivalism
Everett, Edward, 105

Faber, George S., 57
Fillmore, Millard, 105
Finney, Charles G., 13-14, 208
Fish, Henry Clay, 11, 71, 100
Fisher, George P., 136-37

Fogel, Robert W., 94
Forney, John W., 21
Foss, Cyrus D., 56, 159, 230
Foster, Charles I., 16
Fourierism, 12, 60
Foxe, John, 3, 4
Frederickson, George, 105, 125
Freedman: colonization policy for,
    107; in Reconstruction era,
    119–20, 121; postwar condition,
    124, 181, 206–07; suffrage,
    185–88 passim; education for,
    201, 205
Freedmen's aid societies, 67–68, 117
Freedmen's Bureau, 68, 189, 192,
    193, 194, 205
Freedmen's relief association, 67
Freedmen's Union Commission, 205
Free Soil party, and slavery issue, 18,
    90. See also Political parties
French, Austa M., 114, 115
Fugitive Slave Act, 15, 18, 25, 91,
    93, 144, 171
Fuller, Richard, 88

Garrison, William Lloyd, 15
Gaylord, William, 53
Goodell, C. L., 55, 119
Goodrich, William H., 52, 73, 98
Goodwin, Edward P., 223
Gordon, Adoniram J., 173–74
Government: Protestant view of,
    13n, 14–15, 132; Congregational
    concept of, 133; Presbyterian view
    of, 134; Hamiltonian vs. Jefferson-
    ian, 137–38; Confederate, 143.
    See also Democracy
Gradualist philosophy, for freeing
    slaves, 87–89, 92
Grant, Ulysses S., 209, 210, 211
Great Awakening, 4, 21
Greeley, Horace, 21
Grierson, Francis, 22
Gulliver, John, 186, 195

Hall, Nathaniel, 113

Hamilton, Alexander, 137
Hamilton, D. H., 167
Hamline, Leonidas L., 14, 99
Harris, Samuel, 129–30, 164, 168
Hatfield, Edwin F., 62
Hatfield, Robert M., 177, 229
Haven, Gilbert, 15, 33, 75, 76, 81,
    94, 126–27, 128, 157, 176, 211
Hickok, S. P., 231
Hillman, S. D., 220
History: Protestant concept of,
    49–56, 95, 233; Civil War in, 56–65
Hitchcock, Roswell, 46
Hodge, Charles, 31, 178, 180
Home mission movement, 17n, 197,
    203, 207, 214
Hopkins, Samuel, 86
Hough, J. W., 73, 74
Houghton, Walter, 229
Hovey, Horace, 165
Howard, Oliver O., 68, 192, 193
Howe, Julia Ward, 56, 79, 228
Humphrey, Heman, 32
Hurd, John C., 132n

Ide, George, 48, 51–52, 79, 113,
    147, 186, 188, 195
Immigrants, perceived threat of, 222,
    227, 241, 242
Impeachment, issue of, 208–10
Independent, 29, 33, 34, 38, 40–50
    passim, 63, 69, 73, 101, 118,
    121–22, 144–48 passim, 156, 173,
    185, 200, 209, 235
Individualism, Protestant view of, 49,
    130–31, 132n, 162
Ingersoll, Robert G., 237
Interdenominational activity, 16–17,
    65–69, 92–93, 117, 231–32
Israel, symbolic imagery of, 5, 44,
    46, 47, 51, 55, 78, 100. See also
    Millennialism; United States

Jackson, Andrew, 138–39
Jacksonianism, 44
James, William, 232

Jefferson, Thomas, 135–36, 137–39
Jeremiadic tradition, 43, 44–49, 99, 225
Johnson, Andrew, 177; Reconstruction policy of, 182–84; and Negro suffrage, 193–94; issue of impeachment, 208–10
Johnson, Edward, 3
Johnson, H. M., 72

Kansas-Nebraska Act, 91, 93, 96
Kimball, Henry, 99
Kirk, Edward N., 123, 181, 216
Kohn, Hans, 129

Land reform, 121–25, 194–95
Latitudinarian position, on slavery, 84
Leeds, S. P., 78, 157
Liberia, colonization of, 104–05, 107
Lieber, Francis, 132n
Lincoln, Abraham, 23; Emancipation Proclamation, 96; and colonization schemes, 105; war policy of, 150; campaign of, 155; as martyr president, 174–76, 180
Literature: English vs. American, 170; religious novels, 239, 240
Livermore, Mary, 228
Lovejoy, Elijah P., 91

McCabe, Charles, 79–80, 239
McClellan, George B., 156, 159–60
McGill, A. T., 107
Madison, James, 150
Magie, David, 126
Manifest destiny. See National purpose
Manning, J. M., 222
March, Daniel, 53, 65
Marsden, George, 9
Marshall, James, 112, 149
Materialism: jeremiadic interpretation of, 48; Protestant attitudes toward, 109, 146; postwar concern about, 224–26, 231

Mather, Cotton, 226
Melting pot, 129, 166–67, 223, 232
Mead, Sidney, 12
Melville, Herman, 43–44
Methodist Episcopal Church, 141, 185
Methodist Freedmen's Aid Society, 215
Methodist Quarterly Review, 26, 30, 160
Methodists: and evangelism, 71; and slavery issue, 86, 87, 92, 104, 126; Holiness wing of, 99; Western Advocate and Journal, 102–03; in postwar South, 118; on disloyalty, 152, 153–55; and mission in South, 199, 203–05; on Reconstruction, 209; postwar reunification of, 213; and failure of evangelism, 238
Meyer, Donald H., 95
Military power: Protestant view of, 75, 76–77; and evangelism, 80–81; and abolitionist position, 100–01; clerical support of, 158, 240
Millennialism: literature dealing with, 1n–2n; roots of belief in, 2; of Harriet Beecher Stowe, 19; logic of, 53; and significance of Civil War, 54, 55, 61; imagery of, 74 (see also Israel); cataclysmic answers, 83
Millennium: interpretations of, 8; antebellum speculation, 57–64; Hollis Read's prediction for, 59–60; implication for slavery of, 89
Miller, Perry, 44
Millerites, 9, 57
Moody, Dwight L., 2–9, 241, 242
Morris, Thomas A., 37, 71
Mott, John R., 242
Mulford, Elisha, 234

Nadal, B. H., 55
Nationalism, symbolism of, 130, 169–70

National purpose, concept of, 15-16,
    129; antebellum views of, 22; re-
    vised conception of, 43; and moral
    rebirth, 74-81; romantic view of,
    132n; postwar view of, 230
National Reform Association
    (NRA), 141, 142
Nativism, 223-24, 241
Nevin, John W., 132n
Nichols, Starr H., 48, 99
North, attitudes toward blacks in,
    200, 216
Novels, religious, 239, 240

Ottman, Sefferenas, 34

Paine, Levi, 46, 138
Palmer, Ray, 168
Patriotism: antebellum, 15; early
    Civil War, 36, 41; of Protestant
    clergy, 74, 163; during Civil War,
    80, 145; during postwar period,
    133; war as act of, 147; clerical
    support of, 149; symbolism of,
    168; literature and, 170; postwar,
    198
Patton, William, 71
Peck, George, 46, 118
Perry, Lewis, 12n-13n
Personal liberty laws, 25, 32
Peterson, Merrill, 135
Phelps, S. D., 149
Philanthropy: during Civil War,
    68-69; wartime criticism of,
    157-58
Political equality, concept of, 191
Political parties, 23; and abolition-
    ism, 18; and slavery issue, 90; and
    1864 presidential campaign, 155;
    in postwar period, 236
Post, Henry A., 163
Post, Truman M., 133, 134, 203
Postmillennialism, 9, 21n
Prayer meetings, 69-70. See also
    Revivalism
Premillennialism, 9, 57, 238

Prentiss, George L., 49, 50, 51, 161,
    185, 186, 188
Presbyterian, 25, 26, 27, 42; on
    beginnings of Civil War, 45;
    skepticism of, 63; postwar policy
    of, 180, 203, 224; on missionary
    campaign in South, 197
Presbyterians: and slavery question,
    16, 31, 86, 87, 92; and Plan of
    Union, 17n; press, 48, 62-63;
    evangelism of, 71; on disloyalty,
    152; on freedmen, 187, 193, 206;
    mission in postwar South, 207;
    postwar reunification of, 213; and
    national destiny, 230
Press: suspension of freedom of,
    150, 159; Republican, 151; Prot-
    estant, 243. See also specific
    newspapers
Princeton Review, 31, 62, 89, 107
Prophetic Times, 57
Protestantism: predicted spiritual
    rebirth for, 73-74; response to Civil
    War of, 81; and slavery issue,
    83-96; of North vs. South, 110; of
    American culture, 125-28; view
    of democracy, 133; authority of,
    141; Reconstruction economics
    of, 161; middle-class, 226;
    escapism of, 242, 243, 244.
    See also Clergy
Puritanism, 3, 4, 43, 109, 110

Quakers, anti-slavery position of, 85
Quint, Alonzo H., 111

Racism: and colonization policy, 87,
    105-09; of Copperheads, 151;
    anglophilia, 166-77; and Recon-
    struction government, 189-90; of
    postwar period, 120n-21n,
    124-25, 241
Rankin, J. E., 103
Read, Hollis, 59-62, 106, 107, 108
Reconstruction: concept of, 101;
    expectations for, 112-25, 132,

188–89; freedmen during, 119;
land reform during, 121–25;
economics of, 161; politics of,
178–96; radical approach to, 184,
201, 235; failure of, 201–03, 208,
217, 243; clerical view of, 212
Reconstruction Acts, of *1867,* 187,
194, 196
Religion: role in democracy, 12;
conversion of soldiers, 70; secularization of, 77–78, 79, 231. *See
also* Protestantism
Republicanism, 11, 174. *See also*
Democracy
Republican party, 18, 22, 23; in
postwar period, 216*n,* 236. *See
also* Political parties
Republicans, radical, 101
Revivalism, 4; and economic crisis,
20–22; antebellum, 61; during
Civil War, 70, 71; postwar, 239.
*See also* Evangelism
Riesling, James F., 137–38
Rights: states', 137; inalienable, 146.
*See also* Civil rights
Roman Catholicism: seventeenth-
century attitudes toward, 3;
support for McClellan, 159–60;
fear of, 207, 218, 219–23; per-
ceived threat of, 241
Roosevelt, Theodore, 144–45
Rose, Willie Lee, 115
Russell, Charles T., 238

Sanitary Commission, U. S., 67, 69,
147
Sankey, Ira, 239
Schaff, Philip, 5, 11
Scriptures, sources for millenarianism
in, 58, 62–63. *See also* Eschatology
Sears, Barnas, 54
Secession, 23; initial response to,
24–35; legitimacy of, 38; millen-
nial interpretation of, 63. *See also*
Union
Sectionalism: and slavery issue, 30,

95*n;* origins of, 110; and mission to
South, 212–13
Secularization, 77–78, 79; postwar
view of, 231
Seward, William, 15
Simpson, Matthew, 145, 198, 213
Slavery: question of, 7; debate over,
16–17; Lincoln on, 23; Pres-
byterians on, 31; jeremiadic
interpretation of, 47–48, 99;
Protestant attitudes toward, 83–96;
economics of, 84, 85; gradualist
approach to, 87–89, 92; economics
of, 94; and federal armies, 102; as
antichrist, 102–12; and Protestant
ethic, 111. *See also* Emancipation
Smith, Adam, 84, 94, 162
Smith, Gerrit, 195
Smith, Henry, 49, 119
Smith, Henry Boynton, 69, 93, 177
Smith, Moses, 117
Social compact theory, 136–37,
139
Socialism, perceived threat of, 241
Social reform: and evangelism, 14;
antebellum, 18, 81; late nineteenth-
century, 236
Soldier-martyr, image of, 148–49
Soldier's Aid Society, 67
South: slavery issue in churches of,
87, 88; missionary campaign in,
116, 196–217. *See also* Re-
construction; Secession
Spear, Samuel T., 75, 116, 145,
190, 209
Speer, Robert E., 242
Sprague, William B., 64
Spring, Gardiner, 36–37
Sproat, John, 234
Stanton, Edwin, 117
Stanton, Elizabeth Cady, 228
State suicide, doctrine of, 101
Stearns, William A., 163
Stevens, Thaddeus, 187
Stiles, Ezra, 5
Stone, A. L., 39, 45, 126, 136

Stowe, Harriet Beecher, 1, 19, 21, 105, 118, 124
Strong, Josiah, 241
Stuart, George H., 65
Student Volunteer Movement for Foreign Missions, 241–42
Sturtevant, Julian M., 124–25
Suffrage: urban vs. rural, 160–61; for ex-slaves, 185, 186–88, 190–91; clerical support of, 196; women's, 228
Sunderland, Byron, 45
Symbolism: national, 130, 169–70; biblical 156, 177; dissonant, 172. *See also* Israel

Tappan, Lewis, 97, 100, 115
Tarbox, Israel, 124
Tawney, R. H., 162
Temperance movement, 226, 240$n$
Thome, James, 112
Thompson, Joseph P., 28–29, 96, 232, 234
Thompson, M. L. P., 47, 109
Tilton, Theodore, 64
Tocqueville, Alexis de, 160
Tourgée, Albion, 201–02
Trachtenberg, Alan, 171
Tract societies, 68, 80. *See also* American Tract Society
Transcendentalism, 60
Treason, 150, 152–53, 181

Union, preservation of, 15, 24, 26, 27–28; clerical attitudes toward, 33, 36–41, 143, 144. *See also* Secession
Union party, Lincoln's, 155
United States: as successor to Israel, 3, 4–5, 20–21, 43–44, 46, 47, 61, 78, 100, 177, 217, 232, 243; moral rebirth of, 65–72; future mission of, 72–77; as redeemer nation, 128, 218; historical role of, 163–64

United States Christian Commission, 65–66, 67, 68–69
Urbanization, 234, 243

Vallandigham, Clement L., 150, 159
Van Dyke, Henry J., 25, 127–28
Vincent, Marvin, 48
Voluntary organizations. *See* Benevolent societies; Philanthropy

Walker, George L., 82, 125
Wayland, Francis, 15, 40, 88, 89, 96, 123
Webb, Edwin, 174, 175
Webster, Daniel, 15, 24, 105
Weed, L. S., 57–58, 59, 63
Weibe, Robert H., 236
Wesley, John, 86, 238
*Western Advocate and Journal* (Methodist), 102–03
Whedon, D. D., 30, 33
Whitman, Walt, 132$n$
Willard, Frances, 228
Williams, Lester, Jr., 27
Williams, William R., 166
Willson, Edmund B., 36
Wilson, Edmund, 133
Wilson, James P., 135
Winthrop, John, 44
Wolcott, Samuel, 197
Woman's Central Relief Association, 67
Women's Christian Temperance Union, 228, 239
Women: wartime activities of, 67; postwar view of, 233
Women's movement, 228–29
Wood, Gordon, 5
Woodhull, Victoria, 228
Woolman, John, 85
Woolsey, Theodore, 225, 228

Young Men's Christian Association (YMCA), 20, 21, 65, 241

Zilversmit, Arthur, 85

**DATE DU**

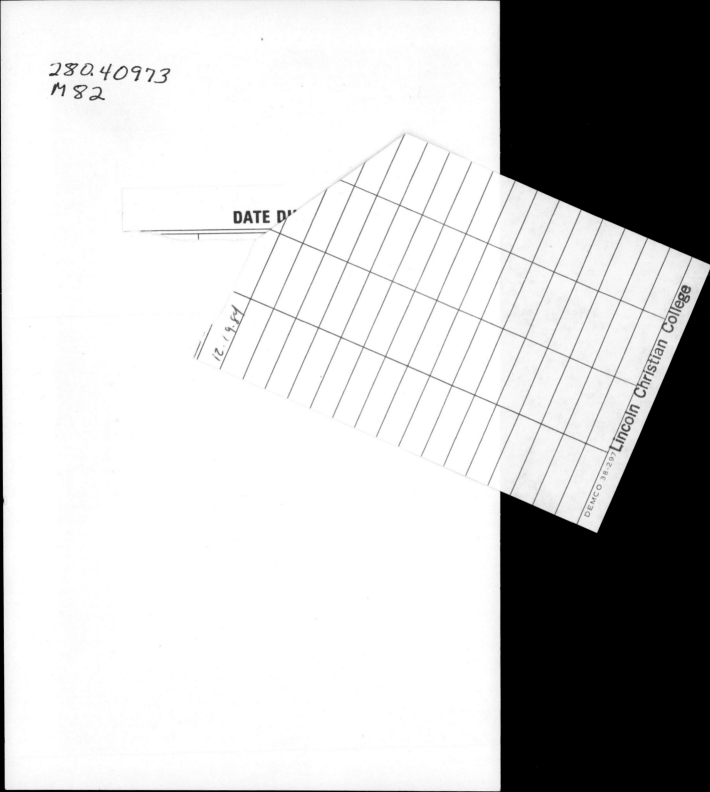